A Bridge To Cross

By

Hans Berger

Best wishes

A BRIDGE TO CROSS

First Published in Great Britain 2014 by Mirador Publishing

First edition: 2014
Second edition: 2016

Any offence the references produce is unintentional.

A copy of this work is available through the British Library.

ISBN : 978-1-910104-28-6

Mirador Publishing
Mirador
Wearne Lane
Langport
Somerset
TA10 9HB

ACKNOWLEDGEMENTS

I want to posthumously thank my mother for keeping a journal during our difficult time towards the end of the war. I had a desire to write this book for many years. I just never found the time to sit down to recall the past. It is my duty to tell future generations of the horror, we, as a family experienced during, and toward the end of WWII.

I am grateful for my sister Herta, who still recalls the horror as we children were caught in the middle of Russia's offensive to destroy Hitler's Germany. I very much appreciate my wife Jeanette for helping to get this manuscript published. She was the one who encouraged me to write the story and has been very patient putting up with me when I typed for hours at a time.

I have been attending a writing class, 'Write for Publish' led by Janice Stevens, an author of many books. She has been a great help and encouragement to write my story. Ginger Niemeyer first edited my writing, a special thanks for her editing skills. Monica Stevens did the final edit and a big thank you, Monica. Gayle Taylor helped me edit my synopsis. A special thank you goes to my class for helping me in grammar and critiquing my work.

It was painful to write of the atrocities we endured. During my childhood years, my mother told me stories I filed into my memory bank. My oldest sister Herta was nine at the time and has vivid memories of our struggles.

Many of my stories came from my mother's war journal. She kept a day to day log of our indescribable suffering.

When I began to write, I was unaware that my mother wrote many of the experiences in vivid details. It hit me hard when I read how close we came to death. Only God saved us.

My sister Herta resides in Germany and wrote a book about our lives towards the end of the war and how we miraculously survived. My mother and father have passed on, and if we, as children, don't write about the chaos and evil which had engulfed Europe, we would be doing disservice to our children and grandchildren.

I am honoring my mother; she will always be my hero. She had total disregard for her own safety, and put herself in harm's way many times to keep us safe, as well as others who relied on her courage.

I will be forever thankful for having had the opportunity to immigrate to this blessed land and the good life I have had.

TABLE OF CONTENTS

1

OH, HEIDELBERG

It was May the 23rd 1944; Papa took us to the bombed-out train depot with little time to spare as we fled the Nazis. It was late evening, the fog rolled in, hiding us from the dreaded Gestapo.

The trains left and arrived on time, not one minute late. We couldn't afford to miss ours. The last train leaving for the east was that night. The Germans are known to be punctual. The train station was heavily bombed by American as well British bombers, but the Germans repaired it so it would accommodate limited traffic.

While Mama and Papa were buying tickets, they were constantly keeping their eyes open for these vultures. Papa got us seated on the hard wooden benches, and made us as comfortable as he could. From the stress and lack of sleep, we were ready to go to sleep at any moment. My oldest sisters knew what was happening all along, and they tried to stay awake, but it was a losing battle. Papa bent over and kissed each of us goodbye, and the girls pleaded with him not to leave them. *Bitte Papa bleib bei uns* "please, Papa stay with us" was their cry. We were all weeping and hanging onto Papa for dear life. Papa, however, assured us we would see him again soon. He was praying this wasn't the last time he would kiss us.

The train started to inch forward at a slow pace, gaining momentum every second. At the same time, we saw the pitch black smoke coming out of the chimney of the locomotive, which was even visible through the dead of night.

As the train gained speed, Papa jumped off, taking the risk of falling under the wheels. Thank God he landed on both feet. It was a very emotional moment as he longed so much to be with us for just another minute, but time had run out. With a heavy heart, Papa walked back to the apartment. His spirits sank low as he pondered if life was worth living.

The war clouds had gathered over Germany, and Heidelberg was faced with the possibility of being destroyed and losing its special place with its romantic old section of town. The towering castle was the guardian of the city. Below the castle, the swift Neckar River snaked through the middle of town as it had done for eons of time.

Heidelberg is famous for having the oldest university in Germany, which was founded in the year of 1386 and has produced many renowned scholars of Europe, including five chancellors of post-war Germany, the latest being Helmut Kohl.

The Berger family lived on Wieblinger Strasse. Mighty chestnut trees surrounded our apartment, and life was like a fairytale. We truly lived in an incredible place. Walking through the old town, one was thrown back into the Middle Ages. Ancient buildings lined the boulevards with towering churches, almost a thousand years old.

Our home was in a modest apartment on the bank of the Neckar River, teeming with many ships and boats, traveling to various towns delivering goods and services. The family was blessed with four beautiful children, three girls and a cute boy. I was the youngest of the children that made the family complete. Mama and Papa finally had the boy they wanted.

My sisters and I were born in tumultuous times and the future was anything but certain as the winds of war gathered over Europe.

Papa was employed at the University of Heidelberg where he worked as a pathologist.

Mama was busy looking after us four children and doing all the work a housewife and mother has to do. She was raised in East Prussia, in the town of *Küstrin*, which is now in Poland. She was an attractive, tall lady of five feet and seven inches, blessed with thick, dark-brown hair reaching to her shoulder blades.

Her piercing eyes made a lasting impression on anyone she met. She had a confident walk and when she entered the front door, you felt the floor vibrating even at some distance from our apartment, an early warning of her arrival.

Papa was born in Hamburg on the North Sea, the largest port in Germany, and third biggest in Europe. He was the opposite of my mother, gentle and never causing anybody trouble. He was slow to anger, and appeared to be in a good mood most of the time. He was not as tall as Mama, but don't let the size fool you. He was strong, and could out-run anybody on planet Earth.

He had blond, naturally wavy hair and was altogether a handsome kind of guy. Women liked him for his gentle nature and warm personality. Mama didn't have to worry about competition, she was a beautiful lady, and Papa was lucky he had found her. Had Mama ever suspected anything, she would have made quick work of him, and Papa was well aware of that.

They met while attending a Lutheran Seminary at the city of *Bielefeld* in northern Germany. Mama was studying to become a Lutheran nun but her hearing impairment kept her from finishing the studies. Papa was studying to become a Lutheran pastor.

In addition, Papa pursued a medical career, studying pathology which included performing autopsies. He came home with the most fascinating stories, and we were always ready to listen to what occurred at the hospital.

One particular day, as the staff was preparing a corpse for an autopsy, they proceeded to open the chest cavity of the "lifeless body". The man had no pulse or any other signs of being alive. Then, all of a sudden, he began to breathe and his pulse returned. Talk about being shocked! They rushed the man by ambulance to the nearest hospital; it was a close brush with death. After he recovered, he lived a long fruitful life.

Another time, Papa was in charge of mentally disturbed patients when he worked in the mental ward of the hospital. One of the men got away, and Papa chased him clear into a cabbage field. When he caught up with the patient, he wrestled him to the ground and restrained him. I knew my dad had good legs, and ran fast, but I never thought of him as the tough guy.

My oldest sister Herta was seven when I was born. She had the responsibilities to look after her two youngest siblings, namely me and Helga, the youngest of my sisters. Herta was a bright brunette with blue eyes and pretty as a picture. She never complained doing her chores, and Mama appreciated her for all she did.

Next to her was Gerlinde, she was two years younger. She was a blonde, and unlike us, had brown eyes. We always wondered why she didn't have blue eyes like the rest of us. She was a stunning young girl, and a little more sensitive than us. Mama entrusted her to help with everyday chores as well, but Herta's main responsibilities were to look after Helga and me.

Helga was two years older than I, and cute as a button. She was blessed with dark, brunette wavy hair and with stunning, beautiful dark blue eyes. The Russian soldiers admired her, and loved being in her company. At one point, she saved all of us from being transported on a truck to Russia. After we returned to Heidelberg, now under American command, you couldn't keep her from the American soldiers.

Herta's responsibility was to feed, and give me baths. She would have rather played with kids around our apartment instead of playing mommy to her baby brother.

Mama was busy with four children and needed all the help she could get. Besides, it was good training for my sister. Herta took me for rides, pushing my baby carriage around our neighborhood. This gave her an escape from doing other chores around the house.

She found peace among the beautiful flowers in the park, observing the ships and trains, and imagining where they were headed. One afternoon, she took me for a ride in the buggy, and was temporarily distracted by a bookstore. Reading was her passion, and while she was indulged in the books, she forgot I was in my stroller parked on the sidewalk underneath a shady tree to keep me from getting too much sun.

She was occupied with a fascinating book when she remembered leaving me unattended outside. Panic set in, and her heart almost stopped when she discovered that I had disappeared. She was gripped with fear that she might not ever see me again. Herta's heart was racing, and she ran as fast as she had ever run in her life to tell Mama what had happened.

She wished this would have never happened. All she could think of was to find her little brother. She pondered what she might do if I was never located, but she tried to wipe that thought out of her mind, it was too awful.

There was still a flicker of hope I would be found nearby, but that didn't calm her. Mama, Papa, and my other sister Gerlinde followed Herta to the location where she had left me. A search party was quickly organized, including many people from our apartment.

In the distance, kids were laughing and having a good time. That was reason enough for Mama to investigate. Kids found this cute, chubby baby boy "me", removed my diaper and played Mama. They were pretending to be mothers, but this did not amuse Mama, who promptly extracted me from them.

There was no call to the police. Everybody was happy they found me, especially Herta. Needless to say, when we reached home, punishment was waiting for my sister. But that was quickly forgotten as we heard the sirens blaring, warning us of an impending aerial attack by the Allies.

Mama took me under her arms, followed by my sisters, reaching the bomb shelter in record time. The bomb raids occurred mostly during the night as we tried to sleep, and we prayed nothing bad might happen to us while we slept.

Each day we were hoping nothing unfortunate would occur. We tried to go about life as normal as possible. We missed Papa because many a night, he couldn't come home, caring for patients, including soldiers from Germany as well as from the U.S. and Britain. When he did come home, it was stressful due to the constant bombing, never knowing from day to day what was going to transpire.

The men were forced to wear army uniforms. Papa wore his lab coat to cover it up. He hated to wear the uniform and did everything to hide it. One night, after Papa had gone to bed, Mama took his uniform, snuck out the back door, and burned it.

Unfortunately, that didn't help Mama to stay in good graces with the Nazi Party she despised. When Papa woke up the next morning, he looked for his uniform and couldn't find it, so he panicked. It was *verboten* to lose the garment. He said to Mama *wo ist die uniform die ich gestern aufhing.* "Have you seen the uniform which I hung up before going to bed?" Mama nonchalantly answered him, "I burned it in the backyard."

He couldn't believe what came out of Mama's mouth. Hurriedly, he ran to the back of the building, thinking, maybe by a miracle, the uniform had not burned, but all he found was a pile of ashes. Mama made sure there wouldn't be any remnant left. He had much explaining to do, perhaps he used the old adage, and 'the dog ate it'.

I don't know how he got around that one, but his explanation must have been sufficient for his boss. The Nazis didn't tolerate anybody destroying the uniform which was punishable for up to a year in prison or one could be sent to the Russian front, which for all practical purpose meant death.

At 11 o'clock one night, Papa was still at work, when Mama woke us and told us calmly to pack everything. The American and British bombers were bombing our neighborhood, and we had to leave our apartment in a hurry. The girls weren't awake yet. They asked her where we were going, but Mama had no time to explain.

Mama was too busy to answer them as she packed up the things we would need for the next forty-eight hours, such as the dolls and of course the baby bottle for me. As we climbed down the stairs, we heard the planes approaching, and bombs exploding with deafening thunder. Mama carried me under her arm, while my sisters skipped every other step on the way down the staircase.

Mama prayed that none of us kids would get hurt due to the lack of lights. Fortunately, we found a place under the stairs to wait out the aerial attack. The building escaped major damage, but our nerves were rattled.

The lull in the bombing allowed us to get back to our apartment. We were happy to return to our home.

In the meantime, we had heard that a large American bomber had crashed by the clinic where Papa worked, and another one crashed into the Neckar River during the night. Non-stop, the German dive bombers, called Stukas, and the flak on the rooftops were engaging the Allied bombers. It was deafening and unbelievably scary.

My sisters couldn't believe what they witnessed when they walked to school the next day. Herta said to Gerlinde *schau mal an, da liegt ein abgestürtzter Flieger.* "Look, there is a plane that crashed." While walking to school, they had to cross the bridge by Papa's clinic. There, they saw another U.S. bomber that had crashed earlier in the morning, all blackened due to the fire that had engulfed the plane. Men with white coats were standing all around, and emergency personnel placed white sheets on something lying on the ground, probably the remains of the American crew. Both girls were very frightened, and wondered if they should continue on to school.

Herta suggested going back home instead of to school. Gerlinde said to Herta, *das dürfen wir nicht tun.Wenn der Herr Lehrer weis dass wir nicht zur Schule gingen wird er uns wahrscheilich strafen."* Once our teacher finds out we skipped school we will surely be punished." Herta answered her, *das ist alles Quatsch was Du da her redest, geh schnell, folge mir so dass wir sicher heim kommen.* "You are talking nonsense; let's pick it up, follow me, so we get home unharmed."

When they arrived home, Herta told Mama she decided to come home instead of going to school, and Mama said she did the right thing. The bombing intensified, and they flew sorties at night as well as in the daytime. We visited the bomb shelter on a regular basis, and getting a good night's sleep was now a distant memory. We were totally fatigued and very hungry. Due to lack of deliveries, there was no food to purchase at the grocery stores.

Leaving the security of the building would expose us to great danger from the constant bombing and the many fires.

The girls couldn't go outside anymore and felt cooped up. They had to be ready to leave at a moment's notice should Mama give the command. Venturing outside was getting way too dangerous. If we stayed where we were, we would be in danger from the constant bombing and fires that raged throughout the city. Ambulances, and fire trucks with their sirens screaming, were everywhere. During this time, the train station was reduced to rubble, our place of departure from Heidelberg as we fled the Nazis.

We didn't know from one moment to the next when the bombing attack would resume. Mama packed us up again, putting everything of importance on the little cart we used to haul our groceries. We fled to a nearby forest where we found lots of people with children, dogs, cats and anything valuable to help them survive.

For four hours, we sat on the damp ground, waiting out the bombing. Herta, Gerlinde and Helga didn't fuss, but were wet and very tired. It was difficult for them to comprehend what was going on. To leave the safety of our apartment was difficult. We had no choice, whatever Mama said, we did, no questions asked.

Mama didn't have to worry about me since I was always sitting either in, or on top of the small cart. I had plenty of eyes watching out for me. People told Mama *die Flieger haben die ganze Stadt zu trümmern gemacht.* "The bombers reduced Heidelberg to rubble" and Mama was afraid our apartment was reduced to ashes.

Neighbors claimed countless people had lost their lives. We heard wave after wave of bombers. The frightening sound of the plane's huge engines, and the flak going off nonstop was terrifying. The sky was red as blood, caused by German warplanes attacking the bombers, causing them to crash nearby.

We were anxious to find a safer place of refuge when we found shelter in nearby bushes. People around us were praying, hoping this ordeal would soon end. Even the dogs yelped. They sensed what was happening. We kids were sitting on the wet ground with moisture saturating our clothes. We were miserable.

During the turmoil, it was as if the night had turned into day; powerful searchlights flooded the area. They missed the place where we were huddled together; but the blaring sirens wouldn't quit which penetrated our bones. We were told by the authorities that the bombing had stopped and everybody could return home, but nobody knew if their home was still standing. The girls and Mama were more than anxious to get up from the wet grass. Mama grabbed the cart, made sure we were all accounted for and started heading back to our apartment. Mama was aggrieved; perhaps our home would be nothing but a pile of rubble.

Papa met us on the road, calmed our fears and said that just a few houses were bombed. It was good news when we found our home had survived, and we could at last rest our weary bodies and get some sleep. The girls were careful carrying their lifelike dolls and made sure they weren't soiled or damaged during this short excursion. To them, the dolls were the most important items, even if it meant not having anything else.

My sisters were so fatigued that they didn't remember falling into their beds. We slept all night without waking up and having to go to the bomb shelter. We were spared that night and there were no sirens going off warning people of an air raid. Mama and Papa were discussing what options we had. Food was hard to come by since the store shelves were empty and venturing outside was very dangerous.

Mama knew of a little corner store where we might be able to purchase food. The question was did the store survive the last raid? Mama told us to stay put while she checked to see if the store was still open for business. She was pleasantly surprised to find the store intact. Mama bought a few staples like bread and milk. The store owner told her, if there was another air raid, he would be closing the store for good. That meant Mama would have to find food someplace else, but where was the big question.

Twenty-five kilometers from Heidelberg was the large city of Mannheim. It was the home of much manufacturing and was important for Hitler's war machine. We found out later that Mannheim had been bombed out of existence by the American bombers.

Heidelberg had largely escaped the carnage, resulting in just a few casualties. However, the air space was full of smoke and soot. Breathing became a problem. Our area was full of soot carried by the wind currents from Mannheim. Pieces of paper and wood fell out of the sky.

Among the debris, the Americans dropped messages, stating Heidelberg would no longer be bombed. It was going to be the home of the Army's American Central Command. It still is the Command Center for the American Army for Europe, which has kept us out of harm's way for the last 65 years.

Mama despised the Nazis, and when she was awarded the "cherished" mother cross, she threw it at the feet of a Gestapo henchman. Hitler needed more able bodied men to serve in the military and encouraged women to have more babies, preferably boys. That infuriated Mama. The local officials placed her on the blacklist. Papa cautioned Mama not to fall into their trap. It

7

would give the Nazis more ammunition against her. Emotions got the best of her and she couldn't control what she felt deep inside.

Mama and Papa knew what was about to happen, and were making plans should it be necessary for her to flee the Gestapo. After the incident, everything went downhill rapidly. To make things worse, Mama was hospitalized with an intestinal disorder. The doctors had a difficult time pinpointing the exact problem, and would have to do exploratory surgery to find the source of the infection. During the procedure, she was in grave danger of not surviving.

After four weeks in the hospital, Mama came home a weak woman. She never recovered. The stress of war and the uncertainty of staying in Heidelberg took its toll.

Hitler's men were making preparations to eliminate her. Mama and Papa had a radio they used to listen to enemy stations to discover the real truth. They placed a towel over their heads, so no light was seen coming from the dial. The news heard on the German channels, could not be verified and most everything was a lie. Many people resorted to listening to enemy stations such as Radio London. This was a common practice. But should the Nazis find out, it was death carried out by firing squad. Mama and Papa were very careful not to arouse any suspicion.

Papa warned Mama to be careful who she spoke to in the apartment. He suspected there might be a spy among the women. Mama got acquainted with a few of them and they often discussed the war. They knew nothing was true coming across the airwaves Hitler controlled. Mama confided in her neighbor Frau Huber and told her she heard on Radio London we were losing the war.

Unbeknownst to Mama, Frau Huber's husband, an SS officer, was making preparations to have her arrested. There was no reason to distrust Frau Huber. She didn't arouse any suspicion among the women, and they didn't keep anything from her. She was a

> The women discovered they had a spy in their midst who leaked the information to her SS husband.

friendly woman, offering the women coffee and cake whenever they met for

Kaffeeklatsch. After the information leaked out that Frau Huber's husband was high up in the Nazi party, the women kept to themselves, afraid the Nazis might come looking.

It wasn't long until the Gestapo called Mama in for questioning, and when the topic of listening to enemy stations came up, Mama vehemently denied she was involved. She told them she was not in possession of a radio. She knew it would mean death. They also called Papa in but let him go without further inquiries. It was not clear why the Nazis didn't suspect Papa, but only Mama.

Mama and Papa were discussing what course of action to take in light of the recent developments. They both knew time was running out, and she would have to flee the city. It was incomprehensible to accept the thought of having to lose his wife and children. Papa couldn't sleep anymore and broke out in cold sweats.

He was strategizing how to smuggle us out of the city without tipping off the Nazis. The next night when we heard the sirens and headed to the bomb shelter as we had previously done, we were not allowed to enter. Instead, we had to go to the abandoned slaughterhouse across the street. We were classified as enemies of the state, which also included Jewish people and other "undesirables" like us.

Mama was taken to the Gestapo headquarters numerous times where they interrogated her for many hours. We feared she suffered torture and sexual harassment. She would never let us in on what transpired, but she cried a lot and we were very sad for her.

Mama tried not to alarm the girls, and told them everything would turn out okay, but Herta had an inkling something was up. She overheard Mama and Papa's conversations. She was very frightened of the thought of leaving Heidelberg and not knowing where we would end up.

At the end, the Nazis found Mama guilty of using a radio to listen to enemy stations. We were deprived of food and basic necessities for our survival. When she went to buy food, nobody offered to help her. The registers were closed. The store employees, afraid of Hitler, didn't want to endanger themselves. It became clear we could not stay in Heidelberg any longer.

2

FLEEING HITLER

In the summer of 1944, Mama was to appear before the *Ortsgruppenleiter* "administrator", in charge of local affairs. He took pity on the Berger family and relayed to Mama, the Nazis were about to arrest her. We children were to be sent to a Nazi orphanage.

He strongly urged Mama to take items on her journey she could carry without alerting anybody in the apartment. He told her to make it quick; the Nazis were closing in on her. That evening, preparations were made to move out under the cover of darkness.

The time had arrived, and we faced the hard fact, we had to leave our home, perhaps for good. Mama took the girls aside and explained to them the best she could, that we would be leaving during the night. This was very frightening for the girls and especially Herta, who shouldered most of the responsibilities of watching over us, especially me.

Where would we be going on such a short notice? Mama didn't have a destination in mind, but after racking her brain, the only option she thought of, was to go to Berlin where her father lived. However, she hadn't heard from him for a long time.

She wasn't crazy about going to see him since their relationship was somewhat strained. We were desperate to leave, and it was the only option open to us. Mama wasn't about to leave us in Heidelberg without her; who knows what might have happened to us, surrounded by ugly party members who would have thrown us to the wolves.

She kept assuring us children all would be well. We were going to see her dad for a little vacation and we would be safe there. The thought of riding a train on a long journey seemed exciting to the girls who had never left home before. Mama told them, Opa had a little farm with a horse and cows. Herta asked Mama if she could ride the horse, and Mama said, "I don't see why not."

It was a huge responsibility for Mama to look after us, especially during these times. At the same time, there was strength in numbers and that may have helped us in the midst of battle. At times, the Russians had compassion when they saw Mama with us malnourished and defenseless children by her side. In one case it saved all of our lives.

Hitler's surrogates were arrogant stopping at nothing to please the Führer – maybe just to save their skin, or perhaps Hitler might throw some crumbs their way.

After Papa placed us on the train car, he felt suicidal. But what would that accomplish? He pulled himself together and did what he had to do.

His faith kept him strong and he believed God would bring us through this terrible time and make a way for us to come back home in a miraculous way. We had no contact with Papa for better than one year.

The train was mainly used for troop transport heading east to the war front. The young German soldiers were a bit puzzled why a young woman with four little children was traveling with them.

With bitter sweetness, we saw Heidelberg disappear as the city lights became ever so dim, but at the same time our angst subsided. Nonetheless, Mama was careful in choosing her words as she talked to the soldiers. She didn't want to arouse any suspicion that we were running from Hitler.

The soldiers asked her where we were going, and she said that we were on our way to see her dad who needed us to take care of him as he was getting on in years. For the young soldiers it wasn't a joy ride where they were going, and they figured, there was a good chance they would never come back alive.

We were like cattle led to slaughter, which was especially true for these young men as they were forced to fight the vengeful Russians. For the Berger family, the immediate future looked grim as dangers lurked at every turn.

> We were like cattle led to slaughter, which was true for these young soldiers as they were forced to fight the vengeful Russians. For the Berger family, the immediate future looked dim as dangers lurked at every turn.

The German soldiers, merely kids, were frightened as the train moved ever so slowly to the East. We engaged in conversation and discovered that some of the men didn't live far from us.

Something incredible happened when they began to sing and play with their harmonicas they had stashed away in their pockets. My sisters and Mama joined in and the train became a happy place as it traveled through bombed out cities. The music and songs took away the apprehension of fighting in a foreign land.

Mama kept vigil and never let her guard down. There was a real possibility the train would derail. Sabotage was prevalent, especially towards the end of the war. She tried to sleep but it was useless, watching us every moment to make sure we were safe.

We eventually made it to Berlin, and met Opa in *Spreewerder* on the outskirts of the city. The girls thought it peculiar that grandfather's Berlin dialect was difficult to understand. Mama spoke the Berlin dialect without a hitch.

Again, she didn't want anybody knowing where we came from because we were far from being out of the woods. Mama was still on guard, and carefully chose her words when speaking to the local people.

You couldn't trust anybody. Hitler encouraged people to snitch on each other to turn their brothers, sisters, mothers and fathers into the police. They conspired to stay in favor with the local Nazis and to avoid being arrested. It was quite common for the Nazi party to drum up charges against you.

Opa took us on a short boat ride to his place. How exciting. None of us had ever been on a boat. It was a short trip to his home, but nonetheless, it was enjoyable, to say the least. We were sprayed with water, licking the cool drops of water as they landed on our dry lips.

It was a beautiful sunny day, a little on the warm side, which made the trip refreshing. When we were at Opa's home, care packages arrived from Papa, a welcoming sight since we had left with only the basic necessities.

We didn't know Opa, and he didn't know us, but soon we became acquainted and made the place our home. We tried to wipe out the bad memories of the last couple of weeks, and started playing games, keeping our grandparents awake. It was incredible; we played the same type of games as the kids in the U.S., such as hopscotch and hide and seek. What a small world we live in where kids all over enjoy much the same things whether it is in America, Europe or Africa.

We were well-mannered, but every so often my sisters got carried away when they screamed and laughed, just being full of life. In contrast, as we came to Berlin we were shell-shocked, but things were much better now. If only for a moment, it was worth it all! It was a good thing we didn't know the tough times ahead.

My sisters had the time of their life out in the country and not hemmed in like in Heidelberg. We were finally able to eat enough and stay clean. Opa had running hot and cold water with a bathtub. Oh, what luxury!

Herta said to Gerlinde, "Let's go and play with the animals." It sounded fabulous to Gerlinde, and Helga. It was time to investigate, and my sisters checked out the place. Herta led the way to the barn and pointed out the exciting things along the way. They ran across five brown cows in the barn, chickens, and rabbits along with a little red tractor nearby which Opa used to farm the place.

Too bad, I was too little to participate in their adventures. I wouldn't have missed that for anything. My sisters played with the rabbits, reaching into their well-kept cages.

They loved their soft, cuddly fur and their long ears, which they tried to tie into a knot. The rabbits didn't appreciate that, and let them know by scratching them with their sharp claws. Well, it was time to check out other places and play with animals that would be more accommodating.

The girls were frolicking through the rest of the barn, when they came across chickens with nests full of eggs. Herta said to Gerlinde not to touch the eggs in fear they might drop and break them on the cement floor. The eggs were mostly brown and white in color, just like the chickens. Helga couldn't help but touch everything, putting things into her mouth she shouldn't have.

Herta couldn't always watch her. She, herself, was too busy investigating all the exciting things. It was tempting to collect the eggs, but they were afraid of breaking them. Opa knew exactly how many eggs there were out in the barn, and even if one was missing, he would have known.

What my sisters didn't count on were two huge roosters. One of the roosters was plain white, wearing a fiery-red comb, making it look fierce. Herta said to my sisters: *seit vorsichtig,* "Be careful, and don't get too close." The other rooster was mostly brown, with beautiful green and blue feathers throughout the tail, glistening in myriad colors. They all came to the conclusion that it would be best to leave them alone.

Both threatened to attack my sisters with their sharp beaks and talons, which resembled daggers ready for battle. The three of them decided to move away from these menacing animals and seek a safer place around the farmhouse.

There was the haystack in the barn, and a perfect playground. It looked so inviting and it was as though it was calling out to them, "Please play in my soft hay, I am lonely."

It didn't take long; my sisters built tunnels and rolled around in the haystack that made hide and seek exciting. Herta was the quickest; she had built her tunnel in no time.

She gave Gerlinde and Helga a hand to complete their job, connecting the three tunnels. Gophers didn't have anything over them. What a great engineering job, but there was always the danger of the tunnels collapsing and burying my sisters alive.

These thoughts never entered their minds. They were having too much fun rolling around in the hay. The smell of hay penetrated their nostrils and made them sneeze almost nonstop. It was no deterrent until Opa caught up with them, and he was not pleased.

They were having a great time at his expense, however. Had my sisters lost something in the hay, like a bobby pin for instance, the cows could have become very sick had they eaten it. The adventure came to an early end. Nothing could top what they had experienced the last couple of hours.

With sadness, they left the barn, their dresses smelling like a silo, and hay still embedded in their hair that made them look like Brunhilde. My sisters had to retreat into the house and play with their dolls they dragged along. Mama made the dolls. After all, she was a seamstress, and a good one. If you glanced at her creations, they were lifelike.

One could say Opa was self-sufficient. He raised his own beef, chickens, and rabbits. There was no need to go to the grocery store, unless he had to purchase salt, etc. During these days, it was a real plus not having to depend on the stores as they ran out of basic food items. Mama and my sisters wished they could have stayed there to wait out the war, but it wasn't meant to be.

We stayed with Opa a few more days when our relationship became strained. I can totally understand that. We had turned his life upside down. Feeding us, probably caused his food reserves to shrink, and there weren't quite as many chickens and eggs around as there were before we came on the scene.

Opa was a bricklayer by profession with extraordinary talents that allowed him to add another room to the home to make it a little more roomy and comfortable. That is where his talents stopped. Opa was a mean man who spanked my sisters with the least provocation, especially Helga who was three years old. She would annoy him to no end. Maybe she did it deliberately!

Mama was afraid to stand up to him because he had threatened her with a lumber ax earlier. He made it a habit to beat his sweet, defenseless wife, a kind woman. He took his anger out on his horse, which made the animal mean. At one point, the horse bit Mama in the stomach and reopened the wound she received earlier when she was in the hospital.

We never felt safe living with Opa with his sudden outbursts of anger. It certainly wasn't a peaceful place; any little thing would set him off. I was told Opa would on a regular basis, throw food his wife prepared for him against the kitchen wall in a fiery rage. What set him off is anybody's guess. It made the place appear ghastly; walls were covered with all kinds of food, causing him to paint the kitchen quite often. One didn't have to ask what they had for dinner; you could read the menu on the wall.

All this time, we had angst Opa would turn us into the police, who would have been more than happy to interrogate Mama again. We were by now getting a little uneasy around him, and Mama sought a place where we could go and be in relative safety.

One of Opa's sons perished, run over by a car when he was 5 years old. It was a terrible tragedy that haunted Mama all her life. Whenever she talked about it, her eyes swelled up, and she began to weep. Her little brother Ernst, *"Der Dicke,"* the chubby one, was close to her age, and loved to tell stories to make people laugh.

Whenever she thought about her little brother, she saw his image, which was forever engraved in her mind. He was such a happy-go-lucky kid and full of life. He had a knack for telling exciting stories, although somewhat embellished. His friends and neighbors gathered around him for hours to hear his latest renditions.

One fateful day, January 27th 1914, Mama, who was a young girl of 7, crossed the street with her little brother Ernst in tow. A car traveling through town at a high rate of speed clipped my mother, but drove over her brother, crushing his chest.

He died minutes later in his mother's arms, and his last words were: *Meine liebe Mutti,* "I love you, Mommy," and he breathed his last.

Her other brother Karl was fighting at the Russian front in 1942, so Opa was without his sons to help on the farm. Karl was far away, and no one knew if he would come back from the war front. I am sure these tragedies of losing his youngest son, and perhaps Karl as well, left deep scars which caused him much grief. We heard later, Mama's oldest brother Karl fell on the Russian front February the 24th 1942 and was buried in a mass grave.

One beautiful sunny summer morning, Mama saw her father place me on his bicycle along with his farming gear, including his scythe. His plan was to kidnap me, but Mama interrupted him. The race was on, and she ran after him as fast as she could with all her strength and finally, after closing the gap, she caught up with him. It was apparent he wasn't going to give me up without a fight.

Mama was a tough lady, and it would be foolish to pick a fight with her. She used everything, and anything, to protect us children, much like a mother grizzly to protect her cubs.

She snatched me from his clutches as he fell to the ground. His entire farming implements scattered. He was slower than Mama, and couldn't get to his feet quick enough. By the time he realized what had happened, I was safely in Mama's arms, and the fight was over.

As we were about to leave Opa, Mama and my sisters became sick. Was it something they ate or drank while we stayed with her father? In a miraculous way, we found a doctor who examined Mama and my sisters, only to find out, they had contracted hoof and mouth disease when drinking the milk from Opa's infected cows. I don't know if Opa and Oma got sick, but we were in too much of a hurry to leave and never did find out the result. Later, Opa's cattle were destroyed, and the farm was quarantined.

The doctor gave Mama and my sisters a powerful medication which cured them in a few days, and they were well enough to travel. Opa's kind neighbors invited us to stay with them, giving Mama and my sister's precious time to recover. Our departure was at hand, but where would our journey take us? How would we secure transportation? These were all open ended questions that only God knew. Mama wrestled with these thoughts all night long and decided to travel to *Pommern,* "Pomerania" East Prussia where Mama had close relatives who might offer us a place to stay.

15

My sisters asked Mama where we were going, and how we were going to obtain food. Mama assured us, God would provide. I don't know how she kept going, not sleeping, always alert to potential danger. She was a super mom.

While we were in *Spreewerder*, we saw many young blonde women pushing babies around in their carriages. On occasions, young men walked beside them, who we thought were their husbands. There was nothing unusual about the scene, except, there were too many of them. The majority of young men were fighting in the war. So, why were these young men not fighting on the Russian Front?

We discovered later, Hitler was pairing blond men and women with blue eyes to promote the master race. Actually, it was a baby factory for his Arian race. Hitler was striving for a far superior nation.

We made preparations to travel to *Küstrin* where my mother was born, but to our misfortune, we found the town was used by the Germans as the staging area to engage the Red Army. Going there would place us in even greater danger. The Russians were poised against the Germans in a terrific tank battle where five thousand soldiers from both sides perished and many more were injured.

Küstrin was a famous city where Alfred von Tirpitz was born. He was the secretary of the Prussian Navy under Kaiser Friedrich the First. Also *Küstrin* on the Oder River was the gateway to Berlin. Later in the war, Küstrin was jammed with refugees fleeing the Red Army.

We had to find transportation, and that wasn't easy, most places were bombed by the Russians, making travel hazardous. Fortunately, we located a train station, but to walk there was too far, as my sisters didn't have appropriate shoes, and we were physically exhausted. I was small and always had the luxury of riding on the cart in the summer or the sled in the winter. As long as I held on firmly, all would be well.

We heard that horrible things occurred, as the Russians pushed the German military from their garrison, and made Küstrin their *Kommandantur* "headquarters". A multitude of Germans were transported by trucks to Russia. Their final destination was Siberia, where they were enslaved by the hundreds of thousands.

Mama and we kids boarded the train, hoping it would take us where Mama's relatives lived. The trip was short, and uneventful, for which we were grateful. We sure didn't need any more excitement.

As always, Mama was alert to anything which would place us in danger. After two hours on the train, we arrived at our Uncle Manfred and Aunt Anne's place who were elated to see us. After climbing down from the train car, our tired bodies fell straight into their arms.

The girls enjoyed their home; the house was nice and roomy. The yard was huge, a perfect place to play hide and seek, among other games.

Uncle Manfred was the principal of the school, and as it is common in Germany, the principal lived in the same building where school was held. Uncle Manfred was a true Prussian teacher, patient to a certain degree, and always business like. Most German teachers in those days were strict.

Mama told Uncle Manfred not to be so stern with us children. She reminded him, they weren't in class, and to give them some slack. My sisters were having fun playing in his big yard and doing things any kids love. Uncle Manfred's neighbors knew by now, he had company when they heard my sisters early in the morning laughing and carrying on.

In the morning, Uncle Manfred enjoyed smoking his cigars. It wasn't long before the smoke filled the entire house. Mama approached him and asked him why he couldn't go outside to puff. He told her in no uncertain terms to mind her own business, and if she didn't like it, she was welcome to leave anytime time she wishes.

After being with Uncle Manfred a couple of weeks, things deteriorated even more. Mama continued with her verbal assaults. Uncle Manfred had enough, and threw us out into the street. Now we were homeless again. However, his daughter Monika took pity on us and invited us to stay with her for the time being. She was kind, and allowed us to stay with her, even though she didn't have a lot of room herself.

Monika was married to a *Hauptmann*, "Captain". He was a rather big man in stature, and loved playing with us kids, throwing us into the air and catching us on the way down. The girls loved that, and asked him to throw them high in the air, over, over. This could have continued for hours, had he not worn out, and asked the girls to give him a break.

He had to promise to continue roughhousing the next morning. Mama couldn't get along with Monika either, and we were forced to move out. Couldn't Mama keep her mouth shut for a while longer? We had such a great time; finally we had a big playmate who made things fun again.

Mama broke the news to us that we had to leave Monika's place and we'd be pulling our little cart towards *Küstrin*. Herta couldn't understand why we had to leave, and travel to Küstrin where the Russians were planning to destroy the city. She kept asking Mama why we couldn't stay with Aunt Monika a little longer. Mama was getting a little tired of Herta asking all these questions when Mama told her to be quiet while she was deep in thought, strategizing our future plans.

Being homeless presented a huge problem. There was no place we were welcomed. After talking with people, it was confirmed, *Küstrin* was a likely target for the Soviets.

3

THE RUSSIAN ONSLAUGHT

Instead of traveling to Küstrin, Mama traveled to Trabuhn. Due to the chaotic conditions, we could not stay in *Trabuhn* either. We hitched a ride on a train which took us to *Königsberg*, East Prussia; it is now part of Russia.

Mama kept her eyes open for the Gestapo, still operating in the war zone, but seen less frequently now. For reasons unknown, the Red Army largely spared *Königsberg* for the time, whilst other towns west, were destroyed.

We lingered in *Königsberg*, and the Russians retreated, due to isolated victories by the German Army. Again, the farmers plowed their fields and planted for the coming summer harvest.

Hitler's propaganda chief Göbbels, told the people not to worry, no Red Army soldier will set foot on Prussian soil. A similar scenario played itself out in WWI when the Red Army retreated and never returned. An uneasy peace returned, the kids were back in school, and the shuttered businesses reopened.

The Germans were shocked, when on October the 21st 1944 the Russians crossed the border, and this time in force. They were ready for a fight the Germans weren't prepared for. It was too late to flee, and as a result, people were slaughtered by the thousands. The Red Army didn't spare any town. How wrong was Goebbels when he stated that the Germans had nothing to worry about!

> In October of 1944, the Russians crossed the border, and this time in force. It was too late for the civilians to flee; the result was they were slaughtered by the thousands.

It wasn't long after we had left Monika's home, when *the Russians overran the German military base, and the town of Neudamm by Küstrin was leveled, January 30th 1945.*

Mama attempted to contact our relatives, but they were not there any longer. Their homes were destroyed, and what happened to these folks? They were probably shot, or transported to Russia. There was an outside chance they evaded the Russians; I hope to God they did.

February the 4th 1945, we traveled by foot to Darmietzel and were escorted to a house by four Russian officers, wearing white gloves. My sisters were scared to death, knowing the Russians had arrived. Mama tried to comfort us, saying we had plenty of time to get out of town.

February the 11ᵗʰ 1945, while in Darmietzel, the Russians ordered us east, and we were forced to travel on foot. Unspeakable tragedies occurred during the night as we hunkered down in an old, dark, rat infested cellar. With God's help, Mama planned to move west when she heard the Red Army was within twenty kilometers. People became nervous with good reason, and panicked. Mama made sure she had everything packed for another long trip, including our feather beds.

February of 1945, it was bitter cold, and during the night, a blizzard turned the landscape into a winter wonderland. Mama wanted to move out after dark, but the mayor of *Küstrin* whom she knew as a young girl, got wind of it, and discouraged Mama from leaving due to the treacherous conditions.

February 11ᵗʰ and 12ᵗʰ, the Russians ordered everybody out of Darmietzel and moved the people to Neudamm. From there, we walked to Landsberg, a distance of forty-two kilometers. When we arrived in Landsberg, we were at the point of collapse. Mama dragged us to an old abandoned schoolhouse.

We arrived in Landsberg at four in the afternoon, Soldiner Strasse 10. Herr Krause, the head teacher, welcomed us to stay with him for the time being. Landsberg on the Warthe River was in engulfed in flames. The old schoolhouse was later converted by the Russians as their command center.

We were trying to flee the Russians, but there was another enemy wanting to annihilate us. Our bodies and clothes were infested with lice. No matter what we did to get rid of them, they always came back with a vengeance.

People were fleeing any way they could. Those that had access to horses, or oxen, were the lucky ones. They pulled their wagons packed high with their household goods.

Mama didn't listen to the mayor, and got hold of a sled that night, with me riding on top, tucked securely in between the feather beds. Off we went into the cold night with much snow on the ground. In spite of it all, we made good time heading out of town. We avoided taking deep breaths; our nostrils froze shut due to the severe cold. Our lungs could have been damaged by the sub-zero temperature. It was time we moved under a roof. We met a young man with a team of horses, who offered us a ride back into town. He convinced Mama the road conditions were getting worse and worse up ahead, and it would be best to turn back to *Küstrin*. We hopped on the wagon with the help of the young man who lifted us and our sled onto his farm cart.

Whenever the Russians went to war, it was in the dead of winter, as the winter was their ally. Both Hitler and Napoleon found out the hard way. The spring was a nightmare as well. The mud made the roads impassable, nothing could move, including the horses. The vehicles sank into the mud and got buried up to the axles in dark, black mud. As for the horses and mules, it became their grave.

A huge mass of people left the city. The Red Army was now at the outskirts of town and everybody who could, left. It was as though time stood still, chaos was everywhere. In a short time, the Red Army overtook the refugees.

Those who could turned back and were hoping for a miracle to escape this nightmare. They were hoping the German Army could push the Russians back across the border like they did at the end of WWI.

There was a long pause by the Russian Army, and it appeared they were moving back across the border. Again, the people returned to their homes and resumed the normal life, briefly interrupted earlier. The children were going back to school, the farmers got ready for spring planting, and everything was back to normal. The Russians regrouped.

GERMAN TIGER TANK

The German Army had a few successes and people were lulled into a false sense of optimism. We lingered for a while until the latter part of spring. The snow had mostly melted by now when Mama secured a cart for future journeys when the roads were clear for travel. It was early April of 1944.

Soon the Russians broke through the German defenses again, and things became even more chaotic. The Soviet soldiers were cruel, and didn't spare anyone who got in their way. We were on our way back to *Neudamm,* where the Red Army met us in force and we were trapped, with no place to go. The city had been leveled by the first wave of the Russian shock troops earlier. Neudamm is part of Poland and its name is Debno Lubuskie in the province of Zachodniopomorski, it was the former German province of Pommern.

> Stalin ordered the troops to rape; kill the German women along with their children.

The Russian forces were similar to the Mongols when they invaded Europe. Stalin ordered the troops to rape and kill the German women along with their children who were considered the enemy of the Soviet Union. They spared just a few. Most women were murdered after they were gang raped. It is estimated that the Russian soldiers raped over two million women.

It was a strategic area for both the Germans as well as the Russians. Another tank battle ensued where the German Tiger tanks were engaging the Russian T 34 tanks in close combat. The Russians were turning out the tanks by the thousands. Hitler could not keep up with that kind of production.

There was absolute chaos wherever you turned. Road jams were everywhere and the going was slow. It was survival, and everybody was looking out for themselves.

Mama was looking for a place to spend the night, when she came upon a big house, where we found refuge.

German refugees, women and children, were trying to warm up and find food. Herta couldn't believe her eyes when she saw a huge Russian tank. It crushed everything in its path. It was a frightening sight, and dreadful, especially at such a young age.

People were fleeing the city any way they could. There were horse drawn wagons filled to the brim with rations they took out of their houses. The road was wall to wall with people and all kinds of wagons pulled mostly by horses and oxen.

The tanks refused to stop, and crushed the refugees relentlessly. The iron monsters flattened the wagons with their tank treads. Mama told me she saw crushed wagons still attached to the horses and oxen. The animals were dismembered by the tanks, along with the women and children. It was pure hell.

Mama was tortured by the tragedy, and asked why the Red Army showed total disregard to civilians who had nothing to do with the war. We were in the middle of this chaos, and with God's help, we escaped.

There was cannon fire all around us as the Russians fired on anything that moved. Soldiers in battle gear followed close behind the humongous tanks for cover. My sisters ran for their lives, followed by Mama who was pulling the little wagon. I was still sitting on top of the wagon and holding on for dear life.

After we traveled for a few kilometers, totally exhausted, we pulled over to the side of the road to catch our breath. We were hoping none of the Russian soldiers would carry us off.

Mama wanted to return to Trabuhn, not far from Küstrin, where my Uncle Karl had his flour mill. Grinding flour for the community was his business. He was a strong young man, and Mama told me he carried two hundred pound sacks of flour without a problem.

My uncle's windmill

We arrived in Trabuhn by train, only to find the town destroyed along with my uncle's windmill from the constant shelling by tanks and cannons as well as bombers. There wasn't much left of the mill, just black giant burned wooden blades, still smoldering, lying in pieces on the ground. The destruction occurred not long before we arrived. We were grateful we were spared.

The mill had only one exterior wall still standing and the interior was gutted by fire. This touched Mama's heart, seeing the destruction. She remembered walking to the mill as a little girl, buying flour for her mom to bake bread and cakes for special occasions. All she could do now was to hang onto the fond memories of yesteryear.

A Soviet refugee truck.

Mama was searching for my uncle's wife and two children in vain; their home was leveled. We don't know what happened to them. She suspected they were evicted by the Russians and taken by truck or train to the interior of Russia. It was an eerie feeling not seeing one soul in the towns overrun by the Russians. Only the ruins were left where once people lived and thrived.

4

HORRORS OF WAR

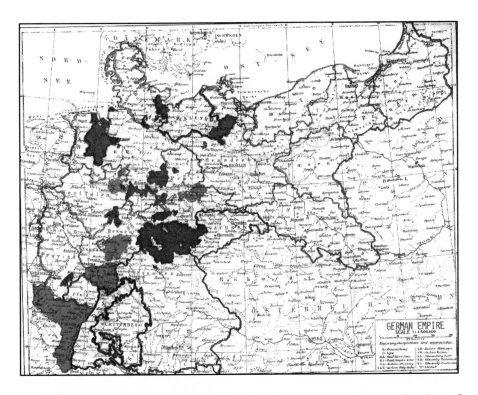

In October 1944 the Red Army broke through the eastern border of Prussia. They were swifter than a leopard and fiercer than wolves at dawn. It was our first introduction to a Russian soldier, scary for everybody.

Helga was four, I was two at the beginning of this hell journey, Gerlinde was seven and Herta was nine years of age, going on ten. We were in *Königsberg* for a short time, when Mama packed us up, destination unknown. No point to linger any longer due to lack of food and shelter. We were very fortunate to have found a house, a place of relative safety for the night.

> The Red Army broke through the eastern border of Prussia. They were swifter than a leopard and fiercer than wolves at dawn.

The house's inhabitants were many single women and their children trying to escape the war. Their husbands were at war and could have been anywhere in Europe, Africa and far away from their families.

After we settled in for the night, and slept in one of the makeshift beds, there was a thump on the front door. We were introduced to Ivan, dirty, drunk and very hungry. He helped himself to the noodle soup prepared by the women. Nobody dared to stop him with his threatening rifle swung over his shoulder.

It didn't take long for many more drunk soldiers to arrive. They made themselves at home, always looking to see who they could rob of jewelry or whatever else they could steal from these women. The children, tucked under their mother's arms, were in a state of shock and sobbing uncontrollably.

Mama was wise to hide her jewelry in the corner of the room. They didn't locate Mama's vital items needed for a time like this. Others were not as fortunate. As the women huddled together, afraid to move, Mama said to them, *habt keine Angst vor den Russen. Ich werde Ihnen entgegend treten, und nichts wird Euch passieren.* "I am going to approach the Russians, and nothing will happen to you." After a short time at the house, Mama approached the Russian soldiers as they came near. She was known as the *Guardian Angel* among the women. She resembled a Prussian general, showing no fear while in grave danger herself. Some of the soldiers, however, did enter the house to secure it, making certain they wouldn't be in danger themselves.

> Mama approached the Russians without fear. The women knew her as the guardian angel.

The Russians were shocked by her lack of fear, which literally disarmed them while they were still carrying menacing weapons of all sorts around their waist and rifles draped over their shoulders. She knew enough Russian by now to communicate to them not to harm these defenseless women and their children. The result was, many of the soldiers packed up and left the house.

God provided her with the courage she needed at a time like this. German women depended on Mama. In spite of everything, there continued to be gross mayhem. Mama facing death, continued to rescue countless women and children from these savages.

Outside of the house, the Russians were driving past with their gigantic military vehicles, vodka bottles in hand, celebrating their victory over Hitler's Third Reich.

The Russians worshipped their vodka and would do anything to get it. Mama traded whatever she had, including cigarettes, vodka, or schnapps for food. I don't know how she obtained the contraband, but it saved us from starving.

These soldiers were undisciplined and unkempt. Blood ran down their faces from cuts of broken liquor bottles. They had no bottle openers, and broke the necks of the bottles by slamming them against their rifles, cutting themselves mercilessly as they drank.

Mama couldn't save all the women from these bandits. The soldiers were inebriated, raping the women one by one. If one refused their advances, she was shot. The women were screaming, and the children were crying for their mothers. Mama was able to help the women at the beginning, but after the Russians had too much vodka, they were unstoppable.

While all this was happening, a neatly dressed, tall Russian officer, obviously not drunk, showed up and this pandemonium stopped immediately. You could tell by his demeanor he meant business.

He ordered the soldiers out of the house and normalcy returned. The children were frantically searching for their mothers in the dark, feeling their way through the blackness. There was much relief as the mothers and their children were reunited and calm was restored, but for how long? After the Russian officer left, unspeakable atrocities returned.

Mama and my sisters heard cannons fired from their big behemoths, "tanks" accompanied by the rattle of their treads as they lumbered past the buildings. The big Russian T34 tanks would not drive around the houses, but drove through them. The result was the houses sustained huge holes throughout. All that was left were the collapsed roofs and partial walls.

An elderly German man came through the door. It looked as though he had been homeless for a long time, much like us. His clothes were soiled and tattered. The jacket he wore was torn at the sleeves. Looking into his face, he had sunken cheeks and the color of his face was a pale grey. Mama saw his plight. She knew he had lost all hope. Mama asked him where he came from, and he said his home was *Königsberg.*

He had been on the run for over a year trying to move west and out of the reach of the Red Army. His name was Otto Paulus, perhaps we were related. He didn't know Mama, but the two were drawn to each other. They grew up in Königsberg, and could have been neighbors at one time.

There was much to discuss, but in the circumstances, it had to wait. The objective was to get this poor man help before the Russians noticed him.

He obtained a few dry pieces of bread along the way and he was willing to share the food with us. A closer look revealed he had no footwear. He said one of the Russians took his shoes and left him in the snow with just his socks. Mama checked his feet to see if he was able to walk with his frost bitten toes.

He was in need of medical attention, but finding a doctor was next to impossible. His toes hadn't turned black yet, but anymore cold, he would lose them and his feet. Mama got hold of some petroleum jelly and rubbed it on his toes. The practice was handed down through generations for curing frostbites. He stayed another night, and improved, whereby he was able to walk without much pain. During the night, a Russian officer came in and the occupants were frightened at the sight. But he had no evil intent. He warmed himself. One of the women gave him a bowl of hot potato soup.

He wasn't menacing, and just wanted to rest and warm up. The Russian officer noticed Otto in the corner of the room and asked him to join him. Understandably, Otto was reluctant. The officer was well armed, and if he wanted to kill him, it would have been easy. He had pity on the man and asked him why he wasn't wearing any shoes. Otto told him, one of the Russian soldiers took his boots.

He told the German, he could have the pair of extra boots he had with him. Otto couldn't believe his ears. He said under his breath, "*Ein Russe gibt mir die Stiefel die er später selbst braucht.* "This Russian is giving me his boots he himself may need later."

The German tried the boots on for size, they were a perfect fit. He was so happy he jumped for joy. His feet started to warm up which gave him renewed hope and energy. Mama was elated for his good fortune, and thanked the Russian officer. A couple of hours later, the officer made his way out of the house and disappeared in the black, cold night.

It wasn't long though before Red Army infantry soldiers came through the door and made themselves at home at the expense of the women and children. Mama was cautious, and prepared as much as she could, hiding anything valuable as she did previously, and made sure we kids were hidden from their view.

Otto Paulus crawled under the staircase, out of the sight of the soldiers, afraid they might detect him. As time went on, the liquor flowed freely. Things got ugly in a hurry. They chased after the women. To them, it was a game just to see which ones they could rape. Each night was much like the night before as lives were lost, children became orphans, and many were without food and warm clothes.

Otto crawled quietly out from under the staircase and attempted to sneak out the back door. A Russian noticed him, and asked him what he was doing here. Mama stepped between the two men, in total disregard for her own life. She explained to the soldier, the older gentleman was just passing through on his way to his home.

The soldier didn't buy the story for one moment. The Russian noticed he was wearing a pair of brand new Russian military boots which sealed his fate. The soldier asked him how he obtained them. Otto told him a Russian officer gave them to him.

We watched in horror, when we saw the soldier take his pistol and shoot the poor man point blank. He fell to the ground outside of the door, mortally wounded. Mama and my sisters wept bitterly as they witnessed an innocent man die. In spite of it all, she had to stay strong to live another day.

When the morning came, we were on our way to the next town. We entered *Skeuditz* in mid-morning. Mama was always looking for a place to stay. It was never too early to find a refuge for the night.

Mama located a house hidden behind tall trees and shrubs. It was as good of a place we could have found. Mama stowed her sled behind the house within easy reach in the event we needed to flee. The evening came, and to our surprise, it remained relatively quiet even though everybody knew the Russians were fighting the Germans close by. The women were praying for God to protect them from these savages.

The town's people didn't have to wait long. The Red Army troops arrived in troves. It was the same story all over again. They made a mess of things, breaking furniture, and had their way with the women who were cowering in the corners of the house. The children were crying for their mothers who were begging the soldiers to stop torturing them.

5

THE UNLIKELY SAVIOR

We were hunkered down in the town of Skeuditz when a Russian officer stepped into the house. We believed he was sent by God to protect the women and children from these marauders. The officer took a liking to us children and played with us, undisturbed by the war brewing outside. He emptied his coat pockets which revealed bread and meat he shared with us which by now were as hard as a rock. Perhaps, he also wished there was no more war and this destruction and killing would stop.

He spoke with authority, but when he was playing with us, he was gentle. At times, he cracked a mischievous smile. He was playing with us and teasing my sisters by hiding candy in his fist just to see who was the quickest to locate the sweet morsels. He threw me in the air, and caught me in nick of time on the way back down. Now this was fun, and for a few moments we forgot there was a war just yards from us. Just in time he saved my sister Herta's life, pushing her out of the way of an incoming tank round which landed inches from her head. Had the officer not moved her away, just one second later, it would have ended in tragedy.

> The Russian officer saved my sister Herta's life by pushing her out of the way from an incoming tank round that landed inches from her.

He told us in German, ich *muss jetzt leider wieder gehen, aber später werde ich wieder zurück kommen.* "He must leave, but he'll be back later to check on us." We never knew his name. We just called him *Herr Offizier* 'Officer'. After he left the house, more soldiers arrived looking for food and schnapps, which was left untouched by the previous bunch. The Russians drank until they passed out. We found them slouched all over the place with their rifles lying across their unprotected bodies. How easy would it have been for one of the women to shoot them? But that would have been sheer suicide.

Some of the women were kidnapped by the soldiers when they left. Their children were cared for by other mothers or grandmothers. These women were never heard from again. They were most likely used to help the Russians cook and clean their clothes, etc.

If a woman put up a struggle, she was killed, and left in the snow to rot.

At times, military vehicles driving through town ran over corpses hidden in the deep snow, packed down by heavy vehicles.

Mama was constantly looking for food and where to spend the next night. She engaged Russians and asked them to share some of their rations with us. They were hungry themselves, and they were looking for food themselves wherever they could find it.

Horses were used by the Russians to pull their howitzers and other military equipment. The animals were malnourished and could no longer function. They collapsed under the stress. In many cases, they were severely injured from hand grenades and other projectiles. These animals were later turned into goulash or soup.

German troops, on the other hand, fighting on the Eastern front, were forever searching for a bite to eat as well, which at times included wild game, grey Russian wolfs and other wild animals. I was told by German soldiers that their experiment making stew out of wolf's meat was a failure and tasted awful.

Mama was forced to cook for the Russian soldiers one particular day, which saved her from attacks, and had she resisted their advances, no doubt, she would have become a statistic. Thank God, Mama was not attacked. My sister Herta was groped by one of the soldiers. She struck him hard with her fist, and he left her alone. With urgency, Mama went looking for another place, less hostile, but where, was the big question? There was no place to hide from battles.

We were caught in the midst of a firefight, with tanks all around us, hearing and seeing the *Stalin Orgeln* whizzing by. In German, *Orgel* is a musical organ. These rockets produced a sound much like an organ after they were fired. It wasn't music to their ears but certain death.

These anti-tank weapons were feared by the German Army. Once they homed in on a target, it was all but over, the rounds penetrated the tank armor and the crew most likely burned to death. To counter their anti-tank weapons, the Germans had one of their own, feared by the Russians, it was the *Panzerfaust*, translated 'tank fist'.

As we walked past burning tanks, Mama saw soldiers on fire trying to escape the incinerated vehicles. It was hell around us as soldiers fired at each other with all sorts of weapons, including tank cannons, rifles and howitzers.

There were mutilated bodies of Germans, as well as Russians, covering the frozen ground. I am certain, some of the soldiers on both sides met their end by land mines as they either drove or walked over them. I can't imagine for one moment, how horrible it must have been for these young men to die like that.

God was with us, and protected us from harm. Not one hair on our heads was singed as we crisscrossed the battlefield. Mama stumbled onto a letter that was near the body of a German soldier killed in battle. At first, she was reluctant to retrieve it, when she saw half of his face was blown off. After she gained enough courage, she picked it up and read it.

Writing to his wife it said: *"the Germans did terrible things to the Russians and the Poles as they conquered their land. They did horrific things to the civilians who were utterly helpless against the force that at the time was unstoppable. It was payback for the Germans, who committed the same atrocities to their people as they were experiencing themselves now."*

After a long journey by foot through the deep snow, we arrived in Darmietzel one more time, where some of Mama's other relatives lived, but found everything destroyed. Mama suspected many of her relatives were raped, shot, or transported to Russia where they were imprisoned.

It was the epitome of brutality as a number of Russian soldiers took a pregnant woman out into the field, raped her repeatedly, then cut her stomach open took out the baby, and bayoneted it. The poor woman was left to die, and then buried in an unmarked grave with the baby. War was hell.

On another occasion, Mama witnessed Polish soldiers take German babies from their mothers, throw them into the air, and on their way down, they were impaled by the soldiers' bayonets. These practices were rare, but they happened.

We didn't find one soul in the Bürgermeister's house and Mama surmised that he, along with his family, were evicted, taken away, or shot. We ventured into their bedroom, and found soft beds still intact and clean. Our tired bodies fell into the soft beds. Mama kept alert, looking, and listening for soldiers who might be coming in to rest their weary bodies, but none ever arrived.

We wished we could have stayed at the mayor's house which had all the comfort of home, but we had to move on, towards the West! We were constantly on the run, never staying more than one night in a particular location, afraid of the Red Army soldiers for obvious reasons.

The Russian women soldiers were rough and tough and liked their vodka, but wouldn't rape anybody. There were times, the Russians kept us alive by sharing their bread, but we had to drink their vodka, and if we refused, they turned angry.

To them, drinking vodka was regarded as a spiritual experience. Without a doubt, if it had not been for the Russians, we would have died of hunger. Some of the Russians were kind, and didn't look to shed innocent blood.

I was too young, and all I can remember was a dark train station, a burned out truck, and the sky turned to blood, probably the result of burning aircraft, or it may have been a town set on fire by the bombers. I was a chubby toddler of two when we left Heidelberg, but during this awful time, I lost much weight. It didn't keep the Russians from playing with me; perhaps it brought back memories of their children they left behind in the motherland. The Russians came up with a new name for me, Ponne. My sisters, relatives and friends still remember me by that name.

Mama found a house late in the afternoon where many Russian soldiers resided. She hesitated a moment as she approached the house, fearing the Russians might do us harm. It was dusk and the night was rapidly approaching. With no place to stay, we reluctantly entered the house.

The Russians ordered Mama to cook for them, but she needed wood for the stove. The house was surrounded by a thick forest, but to venture to the woods was unsafe and wrought with danger. Nearby, constant artillery fire could be heard placing us in great danger. Mama made the decision to enlist my oldest sisters to look for wood. She knew full well, it was extremely dangerous for them to be exposed to the dangers, but the Russians would not allow Mama to leave. Herta and Gerlinde ventured outside pulling the sled into the pitch black night. It was so dark that they couldn't see their hands in front of their face. One of the soldiers was kind enough and gave my sister Herta a flashlight.

Mama prayed to God to protect the girls from harm and to bring them back safely. She reasoned, if she cooked, the Russians would be inclined to offer us some of the cooked food as well, providing my sisters came back alive. From past experience, we were lucky to get just a few crumbs and perhaps a little bit of soup to settle our stomachs. We were easy to please, and it didn't make any difference if the food fell on the floor first, everything was eaten.

They left Helga behind. She would have been too slow to keep pace with Herta and Gerlinde. A short walk from the house, they came upon a grove of pine trees when they struck it rich. They found a pile of wood, fairly dry, covered with a thin layer of snow, and proceeded to load it onto the sled with life giving wood. They loaded the sled with much wood but it was hard for them to pull it through the deep snow. Gerlinde pushed, and Herta pulled.

My sisters' dodged bullets and tank shells as they crisscrossed the battle field. They witnessed things children should never experience. It was dreadful for these young girls as they walked through the battlefield. I could have lost them easily by enemy or friendly fire. This was terrifying for my sisters who never forgot what they had experienced.

Thank God Herta and Gerlinde made it back to the building in one piece where Mama was waiting anxiously for the girls. It was a joyful reunion. They hugged and tears fell to the cold wooden floor. Mama and my sisters dragged the wood inside and didn't waste any time starting up the fire in the stove.

On one of our outings, we found a German helmet, and as Mama turned it over, half of the skull was still encased. We were shell shocked to the bone by what we experienced. It numbed our nerves, nothing stunned us anymore.

There must have been horrific battles. Rifles and other weapons were strewn about. What was heartbreaking, no one was there to give the German or Russian soldiers a proper burial, much less removing their bodies from the battlefield.

It was horrific to see these men from both sides die agonizing deaths. They had parents at home, waiting for their return in vain. There was no one to claim their bodies as they lay on the frozen tundra resembling petrified wood. Never to fight again!

Mama was forever searching for places where we would be out of harm's way, which was no small task, and where to find food to fill our empty stomachs. She found a bunker furnished with furniture and kitchen utensils. Not a soul was living there, nor was there any food.

Mama surmised the place was used for refuge by the German soldiers. We don't know what happened to the Germans, but they were probably shot, which usually was the way it ended.

6

LOST IN THE BLIZZARD

Early the next morning, Mama packed us up again, and we were on our way to who knows where. Many refugees were in a similar situation, and very few had any idea where they were going. All they wanted was to get away from the danger of the Russian forces which were at every turn.

Everybody wanted to escape the war, and on their journeys, they encountered more Russian soldiers, who, for the most part were brutal, looking to see who they could rape and kill. Many women met their end getting shot or relocated to labor camps in Siberia.

We couldn't travel using landmarks as entire towns were erased and buildings were heavily damaged from aerial or tank fire. Nothing looked familiar.

With the sled packed high, and me 'securely' tucked between the heavy blankets, it gave me a bird's eye view of the white landscape. Mama pulled the sled and my sisters walked beside her. She kept an eye on my sisters to make sure all was well. She wasn't overly concerned about me, thinking she packed me tightly between blankets. After Mama and my sisters walked a few kilometers, the weather deteriorated quickly, covering the ground with much snow.

1944 was the coldest winter on record, and we were ill prepared for these arctic conditions. While walking in the deep snow, Herta was horrified when she noticed that I wasn't with them any longer.

Herta frantically yelled to Mama: *Ponne ist nicht mehr bei uns.* "Ponne isn't with us any more." Mama, upon hearing Herta, said in a trembling voice, *Herrgott, wo kann er blos sein.* "God, where could we have lost him?" When she saw the empty spot where I had been, her heart almost stopped. My sisters began to cry, and feared the worse. Mama was lost for words and told my sisters to look hard for any signs that might reveal my whereabouts.

Tears rolled down her cheeks, turning into icicles on her frozen face. She tried hiding her emotions from my sisters, convincing them I would be found.

The big problem was they didn't know how far back they lost me. The conditions were such, finding me in the blizzard was almost impossible.

Mama turned the sled around and backtracked through the howling wind while the snow blinded her as she wiped the icicles off her eyelashes. She tried to follow the tracks of the sled, but by then the storm had intensified and she lost any sign of them.

She wasn't sure if she was headed in the right direction. Should she turn left? Should she turn right? She was at a loss as she navigated through the fields covered with a white blanket of snow. All the while, she heard intermittent gun fire in the distance that sounded like thunder with the accompanying flashes of lightning.

Mama and my sisters had battled through the countryside for a few kilometers, when Mama noticed something ahead which resembled a fallen soldier or perhaps a tree stump. Mama said to my sisters, *seit vorsichtig, da ist was vor uns.* "Be careful, there is something ahead of us." *Mit grossen Jubel fand sie mich im Schnee begraben.* With jubilation she discovered me buried in a snow drift.

With joy, she said, *Gott sei Dank, jetzt haben wir Ihn endlich wieder gefunden.* "Thank God, we finally found him." My sisters gathered around me, pulled me out of my white "prison" with no ill effect. I was just sitting there, fully expecting for them to come back to get me. Herta told me, all I said was, Herti, Herti as I lifted up my arms so she could pull me out of the snowdrift without shedding a tear.

I am sure the ordeal must have been very frightening even at my young age.

Had I moved from the spot, or had Mama decided to take a different route, my fate would have been sealed. I was safe now. I survived the freezing cold, but how were my sisters going to stay alive, never having shoes that fit, or warm clothes in this arctic-type weather?

The night was approaching rapidly, and the opportunity to find a place to seek refuge was fading. Mama made the decision to stay where we were, and we hunkered down the rest of the night. She had heavy blankets and draped them over the sled, creating somewhat of a tent.

The pillows came in handy to protect our heads from the ice and snow. We crawled under the blankets, laid our heads on the soft pillows, hoping the cold night wouldn't take our lives. The snow was still coming down hard, and the howling wind lifted the corners of our blankets, exposing our feet to the arctic air. Soon, we were under a solid white blanket, actually insulating us from the cold. From the distance, all one could see was a white mound. We heard the howling of the wolves during the night, hoping and praying they would not come to investigate, but they never came near. We heard cannon fire that resembled thunder, and needless to say, we didn't get much sleep. With so much angst and the cold, my sisters, as well as Mama, were shaking like leaves in the autumn breeze.

> The wolves were howling during the night and she was praying they would not come near.

34

The morning couldn't come quickly enough when we dug our way out of the snow. It had reached two feet plus in depth. The day was clear with a beautiful blue sky. The sun welcomed us, warming our cold, stiff bodies. The girls played in the fluffy snow, trying to forget the horrible war. All in all, it was a great night; God's hand was truly upon us.

Mama rolled up the blankets and piled them high on the sled and readied everything for our ensuing trip. I was tucked into the middle of the blankets as before, but much tighter this time. It kept me nice and warm. Everybody was keeping an eye on me nonetheless, making sure they didn't lose me again. We were hungry and thirsty, but had neither food nor water to give us energy.

Mama had dry matches and melted the snow to give us precious water to drink. We relied on God to lead us to a place where we could get nourishment. As the day wore on, we still heard the thunderous cannons fired in all directions. Thank God, the cannon rounds missed us as they passed over us high in the sky. We passed many fresh graves of fallen Russian soldiers adorned with the Soviet red star, hammer and *sichel*.

After a long walk through the deep snow, we found ourselves in the middle of Darmietzel, inundated with debris from bombed-out houses. Mama's aunt and uncle lived in this town, but there wasn't much left that wasn't destroyed. Mama never found out what happened to her aunt and uncle. I don't know why Mama came back to Darmietzel repeatedly. It was her childhood town, and seeing it destroyed must have torn at her heart.

She hoped they made it out alive, ahead of the Russians who were massed on the outskirts of town. We were fortunate to find a place where we could stay for the time to warm up, dry our clothes, and thaw out our toes, bitten by the frost.

Mama had the ability to learn both Russian and Polish quickly. It helped us when we encountered Russian or Polish forces and enabled her to communicate, and tell them what we were in need of. When the Russians saw us four children, at times, they showed compassion and gave us food, even though it was dry and hard as rock from being out in the battlefield for days.

At one point, Mama became ill from an ear infection, but there was no doctor anywhere. The pain was so severe, she was desperate to find a doctor anywhere, even if it meant going to a Russian military outpost. Most German women would not have entertained looking for a Russian doctor, but she was fortunate to locate a Russian physician who gave her medicine, and sent her on her way. Within days, she was well enough to continue on our journey.

7

WAS IT AN ANGEL?

The next day, during the course of our travels, my sisters and Mama were fortunate to find a house with a kitchen and a rusty stove, but we had no food. To obtain food was impossible without endangering ourselves due to military action outside.

Neither did we have wood to warm up the place. To find wood was difficult, everything was covered up in deep snow. We resolved to spend the night without eating, and to keep ourselves warm, we wrapped our wool blankets around us.

We not only had to be careful of running into the Russians, but also of hidden land mines buried throughout the region. The mines were just below the surface of the snow. Again with God's protection, we never stepped on any of them. As if this wasn't enough to worry about, there were many hungry wolves, always on the lookout for a quick meal.

We were in the house for just an hour and contemplating what to do, when something incredible happened. A Russian soldier in full battle gear broke through the door, using his rifle to bust it open. We were frightened when we saw him in his battle gear with the assault rifle firmly held in his hand, and pointed at us. He stood in the middle of the room, looking everywhere, for anything, which might cause him harm. We didn't know his intentions. Would he eliminate us? That would have been easy with just a few shots from his rifle, or tossing a grenade in the room where we cowered in the corner. He proceeded to check out each room with his rifle at the ready. Mama held us tight and comforted us as we cried softly in her arms. He witnessed our obvious fears and was overcome with pity.

> Would he eliminate us? That would have been easy with just a few shots fired from his rifle, or tossing a grenade in the corner of the room where we cowered.

Gazing into our eyes, he knew that we needed food very badly and a fire to warm up our cold bodies. He was a big man, with big Russian combat boots and a heavy winter coat, who had no trouble walking through the deep snow.

After he surveyed the building, he left. We wondered where he was going, perhaps bringing his comrades? Mama was frightened at the thought he would come back with his fellow soldiers and, judging from past experiences that was terrifying.

The girls were too frightened to speak. Herta, Gerlinde and Helga crawled into the corner of the room, hanging onto Mama. We were shaking from fear and the cold. Their mouths were frozen shut from fright. Should Mama pack us up and flee? She was torn between the thought of leaving or of staying. By staying, we could all be killed, and by leaving, our fate would be sealed in the snow. She was tossing and turning as she lay on the hard, frozen concrete floor praying. Suddenly she had peace and decided it would be best to remain in the house.

The Russian came back within the hour by himself, dragging a bundle of life-giving dry wooden branches behind him through the snow that left a long trail. We were relieved. He shook the snow off his boots, took off his steel helmet and leaned the Russian rifle against the wall.

He proceeded to make a hot fire, which thawed us out. Oh, it felt so good. He made a couple more trips to the forest to gather more wood as the hot fire consumed the dry branches like water on a hot stove. Mama got on her knees and silently thanked God!

She knew by now, he was a kind man trying to help us, but she still kept a wary eye on him nonetheless. With anticipation, we watched him as he reached into his deep pockets and pulled out eggs and flour, and proceeded to make pancakes, scrambled eggs and bacon.

Our empty stomachs relished the food and we ate, and ate, until we became sick. Herta tried to make conversation with him, but to no avail. He couldn't understand German and we didn't know Russian. Mama knew some Russian, but for reasons unknown, she never engaged him in a conversation.

Were we entertained by an angel? He stayed all day cooking for us, and half of the night. I believe he tarried for a while longer to make sure we were secure. It was just wonderful; it almost felt like Santa Claus came and gave us a very precious gift. We felt secure, but watched him with much regret as he put on his heavy coat, retrieved the rifle, slid the steel helmet back on his head, and out the door he went, leaving his big footprints in the snow.

We hated to see him leave our company. For a few hours we were safe and secure. The only reminders of him, besides the hot stove still burning in silence were the footprints in the snow. The soldier never uttered a word, not one word, when he came, or when he disappeared into the dark night. We never knew his name, or much less where he came from. Was he there to comfort and protect us from the Red Army soldiers during the cold night?

Mama and my sisters were on the lookout for the soldier; perhaps we would see him in town, but no such luck. He disappeared as quickly as he came to us, never to be seen again.

The next day, we moved out, hoping to find another place of refuge for the night. We were fortunate to find a house, however damaged by shells. We settled in for the night, along with many other women and their children.

Mama heard that Russian soldiers were getting dangerously close, sending shock waves of panic throughout.

Mama assumed the guardianship role and confronted the soldiers prior to them entering the house, but she couldn't stop all, and some slipped past her. It was remarkable, the soldiers passed by Mama without threatening her.

As the Russians came into town, they announced their arrival by burning houses, looting what was left, overturning furniture in rooms and destroying everything there was.

It was a chilling place. Women were crying and begging the soldiers to let them live so they could take care of their children. While all this was going on, Mama was hiding in a place the soldiers never discovered.

Turmoil all over again, drunken soldiers were fighting each other, drawing bayonets, causing the men to be seriously wounded with blood splattered everywhere, clear to the ceiling. My brave mother snuck outside and found a Russian officer to whom she related what was going on inside the house. The Russian officer came in and restored order, and forced the soldiers to leave.

The seriously injured were taken by vehicle to the military field hospital. The women cleaned the place, wiping off the blood, which was all over the floor, as well as the walls. They picked up what was left of the furniture. At the end, the women carried the dead to the back of the house and stacked them like cardboard. The cold wouldn't allow the corpses to be buried. Later in the spring the Russians would bury the cadavers in mass graves.

The chairs had broken legs; the tables were broken in half, rendering most of the furniture unusable. The soldiers left, and for a time an uneasy peace returned. The women cared for the injured as best as they could, giving them first aid. They had plenty of bandages and other emergency kits for the wounded given to them by Russians.

One of the soldiers involved in the melee knew Mama sought help from a Russian officer. He was furious and out to find her. He was searching for her everywhere with his weapon drawn. God hid her from him. If he had found her, I wouldn't be here today. She hid in the basement. The entrance was covered with all types of furniture placed there by other women. He stayed for a couple of hours hoping to find Mama until one of his comrades came to pick him up in a military vehicle.

The next morning, another Russian officer came through the door and told everybody in the building to pack up all their belongings, and follow him to a truck. We climbed aboard a heavy-duty six axle military truck. Mama asked one of the soldiers *Wo wollt Ihr uns denn hin fahren?* "Where are you going to take us?" The Russians didn't reply to her inquiry!

Mama suspected the truck was taking us to the interior of Russia. None of the people were able to get off as it traveled at a high rate of speed through the empty countryside. The cold penetrated our bodies and the freezing arctic wind blew against our frozen faces. We had nothing to eat; the clothes we wore didn't keep the freezing cold from penetrating our malnourished bodies.

The girls were crying; the freezing cold turned their stiff bodies into a pale blue from the feet up. It was a rough ride, and we felt every chuckhole in the road. The girls had a difficult time grabbing onto the hard wooden bench without sliding off. By now their hands were frozen and they had no more strength left. They were screaming when wooden splinters worked their way into their thighs and buttocks. That wasn't the Russians problem. They were merely following orders given to them by the *Kommandantur,* "command center".

We crisscrossed the countryside seeing many burned-out tanks and trucks. Houses were turned into rubble, and had the appearance of Swiss cheese, with big holes in the walls from the shelling. Fear gripped us. None of the Russians would tell us where we were going.

How could we get off the truck? Mama thought of jumping, but that would have been suicide. There was no way she would leave us. Surely, the soldiers would have to take a break to eat or go to the bathroom sometime? It was a miracle when within a few hours, the weather turned warm. It was now March 1944. The warm wind turned the road into thick, black mud. The vehicle's axles became trapped in the deep sludge. This was a blessing in disguise as the soldiers escorted us off the truck and dropped us into the deep sludge with our belongings.

We couldn't pick up everything we dropped on the ground, and some of the things were better to be left anyway. Besides, we could only carry that much, and for Mama, carrying me was a heavy load in itself. The girls were carrying their dolls they held close to their bodies.

We crawled away slowly, but where we were headed, we weren't sure. The thick mud stripped my sisters and Mama of shoes and socks. With each step, they sunk deeper. We were trapped. My sisters walked barefoot behind Mama, forging a trail in the dark, cold night.

It caused their feet and legs to become numb. Mama didn't have a clue of our whereabouts. She figured we were deep in Soviet occupied territory. It was exhausting as they labored, pulling one foot at a time out of the cold mud. Mama was carrying me, making it difficult for her to walk. She was afraid she might drop me and what a nightmare that would have been.

The mud clung to our bodies, covering us from head to toe. The sky was covered with thick clouds preventing the moonlight from guiding us. We couldn't see what was ahead. It was blinding darkness.

There were many bomb craters, hard to spot, especially when there was snow on the ground or thick fog. It would have been a disaster had we fallen into one of the deep holes. Thank God, there was no more snow, just suffocating mud.

8

THE LAST SUPPER

No water anywhere, not even a trickle. We wished we could have found a creek or river to clean up to get rid of that ugly mud. Much later, we found a refuge where we cleaned up and washed our soiled clothes. Not a drop of hot water, and taking a bath with the ice cold water took our breath away. We made do, however, as we got rid of most of the sticky, cold mud that clung to our bodies.

There were no Russians to worry about for the time being. Things could change quickly however. The Russians were chasing after the refugees, hoping to rob or violate them. Other women and children were in dire need of food and shelter, just like we were, and finding a roof over their heads was a priority.

During the night, we found a farmhouse by the side of the road. It was a large two story building with three to four bedrooms. For a change, we had running hot and cold water. How blessed we were, at last we were able to scrub the remaining mud off of our dirt covered bodies. The bedrooms had soft beds and fluffy pillows. In no time we sank into deep sleep, our bodies wrapped in soft feather blankets, and pillows encased our heads with only our hair protruding. Not even the rooster could wake us. We woke up around eight in the morning when we heard animals stirring in the stall below us.

My sisters got dressed to investigate the stall. They were greeted by twenty hungry cattle tied up in the stalls. It was apparent, nobody looked after them. Without anybody milking them, their udders had swollen to the point where they might burst. It appeared not a soul was in the huge house which was recently vacated. Mama found dry wood stacked outside of the barn which she carried upstairs. Mama thought, "wie kann ich jetzt ein Feuer machen ohne ein Streichholz." *How can I make a fire without a match?* She searched all the drawers and found matches. In no time, she had a roaring inferno in the stove.

She was worried the smoke might attract Soviet soldiers who weren't far from us. Mama was weary and told us kids to sit down at the table and with luck, she would make pancakes with the flour she found in one of the cabinets. Mama told Herta to look for eggs in the barn. My sister climbed down the steep staircase looking for nourishing eggs. The disturbed chicken took to flight in the barn when they spotted Herta and landed in the stall next to one of the cows.

Herta struck it rich when she found a couple of nests with white and brown colored eggs resting on soft feathers. She called Gerlinde to help her carry the eggs upstairs, taking great care not to drop them along the way.

Mama, like a magician, stirred the eggs into the batter and produced beautiful, fluffy pancakes, enough for everybody. This was too good to be true, oh, it tasted so good and we didn't want to leave, but in the early afternoon, Mama packed us up for the trip to nowhere, hoping we were headed west into freedom. We were rested up, and ready for our journey. We had walked two kilometers when we saw the farmhouse disappearing in the distance along with fond memories.

We traveled nonstop until mid afternoon, when Mama stopped. We took a rest alongside the road in the middle of a dark forest. Mama rolled some of the pancakes in a towel she packed inside some blankets, and we consumed the cold feast.

A couple of green tractors passed us on their way to plow the fields, and that was nothing unusual. We had not encountered Russian troops as yet, and Mama prayed to spare us from these savages. After our late lunch, and a well deserved nap, we continued our journey.

It was towards evening, when Mama noticed an attractive house in the distance. The last few days, we were blessed, and could this one be like the one the night before? Mama never let down her guard however, afraid the Russians set a trap.

Mama was shocked when she saw the city sign of Landsberg. We must have covered a great distance to have arrived in Landsberg. After a short walk, we were at the front door of the house, and without hesitation Mama rang the door bell. A pleasant woman with a friendly smile, opened the door, and greeted us with, *Ihr seit Alle herzlichst willkommen* "A hearty welcome," and invited us in, in spite of our appearance. It was strange to see this house still intact, while others were bombed and burned.

When we entered the dining room, the table greeted us, covered with a fancy tablecloth. Mama said, *Das ist doch ein Wunder dass alles so schön aussieht.* "It is a miracle seeing everything so well prepared." On the table was a delicious, prepared six-course dinner with all the trimmings.

We were stunned by the elegance of the home. Was this our last supper? The lady of the house had the luxury of running hot and cold water. We were invited to the table to partake of a fantastic meal. The lady of the house prayed; *Herrgott sei unser Gast und segne was Du us bescheret hast, Amen.* "Dear God be our guest and bless what you have provided for us, Amen."

We had ham and chicken with potatoes and gravy. When we were done with the main meal, we were offered dessert, which consisted of apple strudel, cherry torte and rhubarb cobbler. We ate, but we were on pins and needles, ready to move to a place of relative safety at any moment should it be necessary.

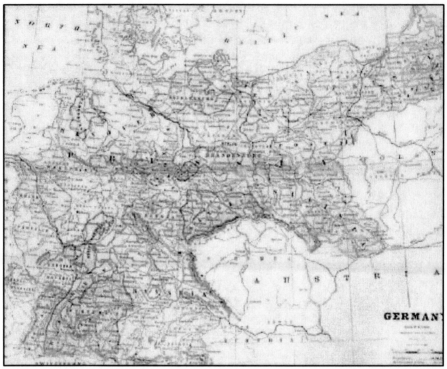

Everything was delicious. We couldn't believe how much food there was. While eating, we heard the rumbling of trucks outside, and an occasional burst of gun fire. After the meal, we were escorted to one of the four bedrooms to get some sleep. The adults stayed up late into the night discussing the war and the devastation. Before Mama came to bed, she, and the owners of the house prayed that God would protect their home and keep everybody safe through the night.

When we climbed out of the bed, the lady made us breakfast. All the while, Russian tanks and trucks still rumbled past their house. We knew it was just a matter of time until the Russians attacked and destroyed the property.

The hospitable couple invited us into their home and treated us like royalty. They knew the Russians would make their presence known soon. I believe they anticipated what was about to transpire, and prepared for their last supper. They meant it to be special, no matter who showed up.

All around us, we heard cannons, and saw the destruction brought on by the war. My sister Herta is still plagued with vivid memories. More mothers with children arrived. Everybody was nervous, and they were in denial about what might happen soon. From experience, Mama warned the people to hide their valuables, if they had any, and to make themselves look as unattractive as possible. The women dragged their clothes through the mud, and tore holes, making them look unappealing.

The women rubbed black soot on their faces to make them look unsightly, with scarves over their heads; they looked like '*Babushkas*' "grandmothers".

Without warning, shells were coming through the wall and were followed by a huge blast. Everybody hid, hoping to shield themselves from this onslaught. Perhaps the Russians thought German soldiers were housed here, so it became an attractive target. The Russians kept this barrage up for three long hours. Lucky for us, the house had not yet caught fire, and we escaped with our lives as we fled with the little green wagon, packed high with our "treasures".

We didn't get far when the Russians told us to stop and turn back. It was a very chaotic scene as we arrived at the house we had our last supper in.

The soldiers rounded up the women including Mama who they escorted to an undisclosed location. We children had no idea if we were going to see her again. We were frightened. My sisters were alone now and gripped with fright, terrified of the thought they might not ever see Mama again.

Thank God, a few hours later, she returned, along with a few other women, but the majority never came back to claim their children. My sisters were overjoyed to see Mama and clung to her like wall paper. What happened to those poor children without their mothers? Hopefully, some of the women, who were left, adopted them. The women, including Mama, didn't say a word about what occurred while they were with the Russians. It was believed, most were raped. Mama's face was as white as a sheet, and she never said anything to anybody about what she had just experienced.

As the night approached, the Red Army soldiers returned. They sought out the remaining women, young or old. It was like all the other nights. The Russians took mothers away who were still able to walk, as well as the nice old man who owned the home. Few returned. The children cried for their mothers.

Nobody knew what happened to these poor women, but I am afraid they took them to give the Russians pleasure, and do their dirty work until they were used up, and then shot them like worn-out horses.

> Nobody knew what happened to these women, but I am afraid the Russians shot them.

During these hellish times, there wasn't much dialogue between Mama and my sisters. Mama was too busy figuring out her next move. She was fearful herself, and had great doubts we would survive this epic journey. It was too painful for her to talk about what had just occurred. Had it not been for us, I know she wouldn't have come back alive.

9

SAVED FROM THE GRAVE

Every day was like the day before, always looking for food and a place to sleep. It was a gigantic challenge, especially with a family of five. With total surprise, Mama took off with my two sisters, Gerlinde and Helga, while Herta and I were left to fend for ourselves by the side of a highway. Where was she going? Nobody knew. Mama probably didn't either.

There we were, by the side of the highway. No food, no shelter, nothing to warm our cold bodies with. We were desperate for food, but no one paid us any attention. Herta thought we were at the end of our lives. She noticed Russian soldiers in a military tent nearby having dinner. The smell of fresh baked bread was unbearable. We had nothing to lose, so, why not walk over to them, maybe the soldiers would have pity on us.

This was another miracle when the Russians invited us to their table and offered us hot soup laced with chicken meat. We each were given a piece of hot bread. We felt blessed that night! We felt angels entertained us and hoped this wasn't going to end. We found refuge and food for weeks at the Russian garrison. One of the men knew some German and we were able to converse. He told us he had a wife and three children at home and hoped to go back home as soon as possible after the war. We were provided food and shelter night after night! We slept in the corner of one of the army tents. We had no bed, but the grassy ground was soft, but cold.

Three weeks passed, and the Russian pulled out with all their equipment, a never ending caravan of trucks and tanks headed in a westerly direction. Thirty days had passed; Herta became frightened with good reason. She was afraid we would never see Mama and our two sisters again. The thought was terrifying; we would have to fend for ourselves. It was a common sight to find children without their mothers by the side of the highway near death. In the winter months, many children froze to death. There wasn't anything their mothers could do to save them. For anyone who found refuge, it was a blessing. It was dangerous not to have a roof to cover their heads. The Russians were looking for anybody who might be a threat. They shot civilians indiscriminately.

It was February the 27th, 1945. Thirty days had passed since we had seen Mama, Gerlinde and Helga. Were we hallucinating? We couldn't believe our eyes when we caught a glimpse of Mama and our sisters as they came around the bend of the road. Within a second, Herta ran to hug and kiss them. It was a joyous reunion, and we were so very happy to see them again. They returned against all odds. Mama didn't say much of their ill-fated journey, only to say, she was happy to have come back alive.

If things couldn't get any worse, they did. The same evening, Mama, Gerlinde and Helga were captured by the Russians as they were walking on the street, just short of crossing the partially destroyed Gerloff Bridge. The Russians released Mama and my sisters after a lengthy interrogation. Later in the week, Mama was interrogated by the Russians for the second time. During the interrogation, Gerlinde and Helga were sequestered in another room.

The Russian soldiers made Mama sit on an old wooden chair for hours. One of the soldiers slapped her, threatened to rape her if she didn't tell them what happened to the Russian officer they found dead. Mama told the Russians she knew nothing of the incident. The Soviets finally released her from custody to be reunited with us.

Mama was in a state of panic and didn't think clearly. She was fearful the Russians were following us. She just wanted to get away. We felt the tension as well. Herta and Gerlinde were frightened of the thought that they might be taken captive by the Russians.

Mama told us: *Jetzt müssen wir uns auf den Weg machen, so dass wir nicht bei den Russen ins Gefang kommen.* "Let's hurry out of the area, the Russians might locate us and take us captive." Just as we rounded a corner, with buildings on both sides of the street, soldiers intercepted us and told Mama to come with them. They packed us into one of their staff cars and took us to an apartment complex. The Russians were in the process of rounding up everybody in the neighborhood, young or old, it didn't matter. In short, we were at the wrong place, at the wrong time.

Nobody knew how the Russian officer died. The Russians thought the Germans murdered him, but that was inconclusive at the time. He could have died of natural causes, or he may have drunk himself to death. The Soviets didn't take any chances, assembled everybody, escorted them to a big backyard and handed each a shovel.

A Russian woman officer made an announcement: *Frauen mit Kinder unter zehn Jaren können weg gehen, aber alle anderen müssen da bleiben.* "Women with children of ten years and under can leave but the rest must stay." Nobody could escape. There were soldiers ringing the backyard, and it would have been foolhardy to try to slip past them. At the same time, there was nothing to lose since they shot you anyway.

The Russians forced people to watch this horror to teach them a lesson. In Mama's journal she wrote, a beautiful young girl of perhaps fourteen or fifteen

As we and Mama were on our way out of the yard, she heard a shot. Mama looked back and saw that sweet girl fall into her grave.

with a blonde ponytail dug her own grave. As we and Mama were on our way out of the yard, she heard a shot. Mama looked back and saw that sweet girl fall into her grave. Mama buried her face in her shawl and wept. Herta and Gerlinde witnessed this horrific scene and wept all the way to the street. Horror stricken, they sunk to their knees, embraced each other, and thanked God for saving us.

We were within earshot of a volley of shots, then, all of a sudden, everything was very quiet. There were approximately forty-five to fifty people murdered. This carnage destroyed Mama forever.

The next day, the ones who were alive and able to walk, were loaded onto a large truck to pick potatoes. Everybody worked until late that night without food. The soldiers watched closely that all potatoes were placed into the sacks provided. After a hard day of labor, and without food or water, the Russians forced everybody to walk back to Landsberg.

Mama and my sisters were dead tired, hungry, and barely able to walk. God intervened on our behalf and we made it back to Landsberg crawling on all fours through the door of the building. Thank God, it was a warm summer day in July 1945.

During this work excursion, Mama sat me down close by her, and made sure I didn't venture off. It was a blessing that I wasn't very active and stayed where she placed me.

When we came back to the house, not the house we stayed in the night before, where we were invited to a supper prepared by the elderly lady, the Russians hadn't returned yet, and we got some sleep. It was a guarantee; the drunken soldiers would find their way back sooner or later. Like every night, it was utter chaos all over again.

It was a miracle; we always found a place to sleep, although it was wrought with ever-present dangers. Most of the time, Mama found food for us, although the portions were meager, but it was enough to barely keep us alive. On occasions, the Russian soldiers offered us bread, and that was a feast for our empty stomachs.

There weren't many places for the kids to play, so children and my sisters played in the streets of Landsberg. The kids tried to drown out the horrible things they witnessed. Playing ball took their minds away from the war, if only for a few moments.

A Russian tank approached and my sisters and the other kids scrambled. A young girl of around eight, apparently unaware of the tank approaching, continued playing with a ball. The driver didn't stop and drove over her. She lay dying in the street with her head crushed, and the rest of her body dismembered. In time, you couldn't even tell that it was a human being as she became an integral part of the street. How the soldier lived with what he had done is beyond me.

46

The days dragged on. Mama heard the Poles were occupying the German towns and the countryside. The Germans were afraid of what the Poles might do to them, but to our surprise, most of these people were kind to us. They saw our plight, and they too had to leave their homes as the Russians took their land.

Mama was attempting to locate a place where we could stay for another night, and, at the same time, find something to eat. While Mama was looking for food, she couldn't help but notice Soviet trucks winding through town with German prisoners of war who appeared malnourished with sunken cheekbones and torn uniforms. Looking into their eyes told the whole story. Another truck was piled high with corpses of German soldiers, arms and legs hanging over the side of the truck, resembling dead cattle. No telling where the surviving prisoners were taken. They were either shot or transported to Siberia.

Everyday, Mama was looking for food, and medication, but it was difficult to find either. We were running a high fever, had diarrhea, stemming from fatigue and a lack of nutrition and sleep. She was hoping we wouldn't come down with whooping cough, diphtheria, or other diseases. I became ill at one point, and fortunately, I recovered. It was incredible; none of us was ever injured, despite all of the dangers around us. To top it off, in the winter, we dealt with severe cold and the lack of food was forever with us. It was a miracle we didn't die.

Mama noticed a group of Russian soldiers gathered by a bridge overlooking the Warthe River. Mama was eager to know what was going on! The soldiers had a lively conversation and were in a festive mood. In Russian, Mama engaged them, and the soldiers told her the war was over, it was May 8th 1945. Their exact words were, *"Voina kaput."* Despite the good news, the Russian soldiers were on their way to Berlin. For them, the war was far from over.

Mama yelled from the bottom of her lungs, *Der krieg ist endlich vorbei.* *"The war is finally over."* There were many obstacles we had to overcome as we fled west. The biggest problem was the civilian population was still harassed by the Russian occupying forces. How were we going to get back to Heidelberg where Papa was anxiously waiting for us? There was at least 500 kilometers between him and us. Our journey to freedom was far from over.

We continued our quest to freedom when we encountered a Russian checkpoint. We were told by the Russian *Kommandantur* "The Russian Command Center", we were to report to the checkpoint early the next day, and board a truck. We thought the war was over and were free to go wherever we wanted, but that was not the case. The Russians were the occupiers.

Red Army trucks offered us a ride, and we knew it wasn't a journey to freedom. The Russians transported hundreds of thousands to labor camps in

Siberia, and for the most part, people were never heard from again, and that included our relatives on Mama's side.

Mama heard from refugees, the Russians were transporting us to the Ural Mountains, or even farther inland. Mama and we children boarded the truck the next day, outfitted with wooden benches, most likely designed for troop transport.

Mama noticed Helga wasn't with us. She told the Russian guard she will not leave without her, whereby we were taken off the truck. But Mama had to promise them we would be back in the morning to continue the journey on another truck. When we returned to the place where we had been staying the night before, we found Helga unharmed.

She didn't seem particularly worried that we wouldn't be coming back to get her. A Russian colonel entertained Helga. She appeared to have had a marvelous time in our absence. She likely reminded the colonel of one of his daughters he left behind.

She was reluctant to leave the Russians. It took much convincing to talk Helga into coming with us. Our journey continued the next morning, but not on the truck. We skirted the Russians, only to find ourselves in the middle of a minefield.

10

SO CLOSE, BUT YET SO FAR

Mama wasn't about to board another truck, even if it meant crossing a minefield. She knew God would not leave us, nor forsake us during this time. She was frightened at the thought of being taken deep into Russia. If that happened, it was a guarantee; we would never return to our beloved Heidelberg and see Papa again. During the night, she packed us up and we fled the area. It was either May or June, the weather was pleasant, a contrast from the horrible winters where we had to navigate through ice and snow. Before long, we were out of town pulling our little green wagon Mama had commandeered earlier, with my sister Helga and me sitting on top of the cart. My other two sisters walked alongside Mama helping her pull the cart.

As we walked along the road, Mama was approached by a Russian sentry who told her, it was *verboten* "forbidden" to be in this area. The checkpoint remained closed to civilian traffic of any kind. She still attempted to get past the Russian guard post. Herta heard the familiar click of a rifle, which meant, we were in imminent danger of being fired on. Mama had a hearing impairment, and didn't hear the sound of the gun. Herta told her what she just heard.

We hastily retreated. A Russian soldier directed us away from the area. Mama kept her eyes on the Russian guard post, and to her surprise, she saw a well dressed young man in civilian attire approaching the Russian, conferring with the guards in perfect Russian.

One didn't see young German men walking around, much less in a business suit. The Russians would have sent him to Siberia, or would have shot him, most likely the latter. With disbelief, Mama observed the Russians open the *Schlagbaum* "checkpoint" and we passed through it without any incident.

While Mama was busy pulling us to safety, she lost sight of the young man. He had disappeared. Mama wanted to thank him for his help. She was convinced that another angel came to our rescue.

As we moved on, we were passed by the Russians moving westward in mass with their military gear. We stayed far to the right as miles of Russian trucks and tanks rolled past us. The column of vehicles never seemed to end as they disappeared in a cloud of dust. At the same time, the Poles were following behind them to occupy the land. It was hard for us to comprehend that all was lost.

In light of everything, we saw light at the end of the tunnel. Every day seemed a little brighter. We were getting closer to the west and out of the reach of the Red Army occupying forces. We were approximately 100 kilometers east of the *Oder, Neisse* line.

The Oder River has its origin in the Czech Republic, and empties into the Baltic Sea. The Oder, and the *Lausitzer Neisse* meet at the city of Stettin. The river serves as the border between Poland and Germany.

Every so often, we stopped to rest and have something to eat from what Mama had tucked away securely among our belongings. My sisters and I were in terrible condition, forever festered by lice, and hadn't had a bath for a very long time. Our clothes were filthy, lice infested, tattered, but the worst thing was we hadn't eaten anything resembling a meal for months.

I am still in awe how Mama gathered the food in the face of the ever greater danger of being taken away, or simply shot by the Russians and now the Poles. The Polish people we met now displayed more animosity towards the Germans than the Russians.

We were anxious to reach Heidelberg, our final destination. We walked many miles without stopping, until we became too weak to walk. We were totally drained of any strength we had left, and couldn't go any farther without food when Mama saw a big red house. She thought Russians occupied it. She knocked on the door, and a Polish officer answered. She was in a state of shock, but hoped the man would be kind and invite us in for the night.

To her astonishment, the soft-spoken man offered us hot soup, with a little meat floating on top, and told us we could all sleep in the barn where they kept their horses. During the night, the horses stirred, and made lots of noise. After a somewhat peaceful night's sleep, we got up early the next morning and started our trek again, heading in the direction of the *Oder, Neisse.*

We traveled hundreds of miles merely walking, and other times, hitching a ride on a train or truck. We survived week, after week, without getting shot, sick, or maimed. We staggered back to Mama's birthplace, the city of *Küstrin on the Warthe River,* and found it leveled by the Russians. We located our uncle's home, in which we had stayed months earlier, and to my mother's surprise, the house was not heavily damaged.

Mama didn't find anybody dead or alive, and we didn't know what happened to them. Deep down inside, she knew they were either shot or taken to Siberia by the Russians, unless they escaped.

We were fortunate to find the heavily bombed-out train station. People told Mama the train would arrive soon, which meant it could be one to ten hours. Eventually, the train did arrive.

Many German refugees had gathered, hoping to climb aboard, heading west and to freedom. It was an old freight train used to haul cattle, but we didn't care as long as we were able to hitch a ride, and didn't have to walk.

We boarded and Mama placed us in a corner close to the exit. We sat on the wooden floor, covered with cow manure and debris, but we made do. It wasn't very comfortable. We had to be careful of wood splinters. The train drove all night. We attempted to sleep, but we couldn't. We saw rats running to and fro, looking for food. Mama sat in the middle and we cuddled up next to her, keeping us warm. Freezing cold air, oozing through the crack of door, caused our teeth to rattle.

We woke up as the sun rays peeked through the door in the early morning hours warming our bodies; oh, how good it felt. Sore from sitting on the hard, wooden floor, in awkward positions, we longed to stretch our bodies and get up, but we were too weak. We needed food, but there was none. As we were huddled in the corner of the car, silence flooded the train. The train slowed down for some unknown reason, and came to a complete stop a few kilometers down the track.

To our surprise, Mama had hid away food. She obtained bread and a little bit of sausage at the last location. We almost attacked her to get to the hard, dried out morsels. It only took a few minutes, and the food was consumed, not even a crumb was left. The reason for the stop, they were switching locomotives. What we didn't know was the Russians had commandeered the locomotive. We waited hours upon hours, but no locomotive ever arrived, then we knew for sure, we had been misled.

At last, after we waited some eight hours, another locomotive did arrive. The crew hooked it to the cars and we finally were on our way again. While we were aboard the train, the Russians helped themselves to jewelry the older women were hoping to carry to freedom, as well as other valuable items. The soldiers separated the older from the younger women. The young were raped, and then thrown down the embankment.

Many women were killed during this unspeakable tragedy, and others were close to death leaving the babies and young children to fend for themselves. We huddled in a corner of the wagon, not far from the exit, just in case Mama and we children would have to make a quick exit. Mama prayed to God, "Please rescue us from these savages."

Mama knew beforehand what the Red Army soldiers had in mind, and prepared for it. She told us kids to act as though we were sick. We coughed non stop, that way, the soldiers would be less likely to approach us.

Our appearance was far from inviting.

> The women continued holding their frozen babies close to their breasts, hoping to revive them.

We had not had a bath for a long time, stunk to high heaven, and our clothes were filthy. Mama was drained of all her strength and looked like death warmed over. She got hold of some discarded paper, and wrote with black ink we were infected with diphtheria.

Hoping the Russians would be able to read German, but Mama didn't have to worry. The news spread quickly throughout the train, and they avoided us like the plague. We were pressed against the side of the wagon in tight formation, and Mama placed herself inconspicuously between us. We were protected through this mayhem, but for others, it was a horrible nightmare.

Unspeakable tragedies occurred and families were separated during that night. The women continued holding their frozen babies close to their breasts, hoping to revive them.

Children perished due to lack of food, as their mothers had nothing more to give. Often the women themselves succumbed to the elements. When the mothers realized their babies were dead, they had no choice but to leave them by the side of the road. With the frozen ground, there was no way to bury them. Our memories were frozen in time.

As the morning dawned, not far from us, on another track, we spotted a train and decided to board without knowing its destination. All we wanted was to get to freedom any way we could, even taking calculated risks. The cars were filthy with manure on the floor, just like the others, and now and then you would spot a rat helping itself to the morsels on the wooden floor.

Would the train be traveling west, or would it be going east to the interior of Russia? We had faith the train would take us out of danger going west. We breathed a sigh of relief. We moved towards the American sector.

We held our breath when we crossed a bridge over the *Elbe River*. Many of the bridges had been blown up, either by the Germans or the Russians, to prevent their armored vehicles from crossing to the other side. If the bridge wasn't totally destroyed, it was damaged to such a degree, that no train should have been allowed to travel on it.

Over time, the track was weakened by rain and ice. Erosion ate away at the railroad ties. Nobody was maintaining anything and all fell into disrepair.

We were at about the middle of the bridge, when the track started to give way. With the weight of the train, the bridge started to sag even more now. The likelihood was that some of the cars, or all, would end up in the cold river below. We made it across, and the people thanked God who held us up with his mighty hand.

The next challenge was crossing the *Oder River*. At last, freedom was in sight and we would be in the American sector of Germany. Everybody got off the train, and walked towards the *Oder River*. It was another long trek, especially for my sisters. It was early summer with much warmer weather making travel easier. We were barefoot, throwing away the old worn-out, ill-fitting shoes Mama obtained as we moved from house to house in search of a refuge.

There were hundreds of thousands of German refugees walking west with no food or a place to sleep. Many were getting fatigued, and the sick, the older people, couldn't keep up the pace. Many perished along the way.

Instead of standing in line with the other refugees, Mama chose a different route. We came upon a village where we found a house that became our refuge for the night. We were given bread and a small portion of potato soup by the residents of the house. They knew we were in desperate need of something to eat.

We bypassed many people who were still waiting in line from days earlier. What chance did we have crossing the *Oder River* when the road leading to it was lined with a multitude of tired, worn-out refugees for many kilometers?

The Russians made it difficult for anyone to approach the Oder Neisse Bridge, and were amused by the human tragedy unfolding before their eyes. I suppose they wanted to exact as much hardship and pain on us as they could. A great number of people became infected with all sorts of diseases, and diphtheria was rampant and to search for a doctor was futile.

Mama had other ideas instead of waiting in line with the rest of the refugees. She entertained the idea of finding her father in Berlin. However, first we would have had to cross the river, and unbeknownst to Mama, Berlin was reduced to rubble.

One morning, out of the blue, Mama told Herta she must return to *Darmietzel*, a hundred kilometer trip east. She placed Herta in charge in her absence, but the big question was: would she be coming back? She took Helga and Gerlinde with her, and why she did that, nobody could ever figure out.

She knew *Darmietzel* was heavily damaged by the Russians, and to go there made no sense whatsoever. Maybe she thought, by some miracle, she would still find some of our relatives there. No such luck!

After Mama left my sister Herta and me to our own devices for the second time, we made it from day to day begging for food. People had compassion, and threw old, dried out pieces of bread our way, that's all they had. My sister did a great job taking care of us both in the absence of Mama.

A Russian soldier ventured by. He looked menacing with his rifle, which by now slid off his shoulder. On his belt, he was carrying hand grenades, a gun, and a *dolch* "hunting knife", with an ornate deer handle.

He bent down, put his strong arms around us, and gave us an assuring hug, as if to say, we had nothing to fear. He reached into his pockets and pulled out life-giving bread with sausage. What a treat from an "enemy" we learned to fear. He lingered a while and observed us intently as we consumed the food. It may have been all the food he had. We couldn't communicate verbally, but when we looked into his eyes, tears rolled down his face. He felt our pain!

> A Russian soldier ventured by. He looked menacing with his rifle, which slid off the shoulder. He put his strong arms around us, and gave us an assuring hug, as if to say, we had nothing to fear.

Mama was gone for three weeks. Each passing day diminished any hope we would see her, or our two sisters again. Herta all but gave up hope! She couldn't believe her eyes when she saw Mama in the far distance with my sisters in tow. Was she imagining things? Was it a mirage? No, it was true, and with joy she ran to embrace them. Tears of joy rolled down their cheeks as they held each other close.

It was a blessing to be together again after a three-week absence. We were very happy to be reunited after all that time. Mama did not find anybody in *Darmietzel.*

The journey was exhausting for her and my two sisters. She didn't anticipate the Poles had occupied the entire area.

She was not welcomed, much less received food or drink, or a place to stay during the nights. She, and my two sisters, had to sleep wherever they could, and that was out in the open most nights.

Mama was in a state of shock when she returned from her journey. She had lost a lot of weight, and my sisters were malnourished as well. Mama couldn't bring herself to smile, and came back in a depressed state of mind. My second oldest sister, Gerlinde, said they encountered horrible things, too awful to describe.

To be with Papa was our longing since we hadn't seen him for over a year, and Papa didn't know if we were even alive. The Oder River was close, but getting across was impossible at this point. We were still 200 kilometers from the American sector and way too far to walk. We hitched a ride by train or truck whenever we had the opportunity. We were forced to walk many miles passing by deserted, bombed-out towns along the way. It was difficult to find a place where we could rest in safety.

Along the way, we saw an attractive house. Perhaps, they would allow us to stay with them for a night. Mama knocked on the door, and we were invited to stay four nights. Oh, what a blessing, being able to stretch and get some rest. We cleaned up and washed our clothes which by now stunk, and stuck to our dirty bodies.

The occupants of the house asked us to vacate the building. How shocking! The Russians quarantined it. The Soviets controlled everything what came in, and out of town. Mama waited for the opportunity to cross the border between the Russian and the American zone. She would have attempted it, had the opportunity presented itself.

Russian military vehicles drove past us, but paid no attention to us, and when it was rainy, the soldiers drove through the rain puddles. The spray of the water covered us from head to toe with dirty, nasty cold water.

Thousands of people were still lined up leading to the Oder River, hoping to cross the bridge to freedom where the Americans were. It was raining; the road was muddy, and hard on our feet. My sisters acquired used shoes along the way, but wore them out during the journey to freedom. Mama obtained footwear for us wherever she could.

Countless children were dying and Mama may even have taken shoes from diseased children. In most cases, the shoes didn't fit. She was resourceful, and cut out the tip of the shoes to make them fit. But to keep out the mud and rain was something else again.

We could hardly believe we made it this far. My sisters had lice in their hair, and that was par for the course among refugees. It was tough to stay clean when you only have one set of outerwear, one set of underwear, and no way to wash the clothes.

Mama saw the demarcation line we hoped to cross. It was so close, but yet so far. We again caught up with the multitude of refugees. Mama was praying for a miracle to get us to the other side, and to freedom. Only God could help us now! Mama pondered what to do. She looked for contraband in her skirt pockets with which to bribe the Russians to allow us to cross the bridge to freedom. She knew if we had to wait for days, perhaps weeks, or even months, we would come down with some type of sickness, due to starvation, and we'd never make it back to Heidelberg alive.

People collapsed, and there weren't any doctors to assist them, or take them to a hospital for treatment. The Russians were crude to them, going to a hospital was unheard of unless you were a soldier, then they were treated in a field hospital. Everybody had to fend for themselves, and survival was only for the fittest. Mama told us kids to be quiet as we passed multitudes of people waiting in line. We just kept moving until we reached the sight of the river. Refugees were getting annoyed as we walked past thousands of people.

We ultimately ended up waiting in line as well, and when we had been there a few hours, Mama noticed a building three to four stories tall. In one of the open windows, she saw a Russian officer waving to her, calling her in German: From Mama's war journal. *Meine liebe Frau, kommen sie doch bitte hoch.* "My dear woman please come up to my office."

She couldn't believe her eyes, and thought he must be waving at someone else. She looked around to see if he was motioning to another person in the crowd, but the officer looked straight at her. In disbelief, she saw he was indeed signaling to her.

She was in shock, but yet delighted. She left us children where we were, and looking at the people around us, she felt we were safe for the time being. With great trepidation Mama proceeded to the building. She did not know what the officer's intentions were. She gathered all her strength she had left to climb several flights of stairs to his office and, with the adrenalin flowing, she literally flew up the steps.

She arrived at the officer's door and knocked. A handsome, tall Russian with wavy dark hair and a black mustache opened the door and invited her in. To her surprise, he spoke perfect German with a heavy Russian accent. He offered her to sit in a comfortable chair, and gave her a strong cup of coffee. His chest was covered with many ribbons and medals, an indication that he was at least a colonel or even a general. She was nervous; her hands were shaking, which made it difficult to hold the cup without spilling it. She tried hard to be calm, but the harder she tried, the worse it got.

The officer had a calm demeanor and that in turn calmed Mama, and her fear subsided. After a few minutes she stopped shaking and regained her composure. He asked Mama how she was doing, and if he could get her anything. The officer was a gentleman, unlike the other Red Army soldiers we had met along the way. He was after all a high Ranking officer. It was obvious he was an educated man and familiar with the German language, which was a help during this time. She said to herself, *Ich habe nur einen Wunsch, dass wir über die Oder kommen.* "She had only one wish, and that was to get to the other side of the Oder."

He inquired about us since he saw us four children standing by her, and asked how we were doing. She told him we went through horrifying events, and were shell shocked. His reply was: *In kurzer Zeit wird alles wieder besser sein.* "In a little while everything will be better."

She was careful not to offend the Russian officer by saying anything derogatory about the Russian forces. He was genuinely interested in our well-being, and for unknown reasons, he chose us out of hundreds of thousands of refugees.

He communicated with his secretary in Russian and appeared to have asked her to hand him two slips of paper which he laid on his desk. The officer made small talk and asked Mama what our names were, and the towns we passed through. In a few minutes, he calmly walked over to his ornate oak desk, and retrieved the two prepared documents. He bent over the desk, and with one stroke, signed the papers, our tickets to freedom.

Mama was in shock as the officer handed them to her, but she couldn't read the writing. It was written in Russian. She was able to communicate somewhat in their language, but writing and reading were altogether different, and difficult. Just in case, she was prepared to bribe the officer with contraband she had tucked away in her skirt pockets. There was no need for that now. Where there was no way, God made a way. People were mocking her as she pressed forward in the direction of the bridge with us kids in tow.

They said she was crazy to even attempt to cross the Russian checkpoint, but that didn't deter her since she had the miraculous slips of papers. But were they the real thing?

She would find out soon enough! Before we reached the Russian checkpoint, Mama glanced at the pieces once more. She still couldn't believe

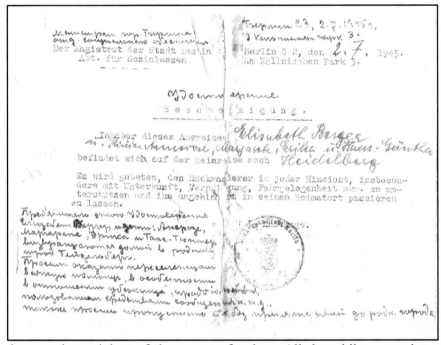

she was the recipient of the pass to freedom. All the while, a number of people tried to dissuade her from moving towards the bridge and yelled at her to get back into line with the rest of the refugees. Mama kept pressing on. My sisters became nervous from all the commotion.

As the situation deteriorated, Herta, Gerlinde and Helga hid partially under the cart for fear of being harmed. There was a possibility a riot would break out at any moment. At that point, the Russians came to our aid and escorted us to the Oder Bridge. The soldiers walked beside us with their weapons drawn. The sentries were alerted ahead, and were told we had permission to cross. Upon reaching the Russian guards, they waved us through after briefly glancing at the documents. This was another time our "enemy" came to our rescue.

11

FREEDOM

The *Schlagbaum* "checkpoint" opened, and we ran non-stop across the damaged river bridge held up by pontoons. Mama was energized, pulling the cart as hard as she could and my sisters were straining to stay with her. It felt as though the cart was airborne, its wheels barely touching the ground as we were flying across the Oder River. I was still sitting on top of the wagon, and hanging on with all my strength.

Mama pinched herself to make sure it was for real and not a dream. As we reached the other side, the Americans opened the checkpoint and, with much joy, we stepped into freedom.

The Americans told us not to linger in the area too long. They didn't have to warn us twice. We wanted to get as far away from the Russians as we could. Upon reaching freedom, Mama got on her knees and kissed the ground. *Ich Danke meinen treuen Herrgott dass Er runs währent diesen Zeiten beschützte.* "She thanked God for being so faithful and for protecting us against all odds during this horrific time."

Mama noted in her journal, we didn't see anybody in the early morning hours. The traffic was light in both directions. We rested on the shoulder of the road and contemplated our next move. We were up all night, and had nothing to eat, but with all the excitement and adrenalin flowing, who needs to sleep or eat?

As time went on, we became tired, and fell asleep on the shoulder of the road. It was wonderful; not having to worry the Russian soldiers would take us away, or confiscate our meager rations. The Russians were concentrated closer by Berlin. Surprisingly, we didn't see any of the Red Army soldiers as we traveled to Leipzig. We found a bombed-out train station, but not many trains were leaving that day because of limited operation. Due to military necessity, the Russians kept the tracks clear to move troops and equipment.

We boarded the train that took us to Berlin. It was a short trip, and upon arriving at our destination, we found the city had been leveled. It was heartbreaking to see the destruction brought on by the war.

July the 4th 1945

The Allies made preparations to occupy Germany. July the 5th, we were directed to a refugee camp by the Russians where we received much needed food. We came across a Russian officer who supplied us with three liver sausage sandwiches and sardines. What we didn't eat that afternoon, Mama hid between our blankets and pillows. The next day, Mama was preparing our lunch when she discovered our food had been stolen.

The refugee camp was located in Kehlendorf by Berlin on Lauchtenberg Strasse. Due to hunger, we weren't able to walk anymore. There we were, the 16th of July 1945 lying on the sidewalk next to the curb begging for food. A Russian officer took pity on us and took us in his staff car to Laukwitz, on the outskirts of Berlin.

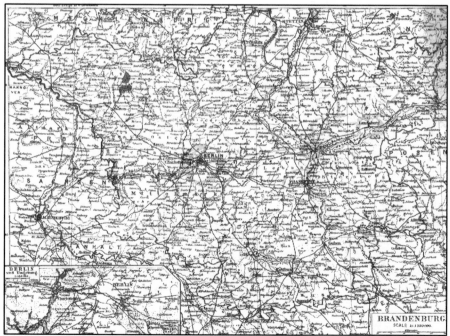

Sunday, August the 19th 1945

We arrived in Eisenach after a long ride from Laukwitz in an open

Russian troop transport truck. We were taken to the bombed-out train station, fatigued and very tired.

We slept on the cold, hard tile floor of the train depot. We read a sign, warning us of a Russian checkpoint four kilometers ahead.

Mama wrote in her journal, she disregarded the warning and traveled on foot to the Russian checkpoint. There, we received much needed food which included cherries, meat and potatoes. We were looking for a way to get to Leipzig where Papa's dad lived.

While in Berlin, we discovered locating Opa would be impossible, the whole city was impassable with streets blocked by debris from bombed-out buildings.

At four o'clock in the morning, we were awakened by Soviet soldiers who took us to Salz Zungen and from there we walked to Orndorf and arrived in Kreuzstadt Vacha early at five o'clock in the morning.

We received no food and had very little sleep. We were at the point of total collapse. Mama had no hope we would ever escape this dilemma. We tried leaning on a door, hoping to get some sleep with our heads in Mama's lap when we were awoken by a Russian tank as it drove past us. Mama said to us, jetzt müssen wir uns aufmachen so dass wir einen sicheren Platz finden. "We had better get going to a safer location."

Monday, August the 20th 1945

We found a farmhouse and were allowed to sleep in the hay barn overnight. We had a restless night. The constant hunger pains would not ease. Our stomachs hurt so bad that we labored getting up in the morning. Mama had a bottle of cognac stashed away hoping to trade it for food, but the Russians took it from her. Our options ran out. We scraped dry bread imbedded in the street and drank water from a bacteria infested pool.

> Our options ran out. We scraped the dry bread imbedded in the street and drank from a bacteria infested pool.

We became very ill from bacteria and were taken to a farmhouse where we met a Russian doctor who gave us medicine to stop our diarrhea and to keep us from throwing up. Mama and my sisters were terribly sick and at times too weak to stay awake, much less able to walk. It took weeks for us to regain some of our strength, but without proper nourishment, we were never at full strength. Gradually we regained some strength and moved to a meadow nearby. We sat in the wet grass, our clothes soaked through and through. On Wednesday 22nd of August 1945 we arrived at the Russian- American checkpoint, barely able to keep our heads up.

There, we received much needed nutrition from the Americans which included bread, sausage, and potatoes. To receive food for our empty stomachs was heavenly. God directed us to the place where we were served by angels.

Thursday, August the 23rd 1945

At six o'clock in the morning, we boarded a truck carrying salt. The vehicle transported salt from the mine in Hattorf. The trip was treacherous; we had no benches to sit on. We held on to each other for the fear of falling off as we bounced on the bed of the truck from the chuckholes and debris on the road. The salt truck drove some two-hundred kilometers through curvy, rough roads in the Taunus Mountains.

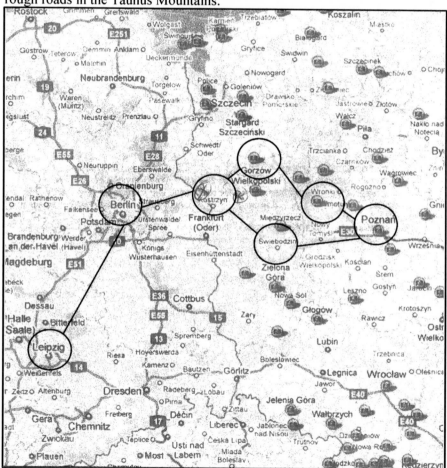

We arrived in Idstein by Frankfurt on the Oder at two o'clock in the morning in the middle of a rainstorm. We thought we still had some of the food tucked away in our small cart. Mama was shocked to discover again, the precious food had been stolen.

In Idstein, we were fortunate; a train arrived to take us to Leipzig. We boarded the train and discovered there were a just a few people taking the trip. This was luxury, and for a change we weren't occupying a cattle car. The car had wooden benches and windows for us to see the countryside as we rolled through the waves of green fields.

All along, we were hoping we wouldn't run into anymore Russians. We arrived within two hours and had no idea if Grandpa Berger was still around. There was no way to call him announcing our arrival.

Mama must have known where he lived, so we began to walk to his place. Ordinarily, it would not have been a problem; we were used to walking for miles, except for me. For Mama and my sisters, it would have been a walk in the park, had it not been for our tired, fatigued bodies. We were close to death.

Mama walked ahead, Herta held onto Helga tightly, embracing her. Gerlinde was very weak and tired as she dragged herself to grandpa's front door. We rang the door bell, hoping he would open the door. We weren't sure of the reception we would receive, since most of our other relatives shunned us. We truly looked like refugees coming from the war zone, dirty, hungry and emaciated.

When he saw us, tears rolled down grandpa's cheeks. He gave each of us a big hug and welcomed us to his place for much needed rest. Grandpa Berger provided us with wonderful food and much-needed sleep. Mama and Grandpa had many things to discuss. He had many questions about our flight from the Nazis and the Soviets. Mama filled him in where we had been, how we returned, and out of the reach of the Russians. The first night, they both stayed up until the early morning hours. He was astonished that we survived.

He asked about Papa, and Mama told him we hadn't been in contact for over a year. Telephone service was non-existent, and that was especially true in the eastern part of Germany. He tried to call Papa, but was unsuccessful.

We were with Grandpa for three weeks, and by then, he was tired of us interrupting his life. We had to move on; hoping our old place in Heidelberg was still standing. We didn't know if other people moved into our apartment in our absence.

We had traveled for almost a full day on foot after leaving Grandpa when we came to a big house in a small village. Mama parked our little cart at the front door. She rang the door bell and a man, the owner of the house opened the door. He saw us children and Mama standing there, and immediately invited us in.

We were still wearing the same old clothes; the girls still had occupants in their hair and clothes. The people made sure we cleaned up first, and offered to wash our clothes. It felt wonderful knowing we had escaped the Russians, and we were on the way to our home! Mama told them the incredible war stories and she stayed up until past midnight.

The Americans did us no harm. On the contrary, they helped us whenever they could, and that was quite a change from the Russians with a few exceptions. We had much to be thankful for, and if it hadn't been for the Americans, we would have never reached freedom. "A big thank you, America."

It was wonderful not having to worry about the Russians anymore; food and shelter were readily available now. We all got plenty of rest and our strength was restored, but getting around was difficult.

Most railroad stations were bombed-out by the Allies and bridges were dynamited by the Germans to slow down the Allies progress. It made it challenging to get back to Heidelberg, and caused us to travel many more miles.

Some refugees from eastern Germany eventually succeeded to reach the west. Those were the fortunate ones, grateful to be alive. Mama told me, every so often, she saw stressed, malnourished German soldiers with their torn uniforms and sunken cheeks.

They were also the fortunate ones to escape the Russians and the Gestapo. Towards the end of the war, if a German soldier walked away from battle, the Gestapo hung him from the nearest tree to tell other soldiers not to entertain the idea.

Mama flagged down a truck to take us to Heidelberg. She paid the driver with German Reich Marks, which were still honored by the banks as legal tender. There was a large amount of Reich Mark money around in the Russian sector. Nobody was able to use currency when the Russians occupied the land. As always, Mama had extraordinary wisdom and foresight. The money she had stored away came in handy and allowed us to buy food and transportation.

When we reached Heidelberg, it brought back many memories, some pleasant, and others not so great. When we left, all hell had broken loose as the Allies bombed the area around *Heidelberg*. Upon our return, the Americans were the liberators

Mama stopped at a *Gasthaus* and bought us sausage and soup. What a delight! We hadn't eaten anything like that for a very long time, and we ate until we were bloated.

Mama looked for a phone to call Papa; her heart was throbbing, we hadn't seen him for so long. She tried to dial Papa's work number, but for the excitement, she momentarily drew a blank and couldn't remember the number. When she dialed the second time, she reached him, and announced to him we were in Heidelberg.

On the other end was a deafening silence. Papa thought he would never see us again, unless God performed a miracle, and he did. His heart was pounding so hard, he had a hard time hearing Mama. He didn't waste any time, and with joy, we were reunited. We arrived at our apartment, and it looked the same as we left it.

Papa was imprisoned by the Americans while working in the hospital, which meant he couldn't leave his work place. He even slept there.

He told us being "held captive" by the Americans was no hardship. He wasn't confined to a cell, but was allowed to work freely as he moved about the hospital taking care of patients. After we had been back in Heidelberg for a short time, the Americans relaxed the rules, and he was able to come home most evenings.

One thing I remember clearly was, whenever he came home, he brought lots of chocolates, like Snickers bars, Hershey and other wonderful treats. Boy, we loved that.

When the Americans came to check on us, they were polite. They even rang the door bell. This was unlike the Russians, who would never ring the bell, but break down the door to make their presence known.

My sisters were still battling the lice imbedded in their clothes and hair. For whatever reason, the lice returned and the girls were tortured day and night. This had to stop when Mama bought strong medication at the pharmacy and got rid of these pests. She burned their clothes and replaced them with new garments she sewed. It was a relief not to be bothered by these pesky insects anymore, and not having to scratch was a huge relief. Somehow, I wasn't bothered by these pests. It just may be my sisters were sweeter than I was.

Mama wrote in her journal: God helped us through the tough times. She was in imminent danger many times, and was even injured by one of the Russians who stabbed her. She experienced forty rape attempts. Mama was close of giving up due to starvation. We were all close to death.

We had been back in Heidelberg for a short time, when Mama met a family at the city park. The woman's name was Brigitte Pschorr who didn't live far from our home. She moved to Heidelberg after Bitburg was destroyed by the Allies, to accept a job as a nurse. She was at the park with her three sons, two were my sister's age, and the oldest had turned thirteen. I was around four years of age.

There were swings and slides for the children's enjoyment. My sisters lifted me up on one of the swings and gently rocked me back and forth. While we were playing, Brigitte and Mama talked about their experiences in the latter part of the war.

In 1944, the Pschorrs lived by the French border, in the town of Seffern, located close to Bitburg. The fighting was horrendous as the Allies overran the area. Brigitte's husband Karl, was fighting in France. As a result, he was wounded during the battle of the Bulge, confined to a wheelchair, and never regained his health.

Bitburg was the staging area for the German troops on their way to occupy France. The town was one big heap of rubble where many civilians lost their lives during the air campaign. Seffern was mostly spared. Many of the Bitburg citizens hurried out of town to seek refuge there.

Towards the end of the war, the Nazis were looking for young and old to fight Hitler's losing war. During the day, Brigitte's three boys hid in the nearby forest, hoping to elude the Gestapo locals who did the dirty work for Hitler. Had they found Gustav, they would have taken him, although he was only twelve years old at the time.

One day, Gustav was talking to one of the neighbors who told him stories of the devastation taking place. One of the party members overheard their conversation. The man who was talking to Gustav was captured by the local Nazis and never seen again. It was said they took him to a yard and shot him in cold blood, as he begged for his life. He left behind a family of four children, and no father to support them.

The Nazis were searching for Gustav, who remained hidden in the forest. Frau Pschorr made sure her son had food, and made trips to his hideout each night, just after dark and carried what she could for Gustav's survival. Her son was holed up in one of the many caves in the foothills of the *Eifel Mountains*. She was very much afraid she would be spotted by one of the local Nazis on one of her treks to the cave. Each night, she wore different clothes and various wigs to conceal her identity.

She carried a flashlight, but turned it on discreetly, making sure that no one was watching her. She selected a different route each night, so, whoever might have been watching, didn't know for sure who the woman was. It was wrought with danger walking alone in total darkness. On clear nights, all she had was the moon and stars as her companions.

In her absence, her other two sons were left alone and anxiously waited for her to return. She couldn't afford to be gone too long. The distance she covered was about five kilometers each way, and it was especially difficult during rainstorms. She walked on the edge of a gravel road, which made it much easier as she avoided the ruts and chuckholes.

Gustav was more concerned about his mother than himself. The Nazis knew where his mother lived, and he was afraid for her safety. He was in a relatively safe location but he wasn't entirely convinced he was secure.

Whenever she returned from seeing Gustav, she was so exhausted from the ordeal, she collapsed on the floor. Her tears rolled down her cheeks like a never ending well, and she cried for her family and prayed to God that He would provide for their everyday needs, and for their safety. Her husband wasn't able to help much. He was paralyzed from the waist down, the result of shrapnel lodged in his back.

Thirty minutes after his mother left the cave, Gustav saw a flashlight in the far distance, drawing ever closer to him. He figured it wasn't his mom since she left not long ago and wouldn't be returning this soon, unless she forgot something. Gustav was getting nervous and accidentally tripped over a rock in the cave, producing a horrendous amount of noise which bounced off the walls, magnifying the sound a hundredfold. Gustav was now able to see a figure coming closer to his hideout, and with angst he crawled into the far corner of the cave and hid behind a big boulder, fearing the worse.

A beam of the flashlight illuminated the area around him. The man called out his name. How did he know his name? It was clear; someone was watching his mother going to the cave and knew Gustav's whereabouts.

There was no use for concealment any longer. The mystery man knew by now, where he was. Gustav made himself visible to the mysterious figure. He emerged from behind the boulder with his hands up in the air. He was afraid of getting shot by the man who turned out to be his neighbor Franz.

At the time, it was difficult to tell friend from foe. Franz talked to the youngster and told him to come into the town with him. He had no choice but to comply with his demand. They walked back without speaking a word. For Franz, he was in an awkward situation. The coward remained silent.

The boy was shocked. Why would a neighbor he had known all his life turn him over to the Gestapo? Franz was a postal carrier, a respected man in town. He was a good friend of his father and visited him often after Karl came home from the hospital. All the while, Gustav kept the option open to perhaps evade the captor armed with a *Wehrmacht* "Army" Luger pistol strapped to his black belt.

In the meantime, Gustav's mother tried to get some sleep on the sofa. She was restless and felt something terrible was happening. She feared for her son's life. The other two boys were sound asleep upstairs. Brigitte paced the floor from one end to the other. Tears kept streaming down her cheeks.

When Franz and Gustav arrived back in town, at around two in the morning, they came to a house on the outskirts of town. There, they were met by two SS officers. Gustav was horribly afraid something awful was about to transpire. They tied his hands and feet to keep him from escaping.

They sat Gustav on a hard wooden chair, and the interrogation process began. To start out with, one of the officers slapped Gustav repeatedly when he didn't answer him. Gustav kept silent and the same officer kicked him in the groin. Gustav fell to the ground with pain shooting through his lower extremities. The two men picked him off of the floor and sat him back down on the chair. The punishment continued. Gustav was in a great deal of pain He blacked out and when he came to, they continued the brutality. The men left for a brief moment when Gustav collapsed again and fell on the cold concrete floor. This continued until after eight in the morning.

When he awoke, the men were back, sitting by a table and eating their breakfast which consisted of hard rolls and ham. The smell of breakfast nauseated him. Gustav was in no mood to eat, he only wanted to get away from this place and nurse his wounds.

The SS officers couldn't get anything of value from Gustav and decided to let him go. They un-cuffed him, kicked him out the front door and into the muddy street. Almost too weak to walk, with each step, pain shot through his legs like a lightning bolt. It was still dark as he dragged himself home through the rain. By now, the deep mud penetrated his clothes.

After two long hours, he reached home but was barely able to stand up as he strained to reach the doorknob with his bloody hands. His mother heard Gustav's moaning and hastened to open the door. She was shocked to see her son with blood streaming down his face, and his mud covered body. She bent down, helped him to his feet, and carried him to the sofa.

She cleaned him, wiped the blood from his face which had dried on his skin. She knew what had happened, and was afraid the Gestapo would be back for her son at any moment. After a few days, Gustav slowly recovered physically from his horrible ordeal, but was very much afraid. The result was, he experienced horrible nightmares and hoping this ordeal would soon stop.

The Gestapo knew where they could find him. Brigitte, his mother wanted to leave and hide at another location, but Hitler's men would probably have been able to discover their hiding place. Would the Gestapo come and drag him off to war? Gustav's mother hid him in the basement. The cellar was concealed with wooden boards, laid on top of the floor, way back in the corner where she piled her clothes, etc. Nobody would have ever guessed that there was an entry to the cellar.

It was now the end of October. It turned very cold with snow on the ground. His mother stacked wood on the outside wall to last for a couple of months, but food was scarce, and most of the chicken they raised had been consumed. The Pschorr's were self-sufficient up to this point, and they hoped the war would soon end.

The Nazis never came back. On May the 8th of 1945, the war was over. Mama and Brigitte continued to share many more horror stories. The women received the worst of the conflict. Life would never be the same for them, but now they had the opportunity to start anew, in great part with the help of the United States. The Nazi regime had run its course.

They parted, and promised to see each other again.

12

THE PRICE OF WAR

We learned later, after our lives returned to normal, many millions of Jews lost their lives in the concentration camps and died a horrible death at the hands of these murderers. Some of the Jews, if they had skills, were used to build airplanes, tanks and other tools of war. Those were the lucky ones.

If they fell ill due to starvation, they were thrown into the concentration camps where they were gassed and buried in mass graves. German companies were using Jews, as well as other "undesirables" to work in their factories to produce the war machinery. Hitler assumed total control of all manufacturing, banks, and other essential services.

Der Führer didn't tolerate other races, including the Slavs. Among them were the Russians, Poles, Czechs, Bulgarians and other people east of the German border. These people were coined *Untermenschen,* "sub-humans". As he conquered Poland, Czechoslovakia and large parts of Russia, his intentions were to use them as slaves to enrich the *Vaterland*, and ultimately rule the whole world.

The insane asylums were emptied; death awaited the infirm as well as Christians. Hitler sent Gypsies as well as hundreds of thousands of Slavs to the camps. Prisons were vacated as well.

If one was found guilty of a crime, or if you opposed Hitler, you were given a short trial, then either shot, or sent to the Russian front.

At the beginning of the Barbarossa campaign, many Russian soldiers were taken captive. It is estimated, the number was close to seven million. Very few ever returned home. The Nazis were starving them, and they ultimately died of malnutrition. Many were used as slaves in factories. For the captives, it was a slow death.

Hitler was arrogant and power hungry, which caused him to be irrational. He inflicted unspeakable tragedies all over the world. Dr. Mengele was a physician, chosen by the Nazis to experiment on prisoners, mainly Jews as well as other unfortunate souls. He used these people as guinea pigs by injecting them with all kinds of viruses just to see how they would react, just to watch them die a slow and painful death.

Hitler even took their gold teeth and melted them down to manufacture industrial products. Annihilation of Hitler and his cronies couldn't come quick enough, but although there were seven assassination attempts, he walked away unscathed. Thank God for the United States who rescued many of the prisoners and set them free.

In 1945 towards the end of the war, the Germans brought their injured soldiers home from the Russian front by the way of the Baltic. It was the only route, since the Red Army closed off the land route to the west.

On a couple of occasions, the ship "Steuben" with five thousand patients and the ship "Goya" with one thousand, were torpedoed by a Russian submarine and sunk with all people lost including the crew. It was revenge.

A luxury passenger ship "Gustloff" met the same fate. Nine thousand refugees and injured soldiers lost their lives. One thousand survived the sinking of the "Gustloff" including the *Kapitän* "Captain".

Hitler was a fraud, and of Austrian birth; not having a father to guide him in his early youth caused him to be insecure and a loner. His real name was not Hitler, but Schicklhuber. In my research I discovered he was part Jewish.

He went to great lengths to level the graves of his relatives so as to not reveal his true ancestry.

The Russians conquered Berlin, their ultimate prize, and lost around seventy-thousand soldiers and three hundred thousand were wounded. The Germans lost around forty thousand soldiers and hundreds of thousands were wounded as well.

Dresden, the Venice of Germany, was leveled by British and American bombers towards the end of the war. Fifty-thousand civilians died in the tremendous firestorms.

Königsberg was a gorgeous city with its old town and the gothic cathedral. The majestic tower could be seen from miles around. The town was on the Baltic and surrounded by thousands of lakes with good fishing and hunting.

The European buffalo, known as *Wisent* in German, as well as moose, were plentiful. It is comparable to Minnesota in climate and geography, but a bit farther north in latitude. Due largely to the war, both species were extinct.

At least one famous person was born in Königsberg: namely Richard Wagner, the famous composer. It was also the place where Kaiser Wilhelm the First was coroneted. *Königsberg* was eventually destroyed by the second wave of Russians, like many other towns. The beautiful cathedral was left intact, and perhaps the Russian soldiers were seeking a place of refuge.

The war was horrible with many lives lost. It is estimated, up to a million Germans from the eastern regions never made it to the American sector. They were relocated to Siberia, where they were interned in labor camps. I have reason to believe, some of my mother's relatives were included in the relocation.

The Germans lost approximately eight million soldiers in the war, and the Russians lost even more. When the Germans first pushed into Russia, they took seven million Russians prisoner. Few of them ever made it out alive.

Due to the air campaign by the Allies, about 500,000 civilians perished on the eastern front, and another 500,000 lost their lives trapped by the Russians. The German government estimates around one and a half million German soldiers were transported to Siberia by the Russians.

Few ever made it back to Germany. Chancellor Konrad Adenauer, the first Chancellor of post-war Germany, arranged to have five thousand prisoners released.

The exact numbers are hard to verify due to the confusion during the war. I am thankful to the United States, Russia, Poland, France and England who liberated the countries Hitler occupied. It is gratifying to know the Führer will never come back.

In 1948, Papa acquired a job in Munich, the capitol of the state of Bavaria. We moved to southern Germany when I was six. From then on, my childhood was like a fairytale, a wonderful place to live.

13

OH, HEIDELBERG HOW WE MISSED YOU

How wonderful it was to be back in Heidelberg with the tranquil way of life, overlooking the Neckar River and the castle still guarding the city below. We began to resume our life we had left behind many months before. By now, I was three years old, and exploring the things around me. I loved sitting at the window overlooking the Neckar River as it wound its way through town, dividing the old and the new.

I was fascinated by all the traffic on the river with its many barges and ships winding their way upstream to Mannheim. Rebuilding had begun in earnest, and construction was evident wherever you looked. Tall cranes lined the river, unloading material for the reconstruction of the cities. There was no time to waste.

Many afternoons, I fed the seagulls flying by our window. I took stale bread, and piece by piece threw it to the seagulls in flight and to my surprise they caught it in midair, and never missed.

I never introduced Papa's delicious creations to the birds. We discovered Papa was a marvelous baker, and on weekends when he was home from work, he baked us delicious pastries for breakfast. The aroma filled the place, and before long it wound its way into our bedroom.

That woke us all quickly. There was no time to waste as we filed out of our bedrooms and indulged ourselves. Oh, they were so good, and we couldn't get enough of them.

Time had a way of getting away, and before long, I turned five, and things hadn't changed much, except we were now a little older. My sisters had gone to school for some time, and had lots of friends who came over to visit, and they played games of all sorts. Games girls play and I was pretty much left out.

They did stuff I wasn't at all interested in, like playing with dolls for hours at a time, dressing and undressing them. Mama sewed different dresses for the dolls, and my sisters had fun keeping them in style.

Mama had the idea of sending me to Kindergarten. She went to the school and asked if they still had room for me, and they were delighted to have me join them. Mama sewed new pants and a starched shirt for the occasion. She took me to the local shoe store to buy me a pair of brown shoes. The shoes were so shiny, I could see my reflection.

I don't remember whether I liked the idea of going to school, but I had no choice, but go. Thinking they might have some snacks for me, especially for a new kid, I walked in, introduced myself to the kids, and I was ushered into a room where the children were making sand cakes.

What kind of nonsense is that? It didn't at all appeal to me, and I snuck out the back while they weren't looking. I hurried out of the building before anybody noticed me gone, and got lost in the midst of traffic as I walked home, covering many blocks. I don't remember how I found my way back, but I did. This could have turned out to be tragic, because I could have gotten lost, or some stranger could have picked me up. Mama was stunned to see me coming in out from the street, and into our apartment. She didn't get mad at me, and was glad that I arrived in one piece.

I was overjoyed when Mama didn't send me back to school, and. I resumed my place by the window as before, observing the river traffic, and of course the seagulls welcomed me back. I remember doing this for hours at a time. How much more exciting can life get? Barges were carrying all types of freight, from building material to vehicles, mainly trucks.

14

POSTWAR YEARS

Things looked tranquil on the outside, but the memories of the war were still fresh in our minds. Herta the oldest, along with my other sister Gerlinde were plagued with nightmares. Their nightmares consisted of Russian soldiers violating them. That was frightful. The horror continued for years, even to today. My nightmares of burning up in a nuclear explosion and Russian planes bombing our neighborhood ended after reaching the United States. I was freed from the hellish images of war.

We left my sister Herta behind when we emigrated to the U.S. It was heartbreaking. She was married and couldn't leave her family. Herta was my idol, she watched over me, during, and after the war. I literally worshipped her. It seemed she knew so much, and had an answer for just about any subject. She did a lot of reading as a child and stored lots of information in her head.

I missed her, but there was no way for her to join us after all these years. I believe both of my older sisters are plagued with post-traumatic stress disorder. In those days, there was little help for them. The term hadn't been invented, but the pain was very real just the same. Herta had the most difficult time; she still has vivid memories of what occurred while we were trapped in the midst of the Russian occupying forces.

If anybody had traumatic stress symptoms, it was Mama. She suffered all her life with horrendous events, etched into her mind. Her nerves were damaged from the vivid memories of the war when she witnessed horrific events. The trip from hell imprisoned Mama forever, and it was difficult for her to be happy. She lacked emotions, even when we kids were playing and having a good time.

Mama took Herta, four at the time, and Gerlinde two, on a walk along the bank of the Neckar River. The waves were crashing against the banks with fury. Papa was working, and had no idea what was about to transpire.

My sisters were frightened of drowning as the waves came dangerously close. Mama intended to toss them into the angry waves. A couple saw what was about to happen, and intervened, rescuing the girls in the nick of time. They took Mama without a struggle and handed her over to the authorities. My sisters were brought home in Papa's care.

She was sent to one of the sanatoriums for observation, and was released after a lengthy stay. The medical staff determined that she no longer was a threat to herself or others. Things returned to near normal, and life went on.

One evening, I overheard my parents' conversation; Papa had an offer to work in Munich at the prestigious Max Planck Institute. I didn't think much about it; I had no idea where Munich was. It could have been in China for all I knew.

On a Saturday, we were having breakfast when they broke the news to us. We are moving to Bavaria. I asked myself, "Where in the world is Bavaria?" I didn't want to leave. I loved living by the beautiful river, and the adorable castle that welcomed me each morning.

It all happened too fast. Mama and Papa started to pack up, arranged for a moving van to pick up our household items, and we were on our way to a land of enchantment. When we arrived in Bavaria, we had a surprise waiting for us as the Bavarian Alps came into view. We had never seen mountains that were this majestic, and to top it off, our new home was at the base of the mountains.

We were blessed to have had the opportunity to move where the Alps greeted us each day. Whenever I have gone back for a visit, it makes me wonder why we left. Our new home was next to the Tyrolean Ache River, with its breathtaking view.

Each morning, the *Hochgern* Mountain welcomed me to another day with its snowy peak that glistened in the evening sun. The river behind our house intrigued me, and you would find me there almost every day, waiting for the river to reveal its secret to me.

My childhood was a dream come true. I roamed the wide open spaces. With the close mountains beckoning us each day, it didn't take long for us to settle in. The earlier days were a distant memory, or were they? My sisters never said much about their experiences from the war, but they were still tormented. Moving away from Heidelberg didn't erase those memories.

At the bank of the river, we found rifles stacked high with other weapons including hand grenades from German soldiers, left there, when they retreated south to evade the Allies. Seeing all the war material, we recalled things we would have rather forgotten.

We played with German *Wehrmacht "helmets"* found strewn about our neighborhood. We tried on the helmets for size, but they were just a little too big. The rims came clear down to our chin. We pretended to be German soldiers, and crawled into the ditches pretending to shoot Russians.

For me, it was just a game. I don't remember much of the horrible war days, only what Mama told me. It may have affected me in some way because when I went to grade school, it was difficult for me to adjust.

When we moved away from Heidelberg, Mama was stressed out. She had to do practically everything to prepare for the move to Bavaria. Papa was working, and wouldn't get home until the weekend. While we settled into our new, beautiful home, she acquired a job at a television manufacturing plant.

The work consisted of piecework and it was very stressful for her. She earned according to what she produced. While she worked at the plant, she suffered a nervous breakdown. Knowing her, she worked as fast and hard as she could, and that placed a huge strain on her. She was still in survival mode as during the war.

Mama became physical with at least three people that I know of. Was this the result of the war, or did she have other problems? The first time, she slapped our landlord while living in Staudach, Bavaria. As a result, we were forced to look for another place to live.

After we moved from the beautiful home, we ended up on the other side of town. The home was more economical. Mama and Papa were still struggling economically and the move freed up precious resources. It wasn't the best place, but we children had no choice. As it turned out, the apartment was a dump, and the landlord was a slum lord. The living conditions were appalling. We had no running water, and the community toilets were filthy and covered with maggots.

On the plus side, the Tyrolean Ache River was our neighbor, and I loved to pay it a visit. We had lived there for a couple of years, when Mama had her fill with the slum lord, and slapped her. It surprised me it took that long. We were forced to move again and ended up in Lorenzenberg, closer to Munich.

While we lived there, Mama was under much stress when she lost control of her anger and pushed a guy down a flight of stairs. He wasn't injured and no charges were filed. She didn't take guff from anybody, whether man or woman. She grew up in East Prussia, and those folks were rough and tough. Her dad was a grumpy old, cantankerous man, and had a difficult time getting along with people. Mama inherited the temper from her dad.

When Mama was a little girl in East Prussia, the Russians invaded the land. Mama and her parents were driven from their comfortable home and relocated farther west to evade the Russians. During that time, her dad was away fighting on the Russian front.

The Red Army leveled towns, much like during WWII. At one point, the German Army got the upper hand and drove the Russians back across the border. The armistice in 1918 ended the war. Opa's home was destroyed, and they were forced to start all over again. This had a cumulative effect on Mama and robbed her of her childhood.

In Heidelberg, we were forced to move repeatedly because she couldn't get along with her neighbors. One of the reasons Mama and Papa wanted to move away from Heidelberg was to recover mentally from the horrible things they both endured. Mama's nerves were kaput, and she had a difficult time dealing with the everyday problems. Even after moving to the United States, she was still tortured by the past. Papa was a kind man, and went out of his way to make her life pleasant.

To my knowledge, Mama was never evaluated by a neurologist, and if she had undergone appropriate tests, perhaps they could have helped her.

15

BAVARIA, YOU'RE BEAUTIFUL

Off we went to Bavaria, the largest state in Germany, located by Austria to the south, and Switzerland directly to the west. I was excited, my life would never be the same, living in a new strange land, and out in the country as opposed to the urban life I was used to.

Leaving Heidelberg was difficult for us children. My sisters had many friends and I missed my Neckar River. The seagulls missed me when they didn't see me sitting by the open window. They probably were wondering what happened to me, when I wasn't occupying my old perch at the window.

Our trip was exciting. The train wound its way through rolling hills on the way to the Bavarian border, passing many quaint little towns along the way. As we came closer to our destination, the landscape became hilly and greener with colorful flowers on the balconies of the big farmhouses. Every so often, the train stopped, and we we'd get out to stretch our legs and use the facilities.

My sisters made sure they arrived looking pretty, and powdered up at every stop. I didn't understand why girls would go through all that trouble. They were pretty without all the make-up. I couldn't care less what I looked like. I hadn't combed my hair in days. Strands of thick blond hair stood straight up like a brush. Who cares, we were on our way to the most beautiful place in Germany. The green seats on the coach had thick cushions, offering us a pleasant ride. It was a relief not getting a sore behind by not sitting on hard wooden benches, or even on the floor of the cars as was the case in the past. We disembarked in the town of Traunstein by the beautiful Chiemsee, the largest freshwater lake in Bavaria after we had traveled for five hours. It is where crazy King Ludwig II built a castle, a replica of the Versailles in France. The landscape was spectacular with the enormous farmhouses meticulously maintained dotting the landscape.

We boarded a second train, a much smaller one this time, taking us to Grassau, located by the Tyrolean Ache River. The trip didn't take but a half an hour when we arrived at our destination. We stepped off the train and the majestic mountains came into view welcoming us to Bavaria, our new home.

Papa was on his way from Munich to meet us in Grassau. He must have been on the train right behind us. This was his first trip to the region and he was taken in by the beauty. From Grassau we walked two kilometers to Staudach Egerndach, by the way of the Ache River Bridge, and arrived at our home resembling the gingerbread house of "Hansel and Gretel".

The hills appeared like velvet among the huge, well-maintained farmhouses tucked away in the valley. What a quaint house it was, with a tall green hedge and pine trees ringing the property. The house was two-story with green gutters. Each window was draped with cascading colorful flowers. The moving van beat us to our new home. The driver was waiting for us and he even helped us unload the van.

Everything was now stacked on the front lawn waiting for us to carry it all inside. We immediately got busy taking our household goods and furniture into our new homestead. Mama was picky where we placed our items. She had it all planned out and when we were done, it looked beautiful. By now, our arms and feet were tired from hauling household items into the house and we looked forward to some deserved rest as we relaxed on the steps in front of our door catching our breath.

The house had lots of room, three bedrooms, one for my parents, one for my sisters, and one for me. This was the first time in my life I had my own bedroom. It suited me just fine not having to share the bedroom with my sisters.

The house even had a sunroom enclosed with glass, allowing for lots of light to get in, warming the room in the summer. In the winter, it was rather cold, and we spent all of our time by the little stove in the kitchen. We met our new landlord, Frau Auer, who welcomed us to our new home with a big hug. We weren't a hugging family, but it comforted us nonetheless. I was so happy, and it was hard for me to keep my emotions in check. I began to sing and whistle the songs I had learned in Heidelberg, by listening to my sisters. I felt like celebrating, and shouting from the bottom of my lungs. I yelled out, "I love my new home."

There was one thing I hadn't given much thought to. I noticed people speaking a dialect I wasn't familiar with, and couldn't understand what they were saying. If I had any chance of making new friends, I had better learn to speak Bavarian.

It was quite different from the official High German. They used different words, and pulled several words together to form a sentence. It was obvious, I wasn't a native Bavarian and it took me a while to get the hang of it. In time, I spoke just like the natives. I made friends quickly, and things were looking up.

The land was magic! The meadows were the greenest of green, the sky was my favorite blue and wherever I went, I was able to sneak into the barns and talk to the cows and horses, providing I got past the guard dogs and roosters. The cattle had always time to listen while they chewed their cud.

They must have been bored, always tied up in their stalls. The only time they saw anybody was when they were milked and that wasn't a pleasant activity. I loved their big brown eyes and long eyelashes. Oh, I was so very happy to witness the magic of farm life.

What a gorgeous place. I awoke each morning with the mountain peaks rising above the valley floor, Hochgern being the tallest. It was the happiest place on Earth. No matter how bad things were, the beautiful mountains made my heart rejoice.

My sister Helga and I made the rounds walking around the hedge that encircled the house when we encountered something strange. I asked Helga if she had ever seen anything like what we were looking at, and she said "never." I couldn't put my finger on it, in retrospect, it was a good thing. We observed the animal for a moment and noticed it had quills all over its body. When it saw us, it curled into tight a ball. After it sensed there was no danger, it uncurled, and ran back into the hedge. Its little head was black, with a pointed nose and little black eyes.

I told Papa what we had seen, and he told me they were hedgehogs. In German they are called *Igel*. I wanted to make friends with my new neighbors. To entice them, I put out a dish of milk, and in the morning they had licked the bowl dry. Not to get punished by Mama, I kept it a secret when I fed the hedgehogs. I sat outside, calling the hedgehogs to come and drink my milk. One by one, they cautiously merged from their nest deep inside the green hedge. At first they were reluctant, and any movement by me, they ran back into their hiding place. In a couple of weeks they had become almost as tame as housecats and followed me around hoping I would offer them food.

In the countryside, cows and horses grazed nearby.

I had only seen a horse and a few cows when we visited Opa in Berlin. It was now a distant memory. I stood by the fence and watched them by the hour. When they came towards me, I backed off afraid of getting bit or kicked. Perhaps they wanted to be friendly, but I didn't take any chances.

Up the street from our house was a quaint farmhouse where I befriended Gustei who was my age. We were full of energy, and together we roamed the countryside. There was much to investigate.

One particular day, Gustei and I had the privilege of watching over a herd of cattle. Gustei's mom packed a lunch for us consisting of rye bread, and a little bit of ham and cheese. It was fabulous! Our job was to make sure none of the cows wandered off. Gustei and I were amazed at the size of these animals as they grazed close by. One cow was nosy, and bumped us as if to say, "Do you want to share your meal?" I knew cows didn't like bread and meat, so there was nothing to worry about. If they would have wanted to do us harm, all they would have had to do is walk over us, and we would have been just a clump of dirt in the middle of the pasture.

After school, Gustei and I wandered from farmhouse to farmhouse. We came across a green Deutz farm tractor. It was beautiful, with big, black rear tires, and much taller than we were. The farmer saw us staring at the machine and came to investigate, wondering what we were up to. He noticed us looking at his new green tractor and we wished we could have taken it for a ride. To my delight, he lifted me high up into the seat. It felt like I had won a million Marks. We had a wonderful time, and never thought it would be this exciting. The farmer invited us into his home and offered us apple cider he brought up from the cellar. Oh, what a treat! It was as smooth as Beethoven's symphonies. Most farmers made their own fermented apple cider. It certainly had a kick and it could have easily knocked us off of our feet.

In Bavaria, people had no direct heat. Only a stove in the family room or kitchen, but it didn't provide quite enough heat for the whole house. The livestock added the extra heat when needed. When I went back for a visit, I was shocked to find that most of the farmhouses still didn't have central heating installed yet.

It always puzzled me why tall manure piles were at the entrance of the houses. I later discovered it was a sign the farmer was successful. The more cattle he had, the higher the pile. That is where we get the saying, "piled high and deep". One drawback was there were lots of pesky flies in the summer, as well as in the winter months, not to mention the smell.

In the spring, the meadows were teeming with the most beautiful wild flowers. The prettiest are the *Schneeglöckchen* "snowbells" which turned the meadows into a white blanket in early spring. The green leaves pushed through the snow, and the white, delicate bells followed. I knew then, spring was at our doorstep.

It was a special evening when my sisters and I were allowed to sit with our landlord past bedtime, along with Mama and Papa. I heard fascinating tales about the Alps. High in the mountains, the Edelweiss and Enzian flowers were hidden in the crevices of the cliffs.

To pick the flower, a young man had to be a top notch mountain climber, even risking his life to come home with one of those beautiful flowers for the girl he loved. All these tall tales fascinated me. I promised, when I grew up and found the girl of my dreams I would fetch her beautiful Edelweiss from the heights in the Alps covered in a velvety white coat. Another beautiful flower was the Enzian, a bell-shaped blue flower, as blue as the Bavarian sky. Some men lost their lives going after these prized treasures.

I asked the adults all kinds of questions and was surprised when they didn't get tired of all my inquiries. One was, where do the cows get nourishing food? Their answer was: after the snowmelt, the farmers walk their cattle up into the Alps. It was a big job, and not without danger. They walked the path carved into the mountain many years ago. Nonetheless, the cows had to climb through thick brush and around boulders. After a hard climb, they reached the destination. The grass was tall and lush green, a gourmet meal for the cattle.

Now the hard job began. The cows were milked in the early morning hours and in the evening before dark. The rich *Milch* "milk" was used to make all types of rich cheeses, like Swiss, Cheddar and other cheeses. Butter was of the best quality, and when spread on a slice of rye bread, it was marvelous.

Mostly, tourists visited the *Alm* "alpine restaurant" to relax and enjoy the beautiful outdoors. I cherished the fragrances of the trees and the flowers ringing the meadows. Mama and Papa took me along to one of the cottages we call the *Alm*. We were tired from climbing all morning and it was a breath of fresh air when we found one of the huts at the rim of the forest.

The green meadows stretched out like a table cloth adorned with blue and red alpine flowers. We selected a table under a big fir tree which happened to be the home of a pair of ravens, anxiously waiting for us to throw them a morsel. The ravens were beautiful birds. Their feathers were a steel blue and the beak like a hammer they use to crack nuts and other types of food.

We ordered Bavarian *Semmelknödel* "dumplings", pork and sauerkraut. Papa ordered a bottle of beer and allowed me the pleasure to take sip. Mama struck up a conversation with the lady manager of the place, who told her she was the wife of the *Senner*. Ordinarily, a husband and wife, *Senner and Sennerin* managed the hütte "*cottage*" that included taking care of the cattle, making the cheese and butter. They also baked breads which required them to get up very early even before the sun was up. They worked day and night. It is even done today, but most farmers employ helpers, especially during the heavy tourist season.

If you were looking for a break from the everyday grind, that was the place. Enjoying the beautiful mountains and eating the delicious cheese and ham between the slices of home baked bread was heaven on Earth. What a dream! The beer wasn't bad either, light or dark. I preferred the dark, it had more body.

I loved the art of yodeling and listening to the singers was a special treat. How in the world did they do that? I practiced yodeling, but I wasn't very successful. I couldn't get my throat or tongue to cooperate. Yodeling was common where I lived. I asked the local folk how the art of yodeling came about.

In the past, the mountain folks of Bavaria, Austria and Switzerland, communicated via yodeling across the peaks and valleys. It was long before telephones were invented. Each yodeler had a different meaning, and if you didn't hear it the first time, the repetitious echoes resonating through the mountains made it clear to the recipient what the message was. It is said, yodeling isn't learned, and one is born with it. On certain days during the year, the locals put on a traditional Bavarian, Austrian show which included accordions, trumpets and *Alpen* "alpine" horn, along with yodeling.

The alpenhorn sounded like no other instrument with its rich tone that could be heard clear down in the valley. It became a happy place, where the trees clapped their hands for joy.

There was no better place to spend the time other than the *Königsee* "king lake" by *Berchtesgarden*. The majestic *Watzmann* Mountain rose out of the lake, and reached into

> It became the happiest place on Earth, where the trees clapped their hands for joy.

the upper heights. On the lake, trumpeters played various pieces of music, producing beautiful echoes, which reflected off of the mountainside.

The music traveled across the lake many times over. I was fortunate to witness the magic when I visited Bavaria thirty-two years later. What delight awaited me; it still resonates after all these years.

On occasions I wandered through the forests, when I came across sure-footed cattle grazing on the hillside of the mountain. The cattle had been up in the Alps all summer. Around mid September, before the snow, the farmers walked the cattle back down the mountains with a joyous celebration.

The cows were decorated with the most beautiful flowers, a big wreath hung around their necks, adorned with flowers, bells and other beautiful ornaments. I heard, and saw the cattle coming into town with their bells ringing through the narrow cobblestone streets. I walked with other kids alongside them, happy that the cows as well as the *Sennerin and Senner* came down safely. I was part of it, and with luck, I was given one of the prized ornaments.

On the other hand, if there was an accident, and one of the cows fell off a cliff, it made the rocks cry out with grief. There were no festivities, the cattle were not decorated. The cows with sad-looking eyes lumbered along, their heads downcast which reminded me of a funeral procession. These experiences are permanently etched into my mind.

It wasn't long before the locals asked me all kinds of questions about my family. They were curious who moved into their neighborhood. I was eager to share stories, especially when the topic was about my "sweet" sisters.

My oldest sisters, Herta and Gerlinde had many admirers, who were hoping to become acquainted with my sisters when my parents weren't home. Everybody in town knew who these boys were, and how often they came for a friendly visit. Boys from around the towns came at all hours with their bicycles and if they were well to-do, they showed up with their BMW bikes. Most drove the 250 cc, a smaller motorcycle but a few had the powerful 500 cc with cylinders protruding on both sides of the bike.

Mama worked away from home teaching young farm girls to sew. She traveled far and wide throughout Bavaria. At times, she was gone for weeks, coming home only on weekends. Papa was working in Munich and was gone all week; you can imagine what kinds of trouble we got into in their absence.

I kidded my sisters Herta and Gerlinde about a particular boy who made a couple of visits. He definitely wasn't the best looking kid in town. I didn't want to miss his visit; his appearance reminded me of an amphibian. asked them when they were expecting "bull frog". I wanted to be there. I had never seen anybody that unsightly with big, bulging eyes. He didn't leave the best impression, and after a couple of visits, I didn't see him come around anymore.

My sisters set their standards much higher, and I was glad of that. They had to kiss a few frogs to find a prince.

It didn't take long for my sisters to find out who was responsible for spreading malicious stories about them around town. One of the stories was who came to visit my sisters and how long they stuck around. From that moment on, they were more secretive when I was around them. It caused me to run out of juicy stories and I was forced to shut down my "Inquirer" press for the time being.

Mama worked hard to make ends meet, but at the same time, we could have ended up as little law breakers. In a sense we were. We took fruit off of the trees from the farmers to nourish our hungry stomachs. In Germany that was not considered theft, it was called *Mundraub*, "mouth thievery".

My sisters were a pain. They loved torturing me. I had to get even with them, especially Helga. In Bavaria we had little, non-poisonous snakes, a little bigger than a night crawler. I captured one of these little cold, slimy amphibians, known as *Blindschleiche*, and before Helga went to bed, I snuck into her bedroom and placed it under the covers at the bottom of her bed. I was waiting for a piercing yell at any moment when she crawled into her soft feather bed, and I didn't have to wait long. Sure enough, I heard a blood-curdling scream coming out of the bedroom. She discovered the cold, slimy snake as it wrapped itself around her ankle. She could have died of a heart attack. I was thankful she survived that scare.

I could always count on a payback, and fully expected it at any moment. I kept vigilant for a good reason when I was around any of my sisters. Helga hadn't forgiven me for the last episode, and I wasn't ready for what was about to transpire.

Helga and I were playing in the backyard when she became agitated at me and threw a tin can right into my face. I sustained a deep cut just above my left eyebrow, and bled like a pig. She was worried I would tell Mama. I assured her it would be a well-kept secret if we worked out some kind of arrangement.

Mama asked me how I sustained the cut, and I told her I fell down the stairs. Her reply was, "Don't be so clumsy from now on." I received no sympathy from her. Covering up for Helga was probably not the wisest thing to do, but I wanted to be a brother who kept his word.

Helga said if I covered up her deed, she would not enlist me to do the dishes for the next two months. What a deal, I couldn't pass it up. Was she going to live up to the treaty? But just as I thought, she broke our agreement early. I thought of another way to pay her back, and the potato field provided me with a perfect tool.

Coming home from picking potatoes, I brought home five field mice I had caught with my bare hands for our cats. Two in each pocket, and the fifth one I held firmly in my hand. I shoved them into my pant pocket, hoping they wouldn't chew their way through the fabric. The cats knew, when I came home, I would have a special treat for them. They were lined up and ready to capture the furry rodents, their favored food. After playing with the mice for a while, like all cats do, they made quick work of them and ate them.

I loved my sisters, don't get me wrong, but scaring them brought me joy. The mouse I kept in my hand was meant for my sister Helga, it was special! It had soft fur and a long tail. I waited until she fell asleep. With the stealth of a cougar, I crawled into her bedroom, bent over her pillow with the mouse in my hand, and "accidently" dropped the little fellow by her side of the pillow.

The mouse leapt from the bed, but not before Helga felt the fur brushing against her soft face. Panic stricken, she too leapt as fast as a lightning bolt, terribly afraid an intruder was in her room. In a way, she was right!

The little mouse hung around and became our pet. We named it Hansi. I was glad it wasn't a rat! The mouse was healthy and became tame as a cat. We fed it the choicest of food and the rodent gained weight. Soon it resembled a furry fat sausage. It was a miracle the cats never caught up with Hansi.

Whenever we called its name, it hurried towards us on its four little legs, barely touching the ground as it ran. One morning, I found the poor thing on its back, with its feet up in the air. It had died. We loved the little mouse, but we probably contributed to its demise, feeding it too much. My sisters and I arranged a funeral for Hansi in our backyard. I gave the eulogy, and my last words were: *Schlaf im Frieden.* "May you rest in peace." We missed the furry fellow a lot and I was looking for another creature to join our family.

I was known as the storyteller around town, and I at times embellished the tales to make them more exciting. Even now, when I go back, they still remember me when I was a kid. It's been more than fifty years. I must have left some kind of an impression.

Things were tough, and the effect of the war could be seen everywhere. The larger cities were bombed-out, but where we lived, there wasn't any sign of destruction. The devastation wasn't noticeable, but we suffered with hunger. I kept my eyes open for food, even if it meant obtaining the fruit off the trees illegally. I knew it was wrong, but when you are hungry, all you could think of was getting a bite to eat. It wasn't too hard to grab a beautiful red plump apple from a tree. I never took anything else from anybody, except food during these trying times.

At home, my parents did their best to keep us fed, although the portions were meager. Mama did her best, creating meals with little.

At times I went to bed hungry. During the night, the pain was unbearable. I would have done anything to get a bite to eat. My sisters went through the same torment most every night, compounded by nightmares of Russians hurting them.

Mama tried to be home as much as possible as she traveled teaching young country girls to sew. She was well aware of our struggles. When she was home, she worked all night sewing clothes for us kids, even our underwear and socks. Had she known how to make shoes and boots, she would have made them as well.

There wasn't food of any kind lying around, and not even so much as a crumb. It was up to each one of us to find food elsewhere to augment our diet. On the way to school, there was a huge walnut tree; the nuts had fallen to the ground, and were ready to be harvested. The last storm knocked them off and the ground was covered with the dark green nuts. This booty was too tempting. I wasn't known for my athleticism. Rather than climbing over the fence, I slid under it and claimed the bounty.

I noticed from afar, a farmer coming at me with his pitchfork. I ran as fast as I had ever run, looking for a place to hide, any place. In the last second, I found refuge in a nearby barn. I feared for my life. My heart was racing, and I was praying he wouldn't find me. It all ended well. The farmer ran past me, still hanging on to his pitchfork and I still had the nuts in my pockets.

The downside, peeling the skin of the walnuts was rather messy. I ended up with stained hands, a tell-tale sign what I had been up to. There was food to be had, but I had to be resourceful, and not afraid of getting caught in the act. I wouldn't pass up the chance when the opportunity presented itself.

One evening, I got into some kind of trouble. Mama sent me to bed without supper and my stomach was killing me. After an hour, I worked up enough nerve to ask Mama for a piece of bread. I feared Mama, and that is why I waited as long as possible before coming out of the bedroom.

I begged her to give me something to eat, anything to settle my stomach. It would have been terrible had she refused. She reached into the cupboard and retrieved a loaf of rye bread, cut off a slice and handed it to me. What a precious gift. I was glad she complied with my request. The slice of rye bread was delicious. With my stomach settled, I went back to bed and slept the rest of the night.

I was happy having Papa around on weekends. When he found time, we climbed the Alps to look for mushrooms. I begged him to take me with him, and promised him I would help to find these delicacies. I was always getting sidetracked looking at flowers and insects hidden in the pine needles and under the rocks. I wasn't much help.

The mushrooms were hard to spot hidden between the crevices of the rocks. The trick was to recognize the good from the bad. The poisonous mushroom could kill you; once you eat them, there were no second chances.

Papa knew most plants and animals by name, even in Latin. He loved nature, and it was great having him around, pointing out the fauna and flora of all types. It was as though I had an encyclopedia with me. He made me aware of the rich wildlife around us.

At another time, Papa and I were on a mountainside in the Alps, surrounded by tall oak trees. We heard rumbling which became louder by the second. What could it be? We didn't have to wait long to see what was about to transpire. Huge boulders came thundering down the mountain towards us at a great speed.

Fortunately, we found two trees to hide behind until the danger had passed. One of the boulders ended up on the base of the tree where I found safety. Now that was a close call which could have ended in tragedy.

When the ovens were hot, the goodies were baking; I smelled them clear across town. It usually came from the Guggenbichler farm, and I didn't waste any time to pay them a friendly visit; perhaps they would give me at least one apple fritter.

The farmers baked their bread in brick ovens which were located in the front yard. Around *Fasching,* "Madrigal", they baked *Fasnacht Krapfen* "apple fritters", and they were so good. The powder sugar melted in my mouth, and as the apple slices slid down into my stomach. They were as smooth as Beethoven's symphony.

During that time, everybody dressed up in all kinds of crazy costumes for a month. On the eleventh day in November, at exactly eleven minutes after eleven in the morning, the festivities began.

All of Germany celebrated with dancing, drinking and eating with whatever food they could find. You'd see people dressed in all kinds of costumes, and that included us. This was a time for people to find relief from the past. It was an escape for the Germans. Everybody was happy knowing the past was the past, and with the Americans close by, the Russians weren't about to come across the border again.

My sisters didn't miss the chance of dressing me up. They made me get into a dress, and I didn't look half bad. They were still trying to turn me into one of their sisters, but I disappointed them.

The Bavarians loved to celebrate, and honor all the holidays with eating and drinking. *Pfingston* "Pentecost" is no exception. It occurred fifteen days after Easter. Festivities took place in every town. Parades were winding through towns; horses were decorated with flowers and fancy collars.

The mayor, along with other town officials, rode their horses and we children walked beside them, enjoying every minute of this spectacle. Around noon, we were invited to a fabulous meal with all the trimmings. Of course, pork was the meat of choice with sauerkraut and delicious rye bread. For us kids, we were served Radlermass, *"Beer"* mixed with lemonade, not a bad combination. The band played old Bavarian music which set the tone for the evening. Just after dark, I gazed towards the mountains; fires were ringing the mountain tops producing a furnace red-glow. It appeared as though, the whole mountain was on fire. What a sight! I never forgot that moment.

The fires signified the red tongues above the apostle's head during Pentecost. It was well-planned by the forestry department, and they didn't have to worry about forest fires getting out of hand due to the many rainstorms the region receives. Germany, as a whole, is blessed with much rain, turning the fields and trees into a velvety glow of green. Casting my eyes towards the mountains, I saw the mighty *Hochgern*. The town of *Egerndach* is nestled in the valley below. The *Schnappen Kirche* "church" in the foothills displayed beautiful gold colored gothic windows, glistening in the evening sun.

I loved our little church in town with its high tower and steep red roof surrounded by the local cemetery. How could I not be happy in a place like that? Even in the worst of times it lifted my spirits.

My happy-go-lucky attitude came to a screeching halt when I turned six. The time had arrived for me to go to school. Mama took me to Grassau to buy a black pair of lederhosen. It was a tradition in Bavaria to wear them. They took a lot of punishment, and were almost indestructible. The pants came in handy when sliding down hills or running through the brush by the river. The short pants were made out of genuine deer leather, with a side pocket designed to carry a knife.

In the wintertime, I wore the knickerbockers, also made out of deer leather with heavy Norwegian wool sox that kept me warm. The shop owner showed Mama a variety of brown and black pants. I chose the black leather, with beautiful green stitching, depicting an acorn.

The brown pants were okay, but weren't as shiny. After I had the pants for a couple of years, I polished the leather with black shoe paste that made them glisten. A great feature of the leather britches was they stood up straight after climbing out of them. In the morning, all I had to do was to step back into them, and I was on my way. It was a common practice to hand the pants down from father to son, generation after generation. The same went for the girls, who passed their dirndl "dress" down to their daughters.

16

THE STING OF THE ROD

My first day at school in Staudach-Egerndach, was downright scary for a kid my age, and approaching the tall building made me feel as little as an ant. Upon entering the building, I was overtaken by the smell coming from some type of sealer that was applied to the wooden floor and stair case.

When I entered the classroom, I was introduced to my new teacher "Fräulein" Knorr. She had a stern face, but a seldom gentle smile. Her white hair was tied in a bun, giving her a strict appearance. She was short in stature but carried a big stick.

I had a gut feeling things were about to change, and I had better tow the line from now on. Boot camp was a breeze if you compared it to the schools in Germany, where rules were strictly enforced. The teachers as a whole went through much suffering during the war, much like we did. There wasn't much to be happy about. The war drained them of their joy as they mourned for the loved ones who perished. Many died on the battle field, and many were still held as prisoners of war in Russia. The Germans were crushed!

I was too young to understand, for me, life was exciting. I was a free spirited individual, and not good at following orders. That was to my detriment at the time, and later on in my life. Having a happy-go-lucky attitude could have gotten me killed.

School was a bore. I thought it was a total waste of my time, and I held the impression, all the work I did was for my teachers. Once I figured out they were only trying to help and prepare me for life, things became easier. If I had realized it sooner, I would have spared myself lots of pain.

I had a hunch; my teacher must have had a meeting of minds with Mama explaining to the teacher what was in store for her. Fräulein Knorr was a wonderful lady. I was told she had never been married. She also lost brothers and sisters in the war. It was a difficult time in her life, and clear to this date, I am sorry to say, I was totally ignorant of all the pain she suffered.

On the second day in class, she discovered I hadn't done my homework, resulting in a spanking. I got the message loud and clear! I started to do my homework occasionally, hoping she wouldn't check. Wishful thinking!

Fräulein Knorr hid her little stick when she wasn't in the room, and that, was for a good reason. I had lots of respect for the rod, and when she cranked it, it sounded like a whirlwind. It was frightening. The spanking would have given me excruciating pain had I worn ordinary pants, and thanks to my trusty lederhosen, they saved me many times. No homework, among other things automatically qualified me for a free spanking with her little vicious stick she always had at the ready. I was the recipient many times.

We boys had a great idea to avoid getting spanked, although if only for a brief moment. I cut the stick half way through, just enough to render the rod useless. The plan worked great, just as I had hoped it would. I watched intently when she got ready to spank one of the boys. She pulled the rod back, and it snapped in half, inadvertently striking her on the thigh.

She didn't waste any time, and got herself another one of those torture rods. She had a way of getting the truth out of us. If she decided not to spank us, we had to stay a couple of extra hours in the classroom while she graded papers. It was sheer torture not being able to play outside. I would have rather been spanked.

When time allowed, I went home for lunch, just to get away for a while. Mama cooked either hot tomato or lentil soup. That was so good, especially in the winter. The hot soup warmed my whole body. It was a marvelous treat. However, there was a price to pay. I was late to class. Mama wasn't on any kind of time schedule.

That placed me into a bad situation with my teacher who didn't tolerate any child being late. I quietly snuck into the classroom, but that was of no use, the door was by the teacher's desk, and there was no way she didn't notice me. The kids were staring at me and giggling. I got a firm reprimand, and I was warned not to let it happen again. Too bad I couldn't blame Mama for being late, but if I had, she wouldn't have cooked any more of the delicious soups.

It was the culture; kids did not speak unless you were asked to speak. If I did have the nerve to speak up, it had better be good. I could never make any demands, or talk back. If I had, I wouldn't be here today to talk about it. During class, we had to be quiet. It was generous of the teacher to allow us to breathe. I could only speak when the teacher called on me. I prayed she would never call on me. Chances were I wouldn't have had a clue as to what she was talking about. Many times I was distracted, thinking of all the things to do after class.

The teacher placed a pencil on top of my outstretched hand, and it had better not roll off. If it did, she would hit me across the knuckles, or strike me on top of the ear with the rod, and did that hurt. When wearing the *lederhosen*, "leather britches", one wonderful by-product was, it softened the blow considerably. If I wanted extra protection, I'd shove a thin book or magazine, preferably a magazine down into the back of the lederhosen, and it would accord me extra protection. It was called *Lederhosen Schutz*.

The book had to be perfect, not too thin, or thick, that way, I hoped the teacher wouldn't notice. Some of the boys didn't hide the magazine or book well enough, and when she saw part of the magazine or book stick out of the back of the pants, she knew what they were up to. She pulled it out of the pants, and the spanking became more severe. Without saying, boys got into trouble every now and then.

I was a happy kid, with a smile on my face. That wasn't well received by my teacher, who said I didn't show any respect. I guess they didn't want happy kids in their classrooms at the time. One of the substitute teachers asked me a math question, and when I gave him the same wrong answer twice, he slapped me. He thought I couldn't be that dumb, and figured I was just a wise guy. The teacher hit me with such force it caused me to bounce off of the blackboard. I sustained a split lip, leaving a trail of blood on the floor as I went back to my desk. I made sure the next time he called on me, I knew the correct answer.

> The teacher hit me with such force which caused me to bounce off of the blackboard. I sustained a split lip, dripping blood to the floor as I went back to my desk.

If a kid didn't answer the teacher, he or she was spanked as well. I didn't know what they had in mind being so strict, but the German schools were known for that, and probably inherited it from the aristocratic Prussians. I didn't bother telling Mama when I was spanked or slapped. She probably would have said, it served me right and I had better shape up. I never received sympathy from her. She probably grew up that way herself.

We had no classroom materials, only a slate board and chalk. Much later, we were introduced to paper and ballpoint pens, imported from the U.S. Most everything you touched said "Made in U.S.A." Before ballpoint pens, we used pens we dipped into an ink well, and had better not ever show an ink spot on the paper, if it did, we were in big trouble.

Paper was a curse. There was no return to our old slate board. We were using paper now, and it had to be neat. We couldn't erase it when making a mistake. Every letter had to be perfect, and if it wasn't, I was punished.

At about the same time, we were given lead pencils for the first time. It would have been easy to erase a mistake, but we weren't issued erasers. I think they had them though. They didn't hand them out to us on purpose. I discovered, by rolling fresh rye bread into a tight little ball, it worked as well as an eraser. That invention served me well, but I missed my slate board.

There wasn't much to be happy about in our school. One thing I was grateful for was that the teachers couldn't get a hold of my parents. We had no phone. There was only one phone in the village; and it was used only in case of an emergency. Teachers seldom visited my home, if ever, and when they did, it wasn't a casual, friendly visit to get to know my parents. One time my priest paid us a visit. Now that was a shocker. My sister Herta heard a knock on the door, thinking I was clowning around, playing games. She called out, "Okay you idiot, I know it's you, come on in," at which time, the priest stepped in. What a shock. We were relieved not to get spanked by Mama. She thought it was pretty funny and we all had a good laugh.

The kids were punished without much provocation. How could anyone study in those conditions, always being under the gun? On another day, one of the teachers, in the same order as Fräulein Knorr, didn't give anybody any slack. She was strict, but fair. Had it not been for her, who knows where I would be today?

The substitute teacher spanked one of the kids. We thought it was uncalled for. While the teacher was out of the room for a brief period, we placed tacks on his seat, partially obscured by the desk. When the teacher came back, we watched as he got ready to sit down in his chair. Suddenly, we heard this horrible scream from behind the desk that could probably be heard in the next town. He must have had excruciating pain from this unfortunate event. I saw tears rolling down his cheeks, perhaps he felt humiliated as well.
When I think about it, it makes me cringe! He figured it was one of us. I must say a brilliant observation by the teacher. We were held over at the school for three hours and forced us to write the German "National Anthem" one hundred times. Mama hated the anthem. It had the lyrics of "Germany, Germany over everything in the world." It reminded her of the time when the Nazis were running wild. I didn't make any effort to learn it, but writing it a hundred times, I couldn't help but remember it. As long as I didn't sing it at home, it was okay. The lyrics of the anthem were changed after we left Germany in 1957.

One day, one of the juveniles went to the bathroom upstairs. The windows were facing the courtyard behind the school. The boy did not use good judgment. He relieved himself through the open window, just as our teacher's wife walked under it.
The student was never seen again. I think he was taken to juvenile hall someplace, and that must have been pure hell. It was a bad thing to do, and he paid for it dearly.

For some reason, my sisters never got spanked, and if they did, I never found out. I should have asked them how they avoided this terrible corporal punishment. They always did their homework, and were seldom disruptive in class. I believe that could have possibly been the reason they avoided getting

91

spanked. Besides, my sisters were pretty with their pig tails and all, and it was much harder for the teacher to let his anger out on them. If I had grown a pony tail, perhaps the teacher would have let up on me. I wasn't going to do that at any rate.

For sheer boredom, I practiced writing in the snow with pretty yellow. I usually wrote somebody's name in the snow I wasn't too fond of. Names kept popping up all over the place and close by the street where everybody saw it. I avoided displaying any of the teachers' names in the snow. That could have given away who the perpetrator was. It made me wonder, why I did those things.

I had the flu which kept me at home. My body was aching and I was running a high fever. Mama had the perfect cure for times like this. In Germany, no one consulted a doctor unless one was close to death. That is one reason nobody was anxious to have the doctor pay a house call. Mama pulled potent schnapps out of the cupboard she had hid away, just for an occasion like this. The liquor burned the flu right out of me. In the morning I had a bit of a hangover, but otherwise I felt just fine. I was eight or nine years of age at the time. This remedy was passed down from generation to generation. I went back to school the next day, and continued where I left off.

One year, I contracted the chicken pox and was forced to stay home for a couple of weeks. In school, I had difficulty reading and wished I could have done a better job when I was called on to read. My dream was, if only I could read. While I was home sick, I grabbed a book, and started to read. No matter what, I was determined to learn, and before long, my fear of reading vanished forever. I conquered the giant. Had I had not become sick I wouldn't have learned to read. When I came back to school, my teacher asked me to read. Without hesitation, I read the assignment without a hitch. The teacher was shocked. Being sick paid off.

Everything appeared tranquil on the surface, but there was still much pain, families mourned, not knowing what happened to their loved ones who never came home from the war and presumably lost in action. Many soldiers were still locked up in the Soviet Union as prisoners of war. Whenever I went to someone's home, they had a picture of the husband, or son on the dresser. The men who made it home after the war, released by the Soviets, or broke out of prison years later, discovered that their wives had in the meantime married another man. It was heart breaking to witness the calamity.

The country was devastated by war, and most everybody was affected one way, or the other. Mama suffered from the effects of the war. Due to my young age, I was shielded from these horrific events, but my two oldest sisters were emotionally damaged, but life went on despite of it all.

17

CHILDHOOD IN STAUDACH-EGERNDACH

Every boy carried a pocket knife which was used to carve and build toys of all kinds. How things have changed. We never thought of hurting anybody, not even a bug. At school, every boy had a knife.

I didn't leave home without my pocket knife which I tucked into the side pocket of my pants. Making slingshots, bow and arrows, or building a kite, all required a sharp knife. Mama and Papa had little money, so I constructed my toys out of anything I could find. It made me more resourceful.

That is how life was, either make the stuff myself, or have no toys to play with. I made trucks out of wooden yarn spools. I cut grooves on each side of the spool, giving it the appearance of truck tires. Then I used a portion of a candle and a rubber band, wound it up, and it crawled along nicely.

My farm friends Michael and Fritz had all kinds of toys their mom and dad bought. I was so envious, I couldn't see straight. I asked Mama if she wouldn't buy me a toy truck, and the answer was an emphatic "no." That was the story of my childhood, never having things I wanted. If only I would have had a fire truck or a racecar. I would have been the happiest kid alive. I learned to live without things other kids had, and as a result, I didn't buy the big toys later in life.

The greatest show on Earth came to town. The tent went up on the other side of the Ache River in Grassau. I wanted to see the clowns, the elephants and all the things it had to offer. There was no way for me to get into the circus. Money was hard to come by and to get a part-time job was next to impossible since I was too young.

To earn money, I came up with a clever idea. My sisters snuck out of the house to see their boyfriends after dark, but the rub was, they had to be home by curfew. I decided to charge them a quarter each time they came home late. I waited up, and a knock on the window meant a quarter in my pocket. As they trickled in, I opened the window, but only after they paid up. It wasn't a cash cow, but every little bit helped me to buy candy, and perhaps there would be enough money left over to get into the circus.

I still fell short of the money I needed. The next best thing was to peek under the circus canvas. I found a good spot, and wouldn't you know one of the attendants chased me away. Giving up wasn't for me, so I peeked through another crack of the canvas, but I couldn't see, people blocked my view. The next day, I was hoping that none of the workers saw me casing the tent to find an entry. The show was about to begin, and a large crowd stood in line to enter the circus. I was small and melted into the crowd without being spotted. Once inside the huge tent, I selected a choice seat where I had a perfect view of the venues. I thought, *"How lucky could I be?"* I finally got in. I pinched myself, just to make sure it wasn't a dream. It was for real. I was the happiest boy on planet Earth, and I couldn't wait for the show to start. I made myself at home, when out of the blue, a couple came towards me and said, "I was sitting in their seat." How could that possibly be? They called an attendant who asked me for my ticket. I told the attendant I lost it. His reply was, "Sure you lost it," and without hesitation, grabbed me by my suspenders and threw me out onto the tall green grass.

I went home defeated. It was the worse day of my young life. Why wouldn't Mama give me money to get into the circus? I asked her anyway. I had nothing to lose, and all she could say is no. Well, it didn't take long, and her answer was no. That was the story of my life. I endured disappointments but made the best out of bad situations.

Mama still had difficulties dealing with everyday problems. One Christmas, I received a beautiful car, and to make it run, I had to wind it up with a key. The color was red; it had great speed and skidded across the kitchen floor like a real racecar. I loved the toy, and played with it every chance I had.

While winding up the car, the spring broke. Joachim, my friend from upstairs of our apartment told me, he might be able to fix it. He never got around to it. I was afraid, should Mama discover I broke my toy all Hades would break loose. One of my sisters spilled the beans and told Mama what happened to my toy car. I slept on the sofa with one eye open, afraid of what Mama might do to me. I was just dozing off when Mama went into a tirade. She asked me what I did to the car, and I told her the spring broke while I attempted to wind it up.

Without warning, she threw the car to the ground, stepped on it repeatedly with her heavy feet, and crushed it. She picked up the mangled metal car with sharp edges, and threw it into my face. The sharp corners of the toy cut into my face around my left eye. Fortunately, I didn't lose my eyesight. What I had to show for was a beauty of a shiner and deep fear of Mama.

Mama told me to tell the teacher I fell against the table. Fräulein Knorr did ask me how I got injured and I told her of my mishap. I couldn't look her straight in the eye, because I told a lie. Mama told us kids to never, ever lie. I was confused.

We had no TV and to find things to do was a challenge. There was one game. It was called *Polter Geist.* I used a rubber seal of beer bottles, stuck a screw through it, and tied it to a string. After wetting the rubber seal, it clung to any glass window, and by holding the string tight, and tapping it with my finger, it made a dreadful sound, annoying the people inside the house.

I tried hard to stay out of trouble whenever possible. My friend Helmut in Grassau, was the son of a manager at the train station on the west side of the river. We hit it off, and spent lots of time together playing with match cars, running them alongside the rail road tracks. It was a bit dangerous to say the least.

Herr Hinterhuber was a perfect image of Hitler. He combed his hair, and carried a mustache just like Hitler did. That got him into a bit of trouble. The police became suspicious and kept him under surveillance. His life was wrought with stress, always having to look over his shoulders and afraid the police would arrest him. Had I been him, I would have shaved the mustache off and been done with it. That would have been an easy fix.

In the late fall, I met Anton, and we became best friends. He came down from Munich around Christmas to visit relatives. I introduced him to the snow covered slopes and showed him how much fun it was playing in the snow, skiing and sledding. His parents bought him a pair of skis and with a little practice, he became a good skier. We had so much fun. Too bad, after Christmas vacation he went back home. I missed him. I never saw him again since we moved far away to America. I would've liked to know what happened in his adult life.

During the winter, it started getting dark around four in the afternoon, and time for me to pack up and leave the slope. I skied home instead of walking. It was much faster, and I wouldn't be late for supper. Too bad we didn't have lights on the hills to light the way down the slope. If the slope had been lit, I would have been tempted to stay much longer, but that would have got me into lots of trouble at home. I didn't want to give Mama a reason to get mad, and coming home late, I would have been deprived of supper.

Staudach was a quaint little village in the shadow of the Alps. Everybody knew each other, and there were no strangers in town. When it was time for supper, Mama yelled in a high pitch, P-o-n-n-e. The whole town heard it. I was embarrassed, afraid my buddies would be making fun of me the next day. Her yell drove fear into my bones. I can still hear her voice today.

She sewed everything I wore except my boots which I outgrew. Before long, my toes let me know it was time for a new pair. Money was in short supply, but we made do. My next pair of boots was donated by a neighbor who felt sorry for me when I told him I outgrew my old boots. I was so happy and thanked him over and over for his kindness. It was paramount to have boots that were comfortable to keep me warm and dry.

With the accumulation of the white powder, getting around was a struggle. Just getting out of the front door was a job at times. The snow reached as high as the door jam. At times, we had to crawl out of the window if we wanted to get out of the house.

During the night, it snowed a couple of feet and the wind created snowdrifts up to three feet high. We built caves in the snowdrifts, pretending we were living in a palace. It was surprisingly warm inside, although it was cold outside, minus the comforts of home.

If we were energetic, we built igloos much like the Eskimos. When we were finished with our project, we poured water over the top, it froze immediately upon contact. The outside walls were icy and hard as rock, but once inside, it was warm and comfortable. It was amazing and I never understood the drastic difference in the temperature.

I played on the snowy hill, within a stone's throw of our house. Mama and Papa watched me slide down the hill with my sled, or jump off of the ski jump. Knowing they were watching me, I showed off my best stuff. Another way I spent my time was having empty beer bottles careen down the hill. Too bad, Michael, my cousin Hans and I never found bottles still full of beer. Too bad, somebody emptied them first.

As the empty bottles careened down the hill they gained great speed. We made sure not to have the bottles hit the tires as the cars drove by. It probably would have resulted in damaged tires.

There was nothing more exhilarating than ski jumping. It was a thrill, sailing through the air like a bird. The wind burned my face. I felt my heart pound in my chest, afraid of a crash landing. At times, it was a wreck waiting to happen. I only crashed once, landing on my face. I wasn't hurt badly; only my upper lip was bruised. My biggest concern was the bindings coming loose while in midair, that would have resulted in disaster. Landing was the toughest part, and if I wasn't lined up just right, or missed the exact jumping off point, it was a guaranteed crash landing. There were more than a few landings where I could have gotten hurt.

Without a doubt, winter was my favorite time of the year with much to do. One Christmas, my friend Michael got a toboggan. Boy, did it run, and even had brakes. He outran all the other sleds in the neighborhood. It was like a racehorse on skis. I wasn't to be outdone when my parents bought me a sled.

My new sled was fast, but it couldn't keep up with Michael's. To start the race, we both lined up on the top of the hill, and at the count of three, we pushed our sleds across the starting line. To get to top speed, we ran behind the sled, hanging on for dear life, and at a precise time, we jumped aboard while the sled gained speed. It was a tricky maneuver.

On the other side of town, Michael and I found a perfect spot to get our sleds up to break neck speeds. After walking uphill for two kilometers, where loggers harvested lumber, we took our sleds and let them fly. It was like a bobsled run with lots of ice covering the track. Many of us kids rode our sleds down the hill, much like the lunge in the Olympic Games. It was a super fast ride, and what a thrill it was to see the trees and houses fly by.

It was dangerous alright, some of the kids got hurt badly when their sled left the track and collided with one of the trees. We should have worn helmets for this type of recreation, or we should have never exposed ourselves to such danger. Our parents never found out what we were doing, and if they had, it would have been the end of our adventure. It was a miracle that any of us grew up to see adulthood.

It was spring, the snow had melted. The meadows were covered with the most beautiful flowers, and the nightingales and swallows had arrived from Italy and Africa. They filled the air with the most beautiful melodies. The swallows are fast and elegant flyers. They made it look easy catching flies in midair and not fall out of the sky.

At the local lumberyard, *Pausmühl,* had a railroad track to haul lumber to the mill. My friends Manfred, Michael and I found empty rail cars on top of the hill, waiting to be brought down first thing Monday morning. We had other ideas, however, and didn't wait until Monday. One Saturday, we unlocked the brakes of the cars and rode them down to the lumberyard. Riding the railcars was a thrill as the wind penetrated our nostrils, and the air trapped in the shirt sleeves gave us a lift.

Just before getting to the bottom of the hill, the cars slowed down on even ground, and we were able to jump off and allow the cars to come to a stop. It didn't take long when the owner got wind of what we were doing. The fun was over, and we had to think of some other way to find excitement.

On one of the weekends, we had a car race through town, with cars that only had a seat and four wheels. No motor, no body, just the frame. The cars were owned by the blacksmith Huber. We rode them two abreast, blocking the road through the middle of town. It was like a drag race, but a very slow one. That caused a few problems when people couldn't get around us in their new Mercedes.

In school, we tried to be good kids. If we were attentive in class and did not cause problems, the teacher took us on outings. We had a song, trying to soften the teacher's heart; at least we were hoping it would.

Der Himmel ist blau, das wetter ist schön, wir bitten den Herrn Lehrer spazieren zu gehen.

Translation:

"The sky is blue, the weather is nice, and we are begging the teacher to take us for an outing." In German, it rhymes and flows much better. In the summer, our teacher Wolfgang Klotz, walked us to the rim of the forest to pick sweet raspberries and blueberries. Each of us kids received a small jar, and we were supposed to fill the jar, but the berries went straight into our hungry stomachs, none were saved. In a couple of hours, Herr Klotz blew his whistle, and it was time to head back to class. We had a wonderful time. On the way back, we marched in step singing WWII German military songs.

In the winter, our outings were even better. It was more fun. Our teacher took us to a hill just outside of town. The ones with skis were able to ski, and the ones with sleighs, had fun sledding. I was fortunate to have had access to my skis. I used them to go to school while the roads were covered with snow and ice.

We loved snowball fights. It was fun, but if you had an out with somebody, it became a serious matter. There was one kid who ruined it for everybody when he packed a solid piece of ice into the snowball, and when one of the kids got hit, it left a blue mark. That was considered un-sportsman like, and once we found out who it was, we got even with the person, holding him down and rubbing snow into his face.

18

NO MORE CHERRIES

The spring had come with the beauty of colorful flowers in the meadows and trees with white and pink blossoms. It was paradise living in the valley. The mountains were still covered with snow. As the air turned warm, the snow in the mountains melted, and the trees emerged from their slumber.

I couldn't wait until the sweet cherries and the juicy blue plums were ready to be picked. On the way to school, I passed by Bacher's grocery store, and they had a cherry tree that produced the best cherries in town. Frau Bacher was a sweet lady and allowed me to pick the juicy, red cherries come summer.

Whenever I had a nickel in my pocket, I'd buy a pickle or a handful of sauerkraut to soothe my stomach. The dill pickles and sauerkraut tasted so good, they were even better than candy. The sauerkraut was homemade, and tasted like no other. The huge green dill pickles were home cured. It was a meal in itself. There was no way I would throw away my pickle and made sure the morsel was eaten before entering the school building.

The summers were never too hot, only reaching into the mid-eighties, a perfect time for cherry picking. The Bachers allowed me to go to their back yard and have my fill of the sweet, juicy cherries. I ate until I got sick to my stomach. At that point, climbing out of the tree became difficult without losing the contents of my stomach. When my friend Anton came down from Munich, I introduced him to the cherry tree still loaded with the sweet beauties. With the abundance of cherries, the limbs hung low to the ground. We were afraid of the branches breaking with the load. Actually, we helped the tree, lightening the load. We made quick work of the ones we could reach with our hands. Later in the afternoon, we again climbed into the tree where we feasted until evening. Life couldn't have been better than this.

Living at the edge of the forest had much to offer. There was never a shortage of wildlife. Anton and I ventured into the forest before dark, climbed up a fire-tower and observed the wildlife below. The deer came out in droves to feed on the tender grass shoots. We were very quiet as to not scare them away. To attract the deer, we placed two blades of grass and held them tightly between our thumbs, and then blew between them to mimic the sound of the fawns.

We did this for fifteen minutes or so, until the females came towards us looking for their offspring, afraid they were in distress. The pesky ravens, the deer's best friend alerted them of danger with their loud, deep raspy call. The ravens were intelligent birds and to get past them was almost impossible.

The summer went too fast. A blizzard coming in from the north covered the landscape. It was too cold now for pickles and sauerkraut we usually bought at the Bacher's on the way to school. During the winter months, we sacrificed on food. There was no fruit, no grasses from the meadows, and no mushrooms or strawberries we gathered from the slopes of the Alps. Thank God we had hot sauerkraut and potatoes to tide us over until the summer.

One snowy day, a couple of weeks before Christmas, my buddies and I walked home from school. We were passing Bacher's grocery store when we noticed a beautiful Christmas tree decorated with the most colorful bulbs, in the store window. It was a way to thank their customers for the support throughout the year. For some foolish reason, we wanted to get inside the window, and knock off a few of the bulbs. Kids do crazy things, and that was one of them. We worked a wire through the air ducts of the window and up the tree, and in turn, knocked off a couple of those beautiful hand made bulbs which broke in many pieces when they hit the bottom of the window sill.

While we were engaged in this misadventure, we didn't notice Herr Bacher coming around the corner. He got a hold of me and proceeded to spank me hard. He promised he wouldn't tell Mama. He knew, if he did, there would have been an execution. I paid dearly for that deed. From then on, the cherry tree was off limits, and our relationship was no longer on friendly terms. It was never the same. No more free delicious cherries. From then on, we had to buy our groceries in Grassau, a much longer walk.

19

KRAMPUS

Christmas was a special time for us children. We hoped to receive at least one present, along with food prepared for this special occasion. I didn't know as yet what the Bavarian custom was, and had I known what was coming, I would have run away. In Heidelberg, Germany, Santa Claus wore a bright red suit and sported a long white beard. He distributed wonderful goodies like apples and oranges, and if we were exceptionally good during the year, he handed us a cookie.

Nicholas looked like the pope, with a fancy tall hat and staff. He was accompanied by his helper we called Krampus, who looked like the devil with his black horns protruding from on top of his head. His face was black, and what was really scary, he had a long, red tongue hanging out of his mouth. He was equipped with a whip and a burlap sack designed to carry "naughty" boys and girls off into the cold night.

Saint Nicholas and Krampus visited children December the fifth, and is known as Krampus Nacht. The thrashing of the chain was heard from a long distance. It got my attention. The chain symbolizes the binding of the devil by the Christian church. The rattle of the chain filled the cold, still air as Krampus dragged it in the deep snow. The clatter of the chain brought deep fear to my heart. The rattle resonated as the pair came near our home. It was as though my world was caving in. It was a bad night for me and the worst was yet to come. There wasn't anybody I could turn to. All I wanted to do was to get away, far, far away. My three sisters formed a circle around me, and I couldn't escape. I heard Saint Nicholas' heavy breathing, which told me he was out of shape. By now they were getting very close.

I became as nervous as a bank robber on the front bench in church. I knew

Saint Nicholas didn't bring that black devil along just to keep him company on a cold night.

They entered our home, and my heart pounded hard and fast, I couldn't hear a thing Saint Nicholas said to me. He opened a huge book that resembled a Bible, and started to tell me all the bad things I had done during the year. How could he know, unless he was God himself?

I was trembling with fear, and squirming in the corner of our family room, and hoping this wasn't happening. Was I having a hellish dream? Krampus tried shoving me into his big burlap sack. I struggled for all I was worth and prevented him from dragging me away. My sisters were watching me intently and enjoyed every minute. They were hoping to get rid of me for a short time at least.

Saint Nicholas told me to strap on my skis. They had plans to take me into the Alps, drop me off, and let wolves devour me. I begged him not to take me away, and I said, *Bitte nehm mich nicht weg.* "Please don't take me away." My life passed before my eyes, knowing full well, it was going to end soon.

> My life passed before my eyes, knowing full well, it was going to end soon.

But wait; at the last, a thought shot into my mind that might have saved me that night. I told him my skis were in the shop to be repaired, and it would make it impossible for me to come with him. He bought into my story.

I breathed a sigh of relief, and felt much, much better as they both walked empty handed out of our home. The only visible sign they left were the shoe prints in the snow leading out into the cold, snowy night. They were on their way to ruin other kids' Christmas and to set them into a panic mode.

This happened each and every year. I got sick of the whole charade. From now on, Christmases would not set me into a panic. I discovered Saint Nicholas was our physician, who had earlier saved my finger from being amputated. I never did find out who his black helper was. My sisters had their hands in this. They conspired against me and revealed to Saint Nicholas all the things I had done throughout the year. Never mind all of the good things I did, like shining their shoes each weekend.

They would have left me up in the mountains, if they would have had it their way. My only salvation that night was Mama and Papa.

Saint Nicholas went to a house to see a little girl when things got out of hand. Krampus stuffed her into that burlap sack and dumped her into the shallows of the freezing Ache River. The girl was able to crawl out, but it could have had a tragic ending. I found out much later, my sister Herta had a similar experience. Christmas in Bavaria was long ago, but the memories still haunt me.

20

WEIHNACHTEN

Two weeks later, it was Christmas. Papa dragged home a Christmas tree he cut down in the forest surrounding our home. He always did a great job picking the right one, straight as an arrow reaching the ceiling. Mama did a marvelous job decorating it with beautiful bulbs, mostly red and green in color. She mounted wax candles and placed them towards the end of the branches, far enough out, so they wouldn't burn the tree when lit. It was such a beautiful tree.

When the candles were lit, it was angelic. We sang *Oh, Tannenbaum, Oh, Tannenbaum we grün sind deine Blätter.* "Oh Christmas tree, oh Christmas tree." I loved that song, and we sang it over and over until the fragrance of the green pine needles reached deep into our lungs.

Christkindl "Christ Child" came and brought each of us a present on Christmas Eve as we kids were sequestered in another room, waiting for our parents to give us the okay to come and see what the *Chistkindl* brought us.

Christmas Eve, our family gathered in the family room, and thanked God for all the blessings He bestowed on us. Papa read the Christmas story as we sat around the Christmas tree. We had to be very quiet; there was not a sound in the room. We were reminded of our past, and it was truly a miracle we survived the carnage of war. That particular night, my parents surprised me with a train set. I was so happy; at last, I received from Christkindl the present I always wanted. In the coming weeks and months, I played with it until the wheels came off. The tracks wore out first. They were made of light aluminum, but the cars lasted forever minus the wheels.

After we received our presents, we got up from the floor and moved to the table, decorated for this special time with live pine branches and lit candles. It was difficult for me to part with my train set. I stayed up until late and played myself to sleep. I was fast asleep lying on the floor next to my train set when Mama carried me to bed.

Our Christmas dinner consisted of a couple of hotdogs for each of us and potato salad. That was a treat. If we were lucky we had meat once a week which consisted of sometime moldy *Leberkäse* "liver cheese".

During the winter months, it was tradition for Mama to make her famous herring salad using the old Prussian recipe handed down from her mother. If you liked herring, it was a great dish. However, Herta and I were the only ones who detested the fish and wouldn't touch it. It took all evening to pick out the bones and soon lost its flavor.

One of the reasons I didn't like Herring, was because soon after we came back to Heidelberg from our epic journey as displaced Germans, we had to go to a soup kitchen to receive free food. As we came close, I saw a big bowl with something that stunk to high heaven.

It was soup with pieces of smelly herring floating on top. Ever since that time, I can't stand the fish. Herring was a national dish in Northern Germany and was served a million different ways, similar to our famous Hamburger. My dad consumed the fish raw, rolling it like a burrito with vinegar. He even ate the salty fish eggs, similar to caviar.

One evening, after Christmas, we were gathered in the family room. Outside, it was very cold with a driving snow blizzard. Mama wanted us to have something special, and what could be better than hot chocolate on a cold night?

She cooked a big pot, and when she attempted to carry the heavy pot to our dinner table, one of the handles broke. I am glad she wasn't burned, but the hot chocolate was all over the wooden floor, and disappeared into the cracks of the wooden boards. In time, we got over the loss but left an impression.

21

THE GOOD, THE BAD

It was magic living at Frau Auer's house, our first home in Bavaria. A couple of other families living there made it a wonderful place. We had a great time singing on weekends, joining the adults playing their musical instruments. There were times when we went to the Bauer's across the street, and Anderl, Frau Bauer's son, played the accordion. We sang our hearts out. The whole village was on fire with music.

One day, the sad news reached us that Herr Bauer, a carpenter, fell from a building and was critically injured. He later died at the local hospital. Everybody was in mourning. I wanted to attend the funeral, but Mama felt I was too young. The loss was a great financial hardship for the Bauer's. Mrs. Bauer's sons helped their mother with the finances as much as they could.

Tragedies come in bunches. The Friedman's lived in the same house we did. Their daughter, Wallie had surgery on her leg. She never seemed healthy, but there was hope with undergoing the surgery she would be back to normal. Not long after the procedure, she developed a blood clot which ended her life. She was only twelve years old. I viewed her body at the funeral parlor at our church in Egerndach. It was a traumatizing experience, and realized how fragile life was. I couldn't get over how real she looked in her coffin and I expected her to get up out of the casket at any moment. It was wishful thinking.

Life in Staudach was extraordinary in many ways, especially in the winter when farmers used their huge freight sleds to carry their goods to the market, or transport the freight across town. The huge draft-horses standing up to fifteen hands tall, moved the load with ease, but at times struggled because of the snow and ice.

They were gentle giants, even-tempered, not easily spooked, and that is what a farmer needed. They had to share the roads with cars and trucks. I heard their intense breathing, and saw steam rising off of their backs as they trotted through the narrow cobblestone streets.

> The huge draft-horses standing up to fifteen hands high, moved the load with ease, but at times struggled because of the snow and ice.

The farmers worked the horses hard, and I felt sorry for them. The smaller farms used a team of oxen, and I saw them lumbering through town with their loads. They had great strength, but were slower, and stubborn. Unlike the oxen, I heard the horses from miles away. Each horse wore a collar with bells that resonated through the cold winter air.

In spite of the Bavarian charm, life was still difficult. I remember chasing a dog with a piece of bread in his mouth, and I wasn't about to let him keep it. I grabbed the morsel from the dog's mouth when I caught up with him. I believe the animal slowed down, thinking I wanted to play, and that is when I made my move, and grabbed the bread. I took a big chance by doing this. The dog could have had rabies and bitten me. We did what we had to do to get food, even if it meant getting hurt. Looking for food was a fulltime job.

In our neighborhood was a big apple tree. The apples had already fallen to the ground and began to rot, but it didn't deter me from picking one up and eating it. It was by the grace of God I didn't get sick.

Across the street from us was this beautiful pear tree. The pears were as large as a beer bottle, that is why they were called bottle pears, and eating one of them carried me through the day. What a prize. Due to their weight, they hung low, and it was easy to reach for them without having to climb up into the tree. What a catch.

On Helga's birthday, the youngest of my sisters, I surprised her with a special treat, a piece of bread covered with brown sugar. It was a pure sacrifice giving her the bread when I was hungry myself.

To tide me over, I ate grasshoppers and shared them with Murkel, my cat. I pulled off the wings and legs and that made them slide down much easier. I didn't chew them but swallowed them whole. If I had chewed them, I would have gagged. I was always chubby as a kid, and nobody would have thought I lacked any kind of food.

> I ate grasshoppers and shared them with my cat Murkel.

Murkel ate the grasshopper whole, with a crunching sound. With head first, and legs sticking out of the side of his mouth, he swallowed them with one bite. It was a happy time for both of us. Murkel was a happy cat.

In the summer, I went out in the meadows looking for special kinds of grasses to augment my diet. One was the *Sauerampfer* which had a sour taste, but is nutritious and packed with of vitamin C. The other was the *Kugerutz*. When breaking the long stem, it produced a sweet, milky substance.

We had no idea where the next meal was coming from. One evening, we received the surprise of our lives. We were blessed with enough food for all.

Murkel came home with a big hare. He was proud of this awesome catch, and made sure we noticed it as he dropped it on the door step. In Europe, the rabbits are huge and measure up to three feet in length, and stand two feet tall. Papa skinned it, cooked it, and we had a delicious meal that evening. It tasted a little gamey, but what a treat.

Murkel was a big gray Tom cat, and if there was another cat in his territory, a fight was on, and the fur was flying. Every so often, he got injured during skirmishes. The scars on his ears were a tell-tale sign of previous fights. I can't recall whatever happened to my favorite cat, but if there is such a thing as a cat heaven, I am sure he is there.

I walked from Grassau across the Ache Bridge, when a big German shepherd accompanied me. I was at first startled since my past experiences were not pleasant when encountering these dogs. The dog meant me no harm and we walked together and bonded quickly. The German shepherd stuck to me like glue. I had plans to take care of him, and give him a good home. Perhaps, I would have a pal for the rest of my life?

Mama had different ideas however, and my plans didn't work out. She told me to forget about it, and leave him by the side of the road. The dog could have been sick. Mama was just protecting me. The dog and I formed a partnership. He was one beautiful specimen. Early in the morning, I rushed to the street and hoped he'd still be there, but there was no sign of him. I hoped he found his way home. Was I in danger and did he come to protect me?

It was harvest time. The ground took on a brown, greenish tint with walnuts waiting to be picked. Fall had arrived; cool nights were welcomed after a hot summer. The farmers were waiting for the late fall storms to empty the trees.

My sister Gerlinde eyed our neighbor's tree. The previous night, the storm stripped the tree bare of most of the nuts. While picking up the walnuts and putting them into her apron, out of nowhere, the farmer chased and caught up with her.

> He grabbed her by the pony-tail and dragged her to his house where he threw her down the concrete steps and locked her into the cold, dark, rat-infested cellar.

Our stories are similar, were it not for the ending. I got away, and she didn't. He grabbed her by the ponytail, dragged her to his house, where he threw her down the concrete steps and locked her in the cold, dark, rat infested cellar. She felt the rats brushing against her as she sat on one of the steps. Gerlinde was extremely frightened. She had no idea if she would ever be released from the dungeon.

It was pitch dark; she had no idea if there was a window she could climb out of. She started to move around, but kept falling over boxes, and at one point, she fell on her side when she attempted desperately to get up from the cold, damp floor. All she could hear were chirping noises from the rats.

Mama was getting worried when she didn't show up for dinner and at once started looking for her. She had a hunch where she might be. She had seen her in the neighbor's orchard before, picking up fruit. Mama hurried to the farmer's house and knocked forcefully on his front door. He slowly cracked open the door, and when he saw Mama, he hid.

Mama had a suspicion that he was the kidnapper. Without hesitation, Mama demanded that he free Gerlinde at once. She wasn't open to any kind of negotiation to get her back. He confessed to kidnapping Gerlinde, and didn't waste any time bringing her out of the cellar. It was a difficult climb for Gerlinde to get out of the dungeon. She felt her way up the concrete steps in total darkness. She stumbled as she climbed over the sharp edges of the cold steps which cut her ankles every time she attempted to gain a foot hold.

She was ecstatic when she saw light. The darkness blinded her, and the glow of the bright lights caused her to miss several steps as she, with haste, climbed out of the cellar.

The farmer grabbed Gerlinde by her hair and threw her out the door and into Mama's arms. Mama was ready for a fight, but he wouldn't have any of that. He quickly slammed and locked the door.

From then on, we had no more problems. She came home a frightened little girl, and happy to have escaped from the cold, musty cellar. From now on, Gerlinde stayed as far away from his orchard as she could. I don't know if my parents notified the police. In those days, most people worked out problems among themselves.

After the war, the police were slow to react. Most had bicycles or motorcycles and when there was an emergency, we couldn't call them. Very few homes had the luxury of having a phone. The incident with my sister Gerlinde brought back vivid memories of the war. The farmer behaved like the Gestapo.

Papa befriended a man who didn't live far from us. I clearly remember, Herr Brandl had a big cuckoo clock hanging in the family room, and a giant red deer mounted on the wall. For a hobby, he bred shorthair pointers, and I had fun playing with the puppies, the problem was, their sharp teeth at times drew blood. I enjoyed visiting him at the edge of the dark forest. It was a small house reminiscent of a hunter's lodge with deer antlers mounted above the entrance.

By profession, he was a forest ranger, and on occasions took me with him on his excursions into the forest. His shorthair pointer was leading the way. We ventured out into the swamps where dangerous wild boars were known to roam. As long as he had his hunting dog with us, I wasn't worried. But I was glad he brought his rifle along.

There is a legend in Bavaria about a hunter who met his fate while hunting wild boar. He was stalking the animal, and waited for an opportune time to get off a shot to kill the beast. When he pulled the trigger, he discovered the gun had jammed. The animal was within yards of him. He knew he was in peril, and looking for a tree nearby where he might find refuge. Lucky for him, a tree was close by and he climbed up, out of the reach of the ferocious animal. In haste, he left his rifle at the bottom of the tree but to retrieve it would have been too dangerous.

Had he only brought his gun up into the tree, he could have shot the ferocious boar. Hours passed. The hunter was desperately looking for an escape, but he had no such luck. He prayed that the wild boar would leave so he could climb down the tree and flee.

Hours passed, and with horror he observed the animal using its razor sharp tusks to uproot the tree. The roots were no match; suddenly the tree fell on its side with a loud thump. With all his strength the hunter tried to rise but he had injured his leg in the fall. Unable to run, the boar thrust the tusks deep into the hunter's midsection and the helpless man succumbed to his injuries.

SPIEL HAHN

I had a great interest in animals. I wandered through the forest to discover what it might reveal. I heard the cuckoo, the crows and an occasional owl in the woods. If I was real quiet, I could observe a grazing deer on the edge of the forest along the way.

Among the many animals, the *Auer Hahn* "grouse", had its home in the Alps. It was a rather large bird, and the *Spiel Hahn* "grouse", is a bit smaller.

These birds were gorgeous with their colorful feathers. The *Auer Hahn* sported thick red eyebrows with steel-blue wing feathers. The birds were sought after by the Bavarian hunters who mounted the feathers on their traditional hats. The larger the feather, the more prominent was the man.

It is a tradition of the Bavarians to mount a *gamsbart* "mountain goat beard" on the side of their hats. The *gamsbart,* beard of the goat, was black in color, and the darker the color, the more sought after was the goat. The prominent beard was found below the chin of the animal. The *Gams* "goat" was found high in the mountains, a solitary, sure-footed animal. It was hard to spot, and much harder to shoot.

When Papa had time, he practiced taxidermy, and people from far and wide brought all kinds of animals for him to prepare. I remember when he worked on a Gams, "mountain goat", a deer, an owl, and an *Auerhahn* "grouse". The *Auerhahn* was stunning. He once worked on a barn owl, and when touching the feathers, they were the softest I had ever felt, even softer than goose down.

In those days, taxidermy was a real art. The actual skull was used, not a plastic replica. Papa was good at it, and I was fascinated watching him do his mastery. I wanted to do that as well, but along the way, I was sidetracked and never practiced it.

He did taxidermy for universities in Munich and other places. He then transported the animals by train. He also worked on fish, but they are difficult to prepare. Once the fish dies, the colors disappear, and Papa had to paint the entire fish from head to tail by hand. The most difficult fish was the rainbow trout, with many colorful spots on its sides. After he was done, the animal came to life.

On weekends, when Papa was home, he was busy with us kids. He was interested in what we did at school and at home. My sister Herta was the smartest. She was a confident girl at the age of twelve. On her birthday, Mama and Papa bought her a bike she always kept polished. Even after a year, it still looked new. I even remember the brand name "Standard". It was made in the U.S. Most of the merchandise was made in America.

Herta couldn't wait to try out her new bike. She had her place picked out! In Staudach, at the bottom of the hill stood a *Gasthaus* "guesthouse", known as the *Maut*. It was an eating establishment where one could eat, drink beer, and on weekends, they offered dances. It was a swinging place on weekends.

My dear sister Herta was pedaling home from seeing her friends, but before getting to our house, she had to negotiate the hill. I don't know what happened, perhaps she was panic stricken. When she reached the bottom, she drove through the open entrance of the building and crashed into the back wall. Thank God, she walked away with only scratches.

My youngest sister Helga also had a bike she used to go shopping and other places. I had not yet learned how to ride a bike, and that may have been a blessing, seeing what happened to my two sisters.

I was outside when I heard something crash, and when I looked up, I saw a huge cloud of dust. I thought, my God what was all that about? By the time the dust settled, I saw that Helga had crashed going down the gentle grade. The crash was caused by the aluminum milk can wedged in the spokes of the bike.

Herr Bachmann witnessed the accident, picked her up and carried her to our home. She was as limp as a rag doll as he laid her on the bed. She appeared dead. Mama checked for a pulse. It was weak, but she was alive. We prayed to God for her to regain consciousness. Mama called our doctor, Herr Gruber from Grassau, the next town over. He came at once to assist her in his new Ford.

We were distraught, and hoped she would pull through. Her forehead had gravel imbedded from the impact, but she didn't seem to have broken any bones. The doctor told us, there wasn't much else he could do, and said, if she didn't come around in a couple of days, he would have her transferred to a hospital. We were afraid of her dying in the meantime.

In those days, the very last resort was to call for an ambulance. We held vigil over her day and night. There was still no movement. The only positive thing was she was breathing on her own. On the third day, she miraculously awoke. We were overjoyed, and thanked God she was still with us.

She recovered, with no neurological problems later in life. Her demeanor didn't change any, and she was as feisty as ever.

I was too busy to investigate things around our new neighborhood. One day, walking on the right shoulder of the roadway, and minding my own business, I found myself knocked to the ground by something I wasn't sure of. I was in a sitting position, and when I turned around, I saw a bumper, and four wheels, about to run over me. I was shocked to discover a car knocked me to the ground. How could this have happened? I wasn't injured and I am thankful the car came to a stop when it did. I don't remember anything about the driver, but I am sure of one thing, he was happy he hadn't caused me any injuries. We both shared the same feeling.

When I wasn't busy playing, looking for food was never far from my mind. I recall, during lunch recess, the farm kids were eating their lunches they brought from home. It was torture watching them eat the choicest of food while I went hungry. I worked up enough nerve and asked if they wouldn't want to share their good fortune with me. I never had any offers. Needless to say, I was addicted to food spurred on by hunger.

On a sunny afternoon, my sister Helga and I were walking along the road leading out of Grassau, when we noticed a big farmhouse. There was nothing unusual about the house, except for one thing: looking through one of the windows, we noticed a round loaf of home baked bread, still steaming hot, setting on a table. We would have given anything for just one piece, especially if it was hot and fresh out of the oven. We wanted the bread so bad, we could taste it. We had to act quickly if we wanted to get a hold of the hot delicacy.

We decided Helga should go on the mission to retrieve the life giving loaf of bread. She was older, and pretty fast on her feet. I was too chubby and slow. It worked out perfectly. Once at the building, Helga crept down the hallway, always aware of her surroundings. She opened the door that led to the room where the bread was laying on the table, still good and hot and with one swoop, she grabbed it.

She executed the plan perfectly, and in anticipation, I was licking my

111

chops. Out of the front door she ran, her arms and legs flying; it looked as though she was going to take to the air. Into the ditch she dove with the loaf still tightly tucked under her arm. The venture took everything out of her as she fell into the ditch, exhausted.

We had a feast. I don't ever remember anything tasting that good. I wonder what the farmers thought when the loaf of bread had vanished into thin air.

Papa kept busy collecting things at the laboratory where he worked as a pathologist. I remember he brought home two "ancient" Germanic human skulls he obtained from the university.

I could just see Papa riding the train with two skulls tucked firmly under his arms. I am surprised he came home without being interrogated by the police. I wish I could have seen him sitting there on the bench, holding the skulls in his lap. What a sight!

One night, after I had gone to bed, sound asleep, my sisters came into my room with the skulls in their hands. They moved the skulls' jaws up and down, making an awful sound which woke me up. It made my teeth chatter for fear. They were just having a great time. I uttered under my breath, "You just wait, and tomorrow will be another day."

Mama was getting tired having to move the skulls around when she dusted. One day, she took them one by one, and in a fiery rage threw them to the ground. The skulls broke into a million pieces, and that made me very happy. The torment came to a halt for the moment. At last, the ancient German skulls would never rise again.

That evening when Papa came home from work, he wasn't at all pleased to find his ancient treasures in the trash can. Mama and Papa had very few arguments. But that evening, they had a spirited conversation that could be heard clear into our bedrooms.

While living in Staudach, Papa accepted a job in Amsterdam, Holland, at a hospital as a pathologist. At one point, I didn't see him for more than half a year. When he left, we were crying and didn't want to let go of him. It was another sad chapter. After Papa had been gone for a few months, he was offered a position in Munich, Bavaria. We were so happy, only to lose him again during the week when he accepted a job in Munich but we were happy to see him come home on weekends.

When Papa was home, he thought of something he could do with us kids. One thing I loved to do was to pick blueberries out in the forest. The berries were small and hard to find. After a couple of hours of back-breaking work, Papa noticed my jar was only a quarter full. He asked why I didn't have more berries in my jar. I simply told him, "I ate them."

On another outing, Mama and I ventured up into the Alps to pick wild strawberries; they were so sweet. It was quite a climb to reach the berries, located in the alpine meadows. We traversed boulders, and jumped across small creeks.

What bothered me, I was afraid we might get lost. Mama was forever getting lost, and even got turned around in our home. God was truly with her during the war. We knew that going downhill would eventually get us into our valley.

We stumbled onto a green meadow, sprinkled with red dots all over. Here they were, small red berries, ready to be picked. With the berries being so small, it required lots of bending down. I had the same problem as I did with the blueberries. I ate more than went into the jar, and often I got sidetracked chasing butterflies, or playing with the frogs in the nearby pond. I wasn't much help.

It was a lovely outing. I stood on top of the world viewing the valley below with the large farmhouses and the grazing cows; they looked like small black and white dots. It was breathtaking. My only wish that day was to be a bird, soaring across the mountains and valleys, giving me a bird's eye view of the spectacular scenery.

We had a friendly, young couple living in our house. One day, he was outside chopping wood to fuel his stove. The winter was just around the corner, making its presence felt with thick frost covering the ground in the early morning hours. In the afternoon, Helga and I were playing in the yard when we found a huge lumber ax leaning against a tree stump.

What better things to do than practice chopping little sticks of wood? As it turned out, it was a bad idea. Helga was holding the ax, waiting for me to move the branches where the sharp ax severed them. I did what she told me to do, and that was a mistake. With the weight of the ax, she lost control. My hand was directly under the sharp blade, and with one swoop, she cut my hand. It severed my index finger and made a deep cut into my middle finger.

My index finger was still attached to my hand by a bit of skin. I was in shock. Blood was squirting in every direction. The last thing I saw of my sister was her skirt flying over the fence, and she was gone. My oldest sister Herta was close by, and with horror she witnessed what just happened. She hurried, and packed me into the little green cart we still had from our odyssey.

She placed me into the cart, and laid a board across for the support of my injured left hand. The main artery of the finger was severed and I was bleeding profusely.

There were no ambulances. Herta pulled me for all she was worth across town to doctor Pawalovsky's office. She was weeping; tears rolled down her cheeks, and afraid I may not make it as the blood ran down on both sides of the wooden board, turning it into a bloody, red color. Why Mama didn't take me puzzled me.

We traveled two kilometers from our house to his office and we didn't even know if he was in that afternoon. We had no phone to notify him of our emergency. Herta was worried I would bleed to death. The artery squirted enough blood to fill a bucket.

Herta encountered people along the way, hoping they would help her, and perhaps wrap my hand in a towel and stop the bleeding. No such help was offered. She continued pulling me on a dirt road, full of chuckholes making the cart unstable. Herta prayed, "Please God, let the doctor be at the office."

When we arrived, she rang the door bell. It seemed like an eternity until the doctor answered the door. When he saw us, he rushed to help me get out of the cart. I literally fell into his arms. My strength was gone and Herta was at the end of hers. The first thing he did was to stop the bleeding when he attached a tight strap. He tried to calm me, speaking to me softly, and assured me everything would be just fine. He got with the job of sewing the finger back on as best as he could.

The prognosis was: the joint was severely damaged, and I would never have full use of the finger. He placed a cast on my hand, extending halfway up my left arm. To lift my spirits, the doctor handed me a piece of bread, covered with real butter, not margarine to help ease my pain.

I am sure, he anesthetized the hand; otherwise the pain would have been unbearable. I pulled through the surgery just fine, but I was weak from the loss of blood. Herta brought me back home in the little cart, but turned the board over to the other side to hide the blood. My family was happy to see me come through this ordeal. Herta recently told me, I never shed a tear during this ordeal. I must have been in shock.

For a couple of days, we saw neither hide, nor hair of my sister Helga, and everyone wondered where she might be. Mama figured she was staying with one of her friends in the neighboring town until things calmed down.

She finally came home on the third day, fully expecting a spanking from Mama. Mama took the bloody board and spanked her behind. It traumatized Helga. That was the wrong thing for Mama to do. After all, it was an accident. This accident taught us a valuable lesson, never pick up anything resembling a sharp tool.

I could never figure out why my sisters loved to torture me. On one occasion, they had the bright idea of piercing my ears with a dirty rusty wire. All three held me down while Herta punctured my earlobe and stuck a rusty wire through it. I struggled to free myself, but it was useless. I was screaming bloody murder, which prevented them from getting to the other ear. They were afraid Mama would hear my cry and come to my rescue. They finally let me go, but the damage was done to my earlobe. It was all over but the crying.

Their plan was to turn me into a girl. My sisters thought, one step at a time might move me into that direction, but I disappointed them.

22

GREETING FROM TYROL

We lived with Frau Auer for four years before Mama found another apartment, a much cheaper one on the wrong side of town. It was close to Grassau, by the Tyrolean River, Ache. In spite of it all, it turned out to be a blessing.

The two-mile trip was uneventful as we followed the moving van to our new home. Like the last time, we pitched in carrying our belongings, and were happy to be on the bottom floor. The place was a dump. I had to give up my bedroom. The bathroom was infested with maggots, crawling all over the toilet seat, and the floor was covered with slimy mold. I was afraid to sit down. It was putrid. When I walked into the bathroom, I couldn't help but step on them, and felt them getting squashed under my bare feet. A plus, the bathroom was indoors.

> The place was a dump. I didn't have my own bedroom, much less a bed. The bathroom was infested with maggots, crawling on the toilet seat.

I was careful so not to have the maggots wriggle up my shorts. The stench was unbearable and we were concerned for our health. In those days, there was no health department, and landlords took advantage of the situation. Whenever I could, I went out into the woods to do my business, using leaves or grass to wipe. Our new landlord was a slum lord. I could see big problems arising in the near future.

We had fertile ground, and many types of vegetables were grown in the area. I watched them fertilize the crops, and with horror I noticed they were using the dung from our cesspool. I was surprised nobody ever got sick. From that moment on, I never had another bite of vegetables. It still makes me sick today when I think about it.

Four families lived in the house. Bachmann owned the property, living on the bottom floor. Upstairs was Frau Schroeder, a single mother who lost her husband in the war. She had two boys, Klaus and Joachim. We lived in the back of the cramped house.

Our kitchen and family room was one room. We had two bedrooms, one for my parents, and one for my three sisters, which meant I was without a bed. My new bed consisted of two wicker chairs tied together, and I slept that way until I outgrew this arrangement. It was depressing to say the least. I wished we hadn't left Frau Auer's house.

We were not happy, and neither was Mama. After about a year, I was upgraded to sleeping on the sofa and that was much more comfortable than the two chairs with no place for my legs and feet. All in all, things weren't the best, but we made do. We had no choice! On the other hand, we were fortunate. Not long ago, we were running from the Nazis and the Red Army!

We had no running water and that added to Mama's overall difficulties. At the beginning, I had to lower a bucket into the well to pull up the water using a rope. It was a tough job for a kid. A year later, it was upgraded to a manual pump, installed in front of the house. I had to pump fifty times to fill up the bucket. I didn't mind doing it since my sisters did everything else around the house. Just the same, I didn't look forward to that chore.

To my amazement, the place was perfect with lots of things to do. The river was behind the house, and to the north of us, were the swamps.

In front of the house was a *Buche* "beech tree." It was huge and brought us lots of shade in warm summer months. There is a saying in German: *Die Buchen soll man suchen, und von den Eichen soll man weichen.* What that says is, "one should look for the beech tree in case of thunder and lightning, and never take refuge under an oak tree". In German, it rhymes, and through the translation, something is always lost.

On a nice day, you would find me under that beautiful tree pondering what to do the rest of the day, and one task was to polish everybody's shoes, and the place I chose, was under the beech tree. They called me the *Schuhputzer* "shoe shine boy". I took great pride in doing the job, and when I was finished, the shoes looked like new. I shined everybody's shoes in my family, and at no charge. In so doing, I allowed a perfect opportunity to pass me by. I could have earned myself a bundle had I shined other people's shoes as well.

When I wasn't shining shoes, I'd be down by the Tyrolean Ache River kicking rocks and looking for driftwood. I learned quickly how to skip rocks across the river; I knew the ones that would do the best job. They had to be flat and round to send them to the other side.

Skipping rocks occupied me for hours. I observed the various water fowl visiting the river. The ducks were the prettiest of all the birds with beautiful colors which changed in the sunlight to a beautiful blue and green around their necks and wing tips. I observed rats swimming along the shore looking for food or a place to sleep. The shoreline was busy with life of all sorts, including snakes, the elegant swimmers.

We only had one species of non-poisonous snakes, the *Ringelnatter.* You found them by the river. They got to be a good size and were beneficial to have around. Their main meal consisted of rats, and there were plenty.

In the spring, the river was at flood stage as it wound its way through the Alps. The Ache River had its origin high in the Austrian Alps by Kufstein where it is called the Brandenberger River. Eventually the river merges with the River Inn. Debris of uprooted trees and dead animals of all kinds were swept away by the raging river. On occasions it breached the dikes, but while we lived there, the river remained contained. At times, the water was as high as the bridge and it was in danger of succumbing to the awesome power of the River Ache.

While the treacherous river unleashed its fury, a man was seen in the angry waves and swept downstream. It was determined he was from Austria, many kilometers upstream. The fire department retrieved the body, and notified the next of kin. I wondered why he fell into the raging river!

I went to the river when it was broiling, and viewing the white caps fascinated me. I was standing at the edge when suddenly I slipped, and I was in danger of falling into the torrent. The last second, God provided a branch. Had I not taken hold of the branch, or had it broken off, nobody would have ever found my body.

I kept the incident secret. I knew if I had told Mama and Papa, the river would have been off-limits. I told them the story much later during a conversation at the dinner table. They both told me in no uncertain terms, never to go to the river again while it was at flood stage.

I disobeyed my parents and continued visiting the river. I was hypnotized by the raging water. I couldn't help but return and watch the fury of the cold, icy friend from Tyrol. Papa found me at the river, and proceeded to spank me. It was a reminder not to ever disobey him again.

At another time, I stood on the bridge looking down at the river when I spotted goats in the middle of the torrent. They were still alive, and fighting to keep their heads above water. They were still bleating, only to disappear under the bridge. I felt so sorry for them, but there wasn't anything anybody could have done to save them.

At the beginning of summer, the river calmed down and I enjoyed making little wooden boats out of driftwood I found on the banks of the river. I watched until they disappeared around the bend. I wished I had been aboard, and wondered where the river might have taken me. I carved different types of vessels, one was a sail boat, another a tugboat, and I even made one that looked like an aircraft carrier. I enjoyed doing that, it kept me busy and out of trouble.

After an exhausting day, I lay on the rocks of the river-bank, drifting off, listening to its tranquil melody as the gentle waves licked the bottom of my feet, putting me to sleep.

I found tons of aluminum foil on the banks, dropped by the Americans during the war. The aluminum hid the American bombers from the

German fighters. There wasn't much I could do with it, and left it by the river, its rightful owner. Had I been a little smarter, I could have sold it for scrap.

When I wasn't visiting my friend "The River", I hiked into the swamp. What a place; I saw all kinds of wildlife, including the European deer and birds of all types, welcoming me with their happy songs. At night, I heard the hooting of the owls. That was kind of creepy.

The next day, I wandered back out into the mysterious swamp. I worked up enough nerve to investigate the bird nests. The mama and papa birds were close by watching over their brood to make sure no harm would come to them. While the parents were gone looking for food, the naked birds huddled together, keeping warm.

On one or two occasions, I saw a large baby bird in one of the nests, much larger than it should have been, judging by the size of their parents. The culprits were the Cuckoos. They laid one egg in another bird's nest and when the baby bird hatched it threw out the original brood. The parents raised the lone baby bird, and the adult Cuckoo was home free, letting other birds go through all the hard work of raising their chick.

With all my activities, my crooked index finger still gave me trouble, always getting in the way when reaching for things. Mama searched for a doctor to straighten it out surgically. She found one in Rosenheim, a city of medium size of about seventy-five thousand inhabitants, and only about forty kilometers north from our home. Herta took time out of her busy schedule and we both traveled by train to Rosenheim. After we arrived in Rosenheim, only an hour's trip, she bought grapes sold at a fruit stand. I had never seen, nor eaten grapes. They tasted so sweet, and we consumed them in a hurry. What a wonderful cool treat on a warm day.

After a relaxing walk, we arrived at the doctor's office. The doctor examined my damaged index finger and scheduled me for surgery later in the year. The following September, I underwent surgery. The operation turned out to be a success, and I have a much improved finger, but it remained stiff. I had my finger in a cast for another two months and was careful not to fall, or bang my hand.

Two boys lived in the same house as I. Klaus and Freddie were a year or two older. We loved building tree houses. The tree houses were cozy and the pine branches were like a mat, and soft to sit on. We invited girls to visit us, but none would ever take us up on it

I built a tree house up in a "giant" pine tree. It was hard work getting to the top. I climbed one branch at a time and thank God it had lots of sturdy branches to hold onto. There, I spent hours at a time observing everything in the tree. I was so proud of myself, where nobody could reach me. I was on

118

top of the world. Among the birds and wild animals I felt at peace. Everything was quiet, and a gentle breeze blew through the branches.

In the same vicinity, was a tall electric tower which attracted lots of birds on their migration to the south. One day, I noticed hundreds of dead birds lying at the bottom of the tower. My parents notified the fish and game warden, and they corrected the problem immediately, but not before hundreds had perished. It was a grounding problem, and the birds landing on the wires were fried to a crisp. I picked them up, and their bodies had burn marks all over. The feathers had melted from their bodies. How awful for the birds to die like that.

Walking through the forest, I was forever listening for crackling sounds that might indicate there was a boar near by. Mama sent me there to gather wood for our little stove. What frightened me most were the wild boars and other types of animals hiding in the shrubs. I dreaded it! For good reason, I was afraid to go out into the forest when it was close to dusk. I was afraid that one of these days I wouldn't be coming back. My imagination got the best of me afraid a wolf would haul me away. It was terrifying.

One of my jobs was to get milk from the farmers. Herr Mosbauer had vicious German shepherds on his property. I wish I could have made myself invisible when I approached the farm. One of these days, the dogs were going to get a piece of me. I couldn't explain it, they mostly growled, but didn't attack me. There was one exception.

I walked to the farmer's house like I had done numerous times before. I pretended to ignore the dogs, but angst pumped through my veins. Out of the dogs, one stood out. He was bigger than the others. He had a white chest and paws, but the rest of his body was chestnut brown. The dog sensed I was scared and ran towards me. The German Shepherd was growling, hairs on its back stood straight up and ready to attack me with his protruding sharp fangs.

> The dog sensed I was scared and came towards me growling, the hairs on its back stood straight up and he was ready to attack me.

I ran towards the barn as fast as I could. I was huffing and puffing, and my heart was pounding hard and fast. The dog launched at me from behind baring his carnivorous teeth. He got a hold of my calf and didn't let go. I thrashed about with my arms and finally, the dog released his grip, but not before blood streamed down my leg and into my shoes. I staggered into the barn crying. The farmer rushed towards me and rushed to clean my wound with cold running water. He gently wiped the blood from my leg with a soft cloth from his emergency kit.

Herr Mosbauer then wiped off the remaining blood. The injury wasn't as bad as I thought. It was an open wound and should have been stitched. The bleeding had stopped by now, but I was still shaking from the encounter. It could have been much worse had the other dogs joined in. I thanked God I was still alive.

Mama didn't send me to the doctor and told me all would be okay. I wasn't so sure! Did the dog have rabies? Weeks and months passed, and I didn't display any sign of rabies. The next time when I approached the barn, I made sure the dogs weren't around. I believe Herr Mosbauer locked them up. I prayed: "Please dear God protect me from the scary big dogs."

The dogs weren't the only predators to worry about. The white geese were much bigger than I was and with their outstretched wings resembled angry ghosts. The sound of the wings resembled rushing water. They nipped at my short legs, but didn't hurt me all that much. Just the same, I was afraid they were going to gobble me up at any moment. It was terribly frightening.

First the dogs, then the geese and turkeys threatened my short life. I told Mama about the terrifying animals and let her know I wouldn't be getting any more milk. I shouldn't have said that! She told me, you must be a brave boy and put up with adversities.

I faced the giants again, and again. The geese were just waiting for me coming around the corner, and I believe they were having fun scaring me. I bet they laughed up their wings when they talked about me, "Here he comes, let's have some fun and scare the day lights out of him."

Another time, I ran into the barn, huffing and puffing. The farmer asked me why I was in such a hurry. My reply was, "Your dogs were after me again." Herr Mosbauer seemed not to be overly concerned. It was as though he didn't hear me as he squirted the milk directly into my can from the cow's udder, and within seconds, my can was full of warm, foamy white milk.

I was hesitant to step outside, fearing the vicious carnivores. I looked left, I looked right, but they weren't around. Unbeknownst to me, Mama made a visit to Herr Mosbauer and told him to lock up the dogs next time I came around, and if any of his dogs bit me again, he would face charges. She rescued me!

We had no refrigerator, and at times the milk got sour, but all was not lost. We ate the sour chunky pieces anyway. We sprinkled sugar on the surface, and another dessert was invented. In Bavaria, nobody had refrigerators, and for the most part, that was just fine.

In the summer, the perishables went into the cold, damp cellar to keep cool. Sacks of potatoes, a mainstay, especially in the winter, filled the entry. To cool us off in the hot summer months, beer and soda for us kids was stored there as well. What I liked best was to mix lemonade with beer, called *Radlermass.*

Through the centuries, the Bavarians learned to make many dishes out of potatoes. The delicious potato pancakes were my favorite. Mama ordered potatoes from a local farmer. When it came time to order, they arranged a time. For some reason, the farmer didn't arrive at the agreed time. Later in the day, she noticed a horse-drawn hearse pull into our driveway. Nobody had died recently at our place that she knew of. She was puzzled. There would be no use to have him stop here. The driver approached Mama, and told her the potatoes were inside the hearse and he would carry them to the cellar. Mama wouldn't have any of it, and refused the delivery that day.

We were forever reminded of the war. By the bank of the Ache River, we found live hand grenades. We were naturally curious, picked them up, and looked them over. Klaus, Freddie and I played with them until somebody told us not to ever touch them. Klaus took one of the grenades, pulled the pin, and threw it into the river, creating a huge explosion. I don't know if he knew to get rid of it quickly, but thank God he did.

It didn't have an operator's manual. Had he not thrown the grenade in time, it would have blown us to pieces. Many children were injured and killed playing with these deadly tools of war. I am thankful that none of us was ever hurt. Our parents told us to stay away from these weapons.

Since we weren't allowed to play with hand grenades, Klaus, Freddie and I had to find something else to occupy us. We started to manufacture our own grenades. I was not involved directly. Klaus and the other boys took lime, placed it into an empty beer bottle, added water and sealed the bottle. When the lime came to a boil, it exploded, sending hundreds of glass shrapnel over a wide area. During the blast, we hid behind trees. It was truly a miracle that none of us were ever hurt by the foolish things we did.

Let's do something less explosive. We lined up by my landlord's front door to see which one of us could squirt the highest. As we proceeded with the contest, with shock, we observed our landlord appearing out of nowhere. He grabbed me by the collar of my shirt. I was the closest to him and he spanked me hard. I told him, "Please don't tell Mama." He knew Mama would have killed me or maybe not. I didn't want to find out. .

We had the time of our lives when we observed the Americans conducting military maneuvers in our area. I loved having the American soldiers around. They were friendly towards us and always ready to hand out chocolate and candy. We befriended one of the GI's who came by our place a few times with his shiny green Army Jeep.

It was the prettiest vehicle I had ever laid my eyes on. I liked the body with its cloth top down, and the unusual grill reminded me of shark teeth. The long extended antennas attached to the rear of the vehicle reminded me of a bug.

On occasions, I saw the American Jeeps drive through our town at a high rate of speed, their long antennas almost touching the ground, and disappear in a cloud of dust.

We visited the Americans quite often while they set up camp on the other side of the Ache River, in Grassau.

It just so happened, there was a pond nearby. Herta told me, if I sat there quietly, I could observe mermaids with their long tails sitting on the boulders down below by the water's edge sunning themselves. Since I was naturally curious, I had to investigate. I never saw anything out of the ordinary, other than an occasional rodent and ducks. Herta was telling me stories again.

One very cold, snowy night in January, we had lots of snow covering the ground and were dying for some heat. We knew where to find it. It was at the American camp. The soldiers lifted us up, and sat us on the top of the warm tank. I can still feel the heat coming through the vents, and that felt so good as it warmed our entire bodies.

I was fascinated by the soldiers' starched uniforms, with their colorful ribbons and medals on their chest. The stripes on their upper arms were yellow, and stood out on their green uniform. We couldn't understand a word they were saying, but we knew one thing, they loved us, always reached into their pockets pulling out chocolate bars, candies and chewing gum.

We hated to see them leave after the maneuvers ended, and were anxiously waiting for their return. Whenever the Americans moved out, they left all kinds of food behind, like sausages, bread and other delicacies. Nothing went to waste and we were happy to be the clean-up crew. We found chocolates with candy strewn about, and that was their way of saying they were thinking of us.

I loved having the Americans around our house visiting my sisters. When Mama came home, she inadvertently heard about Herta's escapades. When she was a teenager, and started liking boys, Mama wouldn't have any of it. Somehow, my sisters managed to see them anyway.

Mama was gone quite a bit teaching young girls to sew which took her all over Bavaria. Papa was gone all week, working in Munich, and we were left to our own devices. It was up to Herta to look after me. Herta was glad whenever she saw Mama come back, giving her a well deserved break.

Mama had a short, unpredictable temper. One evening she was ironing clothes, when she became upset with Herta. Out of the blue, she flung the hot iron at Herta, but thank God, she missed her when she ducked in time. My sister was depressed, and lost all hope. She wanted to leave home, but at such a young age, it was not wise. That evening, after she went to bed, Herta attempted to take her life, swallowing a handful of sleeping pills. Mama found her unconscious in bed and arranged to have an ambulance take her to the hospital.

The doctor's prognosis was not good. Herta was not allowed visitors while she was in the ICU unit of the hospital. She laid unconscious in her hospital bed for a couple of weeks. I would have loved to visit her, but even if I would have been given permission, the trip was just too far for me to walk. After three weeks, Herta woke up from her deep "sleep".

We were so happy she pulled through the ordeal and we couldn't wait to see her. Thank God we didn't lose her. It wasn't her time to go. When she was brought home by ambulance, an uneasy peace returned. I was happy to have my big sister back home to whom I entrusted everything.

It was in the early morning hours of July 1952. I was standing in the meadow by our house when I sensed something coming at me very fast. It was some kind of rocket, and it missed me by a couple of feet. It zoomed past me at supersonic speed, and almost knocked me to the ground. I don't know where it landed, but I was happy I wasn't the intended target.

When walking from Grassau to my home, I saw an American military truck with the traditional white star on the doors of the cab. The trailer was filled with soldiers carrying guns as if going to battle. I couldn't believe my eyes when I saw black soldiers for the first time in my life. All I saw were white eyes and teeth. I was scared! I ran as fast as my legs would carry me, hoping they wouldn't catch me. At this time, I was around six years of age.

All winded, I arrived home and told Mama and Papa what I had seen. "Mama, you wouldn't believe what I saw in the American army truck; it was black men carrying rifles. Did they come from a different planet?"

Papa said, "Black people originally came from Africa and were introduced to America by slave traders, and they are no different than any other people, except for the skin color." My fears evaporated, and I enjoyed being with them and accepted their candy and the other goodies they offered.

When crossing the bridge of the Ache River, I hooked up with Hans-Peter as we had done many times before. Out of nowhere, powerful winds began to howl, and the sky turned dark as night. I became frightened, afraid to move.

Hurricane-force winds began to pound the neighborhood. In southern Germany we were used to warm storms, named "Föhn". These storms originate in the Sahara region. If there was snow left on the ground, it melted like butter on a hot stove. I enjoyed these warm winds, and if they weren't too strong, leaning into them was fun. It gave me the sense of flying as the strong winds blew around me, almost lifting me off the ground.

While this was occurring, Hans-Peter and I sought refuge at the local *Gasthaus*. We observed a red ball of lightning bolt enter the Gasthaus, end up at the end of the hall, then shot back out with lightning speed. What a display of power and speed. I had never seen anything that spectacular before, and haven't seen anything like this since.

Hans-Peter had a positive influence on me. Mama encouraged me to invite him over, as she reasoned that his intellect might rub off on me. He was an exceptional boy, and academically gifted. When I visited him at his home, I remember finding discarded ceramic figures all around. Somehow they were damaged during the manufacturing process. His parents owned the ceramic factory where they produced all kinds of neat things. I walked around the pile of ceramics for hours at a time. On one of the heaps I found figurines, coffee cups, saucers, all types of plates and many other creations. How fascinating! It was very tempting to take some home, but they weren't mine, and I left them on the pile.

Hans-Peter was light-years ahead of me academically. A pleasant young man, always cheerful, and when looking at him, I saw the brilliance in his eyes. At the age of 12, he attended the university. His parents were very proud of him, and blessed, to have a son like him.

One day, his school class took a ski trip into the Alps, and whilst there Hans-Peter fell on one of the slopes, and while in the process of getting to his feet, a skier ran over him with the sharp edges of his skis and cut into his neck which severed his jugular vein.

He bled to death on the slope before the paramedics could reach him. I missed him so much, and mourned for a long time. I wondered why God allowed this to happen.

I visited Hans-Peter at the funeral home. It left an everlasting impression on me. He looked so sad lying in the casket, his face was white as snow, and for some reason, his mouth didn't look right. His lips didn't cover his teeth. Oh, it was dreadful! Why did God take him so early from us? I will never know. It was the longest walk home. His death made me aware of how fragile life was.

Mama had somewhat of a mean streak, and told me, Hans-Peter would visit me during the night while I slept. Was this a cruel joke? I wanted to see him again, but not as a ghost. I prayed to God, "Please have mercy on me." Would Hans-Peter seek revenge because we made fun of him? We were jealous of his academic achievements. Kids were cruel, and I prayed for God's forgiveness.

I was terrified to go to sleep. I kept my eyes closed in the dark, afraid I might catch a glimpse of him. All this taught me a lesson. I should always be nice to people and especially friends.

His parents were devastated by the tragedy. After a couple of years, we moved away and I lost track of how they coped with this tragedy

When I walked along the shore of the Ache, it helped me to brush aside the unpleasant things of our lives. I couldn't wait for the river to reveal its secrets each time I paid it a visit. In the midst of the rocks on the shore line were puddles of accumulated water. With amazement, I watched bugs glide on top of the water as though they were skiing. They made it look so easy.

In late fall, the chimney sweep made his rounds to make sure the chimneys were clean of debris. His calling-card was, he rode his bike and wore a black top hat. Everybody in town knew his trademark. His work required him to crawl partly inside the chimney causing him to be covered with black soot from head to toe. I don't believe he earned much money at the job, but kind people gave him food to take to his family.

He always parked his bike unattended in front of the house while he worked, and when he rested. He placed his tall black hat on the bicycle seat during his break. Under the hat, he kept food given to him by his customers. When it came to food, it wasn't safe left alone. Klaus, Freddie and I, milled around his bike, and wondered what might be under the black hat. I wanted to try out the hat, but just as I was placing the soot covered hat on my head, several eggs fell to the ground.

A yellow river was flowing from the seat of the bike to the cement floor. I felt bad about this tragedy. His family may not have had a dinner that night.

Had I known that he stored the eggs under the hat, I would have never done what I did. In panic, I hightailed from the scene of the crime, running down to the river and under the bridge where I knew a perfect hiding place. There was no way anybody would ever be able to locate me. I thought I was safe.

With absolute horror, I saw the chimney sweep climb down the same hill and aim straight for me. I couldn't believe my eyes. Was I seeing things? One of my friends spilled the beans, telling the chimney sweep where I could be found.

He took off his big black gloves and whipped me mercilessly, leaving my face with black soot from the top of my head all the way down to my chin.

I stayed for quite a while until the shock wore off. I managed to clean up with the help of the river who was still my friend, my only friend. After climbing back up, my "buddies" had all but disappeared. One thing I was happy about was, Mama and Papa never found out about this escapade. I learned one lesson, leave other people's property alone.

The following spring, Joachim, my neighbor from upstairs, bought a rubber raft and proceeded to launch it into the river with a couple of his buddies. When they were a few kilometers upstream from the bridge, and in the middle of the river, they realized the swollen stream had full control of their raft.

It wasn't a bright idea to begin with, getting into the raft; the waves were high, and the current swift. The flimsy raft was carried by the angry river at a tremendous speed. The boys cried out for help. When they approached the bridge the boat wrapped itself around one of the huge pillars, spilling everybody into the ice cold torrent.

People on the bridge saw this tragedy unfold and notified the fire department. If it had not been for their swift response, the boys would have been swept downstream and drowned. The fire truck stopped in the middle of the bridge and lowered a rope where the boys were, clinging onto the slick, algae covered pillar.

It was touch and go. The tremendous force of the water made it difficult to secure a line around the boys. They succeeded in pulling the kids one by one, to the top of the bridge. The boys were shaking uncontrollably from the icy water. The firemen wrapped heavy blankets around them to warm up their bodies. They recovered quickly and were thankful they cheated death. The raft was a total loss. I saw the collapsed raft many months later still wrapped around the pillar. It was a reminder of the near tragedy. In time, the raging waters tore it from the bridge and sent it downstream.

Fishermen came from miles around to fish off the Ache Bridge, trying their luck, hoping to reel in a trophy fish. I was intrigued how they rigged the lines and the bait they used. The successful ones used worms. I discovered that some came from as far away as Vienna, Salzburg and even Berlin. It was a beautiful spot indeed with the majestic mountains in the background and huge trees lining the shore.

We couldn't live off of the beauty of the land so Mama searched for employment somewhere else. It took both Mama and Papa's income to make ends meet. She was hired by a television factory in Grassau. The work pushed her over the edge. She was paid by piece work, and the quicker she worked, the more she was paid. Knowing her, she worked frantically to meet, and exceed her quota for the day. It was difficult for her to maintain the speed.

One day, after coming home from school, I was told Mama had a nervous breakdown; an ambulance took her to the hospital in Traunstein for observation. The stress of the job pushed her over the edge. She was drained, and had no more to give. Mama risked her life for better than a year to keep us safe towards the end of the war. Her nerves were shot from all the calamities.

Mama survived two horrible wars, first WWI, when the Russians came across the Prussian border. In 1918, she and her parents were displaced when their home was destroyed by the Red Army. They fled west toward Berlin to get away from the carnage of war. Opa was fighting on the front when the Germans got the upper hand and drove the Russians back across the border. Mama told me, the German army encircled the Russians by the thousands and drove them into the many lakes surrounding Königsberg, Prussia.

Papa was gone all week working in Munich. Without him, it was very demanding and Mama was stressed. She voiced her concern to our land-lord about the unsanitary living conditions. Frau Bachmann told her, "You can always leave." Frau Bachmann didn't appear to be concerned and wasn't about to change anything to improve the living conditions. Mama lost her cool and slapped the landlord. Frankly, I was surprised it took that long. It wasn't long after this episode that Frau Bachmann gave us one month to leave the property. In short, we had to look for another place to live.

It might have been a blessing in disguise. Papa wanted to move closer to Munich anyway. When we lived in Staudach, he made the trip to Munich on Monday and we wouldn't see him again until the weekend. If we moved closer to Munich, he could be home every night. It was a huge plus.

I don't know how Papa managed to travel back and forth to Munich and home all those years. He got up around four in the morning and didn't come home until seven in the evening. His lunch consisted of rye bread and lard. He did this for many years. I don't know what he ate when he stayed in Munich, but I am sure he didn't live a life of luxury.

Papa was a very kind man, and since he wasn't around much during the week, he didn't want to punish us kids when he came home. I never received a perfect report card, far from it. Mama told Papa about my lack of progress at school, and I knew exactly what was coming. I was familiar with the routine, what chair to lie across, and waited for the inevitable. The punishment wasn't bad if you compared it to what I received from the teachers in school.

In a way, I was looking forward to the punishment. After he was done, he pulled out a candy bar and gave me a big hug. Papa had a tender heart and would never fly off the handle even during these unbelievably tough times.

The moment arrived. A large moving van drove to our apartment, and two men began loading our furniture onto the truck. I dreaded climbing into the moving van taking us to Lorenzenberg, fifty kilometers north from Staudach. I bid goodbye to my friend, the Ache River and hopefully not for the last time.

It was wonderful driving through the countryside with rolling hills that resembled green velvet. The huge farmhouses with beautiful murals intrigued me. The colorful pictures on the houses were fairly common, and often times depicted the history of the family living there for hundreds of years. Sometimes it would be of a religious nature.

We moved into a village where farmhouses were 1200 years old and the property was still in the original family's name. Over the years, some of the buildings burned down, only to be rebuilt later. Lorenzenberg and Dorfen were founded around the year 700 and the churches were built at about the same time, or shortly thereafter.

I don't know if the houses of worship had ever burned. Chances were they did. The trip to Lorenzenberg took four to five hours, including potty stops and getting a bite to eat here and there. My sisters powdered up at every stop, just like the last time, when we moved to Staudach from Heidelberg. They wanted to look pretty, just to make a good impression when they stepped off the truck to face our new landlord.

At last, we exited the "Autobahn", and drove on a narrow country road towards our new home. The moving van came to a crawl, and I knew we had arrived. I saw this cute house next to a forest amidst beautiful meadows.

We unloaded the furniture and other household items. The truck driver piled everything on the outside of the house, Mama paid him, and he was on his way. It was our turn to move it all into the house. Without a dolly, the big furniture pieces were the toughest to move. Our new landlord Anderl saw us struggle up the stairs and gave us a helping hand. My sisters moved the lighter items. Anderl, Mama and I carried the heavier pieces of furniture up the staircase.

I was now twelve years old and stronger, lifting furniture and carrying household items into the house. I didn't feel tired and looked forward in anticipation of what was coming. I noticed a boy about my age standing on a grassy hill, curious as to who was moving into his neighborhood. He had black hair, parted down the middle, and a chubby build. Things were looking up; I might have a friend close by to play with. To top it off, our new home was surrounded by green, manicured fields of corn, wheat and oats.

The view from our new home was magnificent. From our balcony, the mountains of the *Wilde Kaiser* "Wild Kaiser" came into clear view, and I realized we weren't that far away from where we used to live.

The green fields of wheat gave the land a look which resembled a soft green work of art. In Staudach, the most common crops were fruit trees and alfalfa. The ground was rocky, and ill suited for growing grain.

Our new landlord, Anderl, a long haul truck driver, loved telling stories about his travels. One of his most memorable stories was, when he was driving on the Autobahn, something wasn't right. Motorists drove alongside his cab motioning to him. Why were all these people concerned? He pulled onto the shoulder of the highway and investigated. A small car had become stuck under the trailer and he had dragged it several kilometers down the highway. He had no idea how this could have happened. Luckily, the person driving the car wasn't seriously injured, shaken up, but happy to be alive.

Anderl was a happy man, and always wore a smile. I can still hear the motor sound of his Adler motorcycle he rode to work early Monday mornings. It sort of sang as it gained speed. He drove to Hohentann where he met his truck. His travels took him all over Europe and he didn't come back for a week or longer. I wish I could have traveled with him, how exciting that would have been.

The first weekend at our new home, Anderl invited us to a *Zitter* performance. He played like no other, and we sang along without skipping a beat. The *Zitter* is similar to a guitar; it is a flat string instrument, and produces the most beautiful sounds. When <u>Anderl</u> played, the music resonated through the town.

Town folks came from all over to see what the occasion was and joined in singing the old Bavarian songs of yesteryear. After a couple of beers, they went home and returned with their instruments. The place was jumping and everybody had a good time. After a delightful evening and much laughter, they picked up their trumpets and walked home. They deserved a much needed rest before getting up to go to church the next morning.

Other times, we played a game called *Ich rieche, rieche Menschenfleisch,* "I smell human flesh". The one tagged had to find another victim, and then it was their turn to find somebody else in total darkness. We played it for hours at a time, past midnight. We climbed over furniture and, in the process knocked over some of the trinkets. Exhausted, we fell into our beds and were happy we weren't devoured by the lion.

After we had lived there for a couple of weeks, I was hoping to meet my new neighbor. He lived on the Heissen's farm, just up the hill from us. The house was huge with a barn attached to the living quarter. I worked up enough nerve and walked up to his place. After I knocked on the door, he greeted me.

I introduced myself to him and he invited me in to meet his parents who welcomed me to the neighborhood. They asked me to stay a while and join them to eat *Kaffeekuchen* "coffeecake". It was out of this world. I consumed a slice, and she offered me another piece. I could have eaten the whole thing. I thanked her, and to be polite, I declined the offer.

After I excused myself, I was introduced to the cattle in the barn, numbering around thirty head. They were milk cows with brown patches and short horns. The cattle supplied heat to the barn, and the rest of the house. The house was surprisingly warm, even in the middle of winter.

Michael's parents asked me where we came from, and I told them we lived south by the Austrian border. My Bavarian was without a flaw, and they couldn't detect that we came from Heidelberg originally. Refugees were considered second class citizens. Actually, we were not considered as such, since we lived in Heidelberg and still had a home after the war.

If I had told the people in the area that Mama and Papa came from north east of Germany, Prussia, and Saxony, they wouldn't have given me the time of day. There was animosity towards people of eastern Germany, primarily due to the religious differences. Catholics from southern Germany didn't like Lutherans. Lutherans had no love for the Catholics either, and that is why there were the thirty and hundred year wars. When we moved to Bavaria, I became aware of the friction between the two Christian faiths. My new friend Michael and his family weren't practicing Catholics, and they couldn't have cared less. I received a warm welcome, and they made me feel at home.

It couldn't have been a better day, and to top it off, I found a friend. Michael was one year older than I, and we were in the same classroom. We attended a country school with no more than thirty kids. Michael was a math whiz and he helped me when I had trouble with arithmetic. I helped him in German, and that worked out well. We complimented each other. Things were working out great.

Most farmers owned dairy cows for milk, and horses supplied the power for harvesting, plowing the fields, and delivering the harvest to the market. Michael's dad was ahead of the game. He owned an old, gray Deutz tractor, and Michael drove the tractor when they worked in the field. There was no room for passengers, so I sat on the narrow fender, just inches from the huge wheel. That might have been a little dangerous. Had I lost my grip, the rear wheel of the tractor would have crushed me.

During harvest time, Michael worked from early morning until dark. In those days, there wasn't much automation, and most everything was done by hand. Everything had to be loaded onto the wagon by strong arms and hands. The evening hours came early and the job had to be completed before dark.

To get the tractor going, they hand-cranked it to get the engine started. It would huff and puff, and huff and puff some more until the motor warmed up. The tractor was kind of like the little train that could. I still hear the gray tractor after all these years.

The farmers cut the alfalfa by hand, then raked the hay by hand, and after a week or so, weather permitting, they stacked it high on the wagon. It was all done with physical labor.

In Germany, it rains an awful lot which limited our outdoor activities, and when there was a break in the weather, you had better take advantage of it. On one particular Saturday, Papa told me to get dressed and said, "We are going to the train station and go for a ride." What a surprise! I couldn't believe he was taking me on a train ride. What did I do to deserve this? I asked him where we were going.

Papa told me he had a special treat for me. We were going to Munich. I never went any place far from home. The only time I saw any sign of Munich was in the evening after it turned dark. The bright lights of Munich illuminated the skyline.

It was hard for me to believe I was going to the big city. I was ecstatic. My heart jumped for joy. The train trip didn't take long, maybe 45 minutes at the most, when we pulled into Munich's *Hauptbahnhof "Main train Station"*. We got off the train and walked towards Main Street running parallel with the terminal. I didn't have to worry about getting lost; Papa knew the city like the back of his hand. He loved to walk, even if he could have taken a bus or train. He didn't divulge what he had in mind before getting to our destination. When he told me where we were going, I couldn't believe my ears. Our destination was the famous Munich zoo. What a treat! When we arrived, there was so much to see, and the time just flew.

The zoo had animals from all over the world. I saw the huge elephants with their long trunks and big ears. People were feeding them, letting them take the food right out of their hand with their huge trunks. Their enclosure wasn't very large. I felt sorry for the elephants. In their native Africa, they had lots of room to roam, but now they were confined.

The lions were awesome with their huge teeth, the males sporting their enormous manes. With their powerful body, I knew why they were called the king of the jungle. Before long, it was evening; the sun slipped below the horizon and bid us a farewell. It was time to catch the train to go back. On the way to the train station, Papa took me to a restaurant to have something to eat and that made it a perfect day.

I had a terrific time spending the day with Papa, just him and I. The ride home was uneventful. Where we were sitting, we observed a family with their three children, two boys and a girl. The youngest of the children was around three, another around five, and the oldest close to eight. I don't know where they were from, or where they were going, but they seemed to have had a good time. Maybe they also visited the zoo.

In a few minutes, we arrived in Assling, got off the train, and started walking home on the winding narrow road. It was very quiet, not a sound in the air. I wasn't afraid, Papa was with me. When I walked by myself, I was in the habit of whistling my favorite tunes I learned in school, drowning out any other noises. By the time we walked through our front door, it was totally dark. Only the stars were visible in the dark sky. I looked north, and there was the skyline of Munich, a wonderful reminder of a perfect weekend.

We climbed up the stairs, and I yelled, Mama, Mama, "Guess what we saw today." She wasn't at all interested in what I wanted to share with her about our wonderful zoo experience. I went to bed and cried myself to sleep.

The following year Papa took me again, and it was just as fantastic. Munich was an exciting town with busy streets and tall, beautiful Rococo buildings, built many centuries ago.

The street cars were packed with passengers. So many people were riding the cars, and there was no more room inside. Some were hanging outside, holding onto the handles by the doors. Now I know why we didn't take the street car. It could have been a frightening experience for me. We were walking on the sidewalk, taking it all in, and with so many things to see, I wasn't paying attention and walked right into a light pole. It made a horrific sound, and people walked over to me to see if I was okay. It proved one thing, I had a hard head.

Papa felt bad, but it didn't slow us down any, and we arrived at the zoo without skipping a beat. When we entered the zoo, I had a big bump in the middle of my forehead. Oh, cool, now I looked more like a primate than a human being. I fit right in. We took off where we left off the year before. I got to see the animals I had only seen in books. This time, we were able to see the other animals we failed to see the previous trip, like the monkeys, chimpanzees, and gorillas.

I saw one of the gorillas throw feces at people as they marveled at the powerful animal. I thought it was kind of funny. I would have been annoyed too, seeing people all day long passing by and staring at me. The weekend had come and gone, and my mind was still in Munich at the fabulous zoo. I cherished the memories forever.

My neighbor Michael and I were together a lot. Where he was, I was, and vice versa. Living in the country was wonderful. It had so much to offer. Michael and I played in the haystack, and crawled through the tunnels we painfully built. We had lots of fun, but his dad didn't like us doing that. He was afraid of us falling down to the concrete floor and getting hurt.

Michael's dad installed a hay loader which moved on a rail, lifting the hay from the wagon and stacking it high inside the barn. Something went wrong. The implement, weighing over a ton fell to the concrete floor missing Michael's dad by inches.

Michael's dad was a huge man, with hands as large as a dinner plate. I made sure I never got in his way, and kept my distance for a good reason. I was so excited when he took us on one of his buying trips. He sold, and bought cattle in the neighboring towns. It was the first time I had ever ridden in an Opel made by General Motors. It was a marvelous trip. To top it off, his dad bought us lunch. While he was talking to one of the farmers, Michael and I did some investigating on our own.

We walked in the barn and saw the biggest bulls. Their heads were huge with a very muscular neck. We kept our distance. Some of the bulls were mean, and it could have been dangerous if we got too close. The farmer also had a couple of draft-horses tied up in the barn. They were tall and powerful, with white curly locks on their necks. Their hoofs were huge and dressed with white strands of hair covering the entire hoof. After an hour or so, it was time to head back home. We climbed into the comfortable Opel and fell asleep, tired from an adventurous day. We drove through the green countryside, and before long, we arrived at his place. His mother greeted us, and asked us to have a seat in the kitchen.

She was the sweetest lady you could ever meet, making me feel at home and offering me something to eat every time I came to see Michael. I can still see her in the kitchen cooking even after she did her work out in the barn.

Michael's dad passed away thirty years ago, and his mom, ten years later, and both were interned in the same cemetery where my home church was.

Michael's sister Anne was quite a bit older than Michael. She outworked any man, mowing the grass by hand, then raking it, and lifting it on the wagon. I had never seen anybody work harder than she did. Anne married a man who didn't like cats. I remember when he took a cat and bludgeoned it to death with a shovel right in front of me. How cruel.

We played in the woods building houses out of pine branches. I had to be careful in the forest. There were poisonous *Kreuzotters*, "snakes", to avoid, but they weren't as poisonous as our rattlers.

In the summer I walked barefoot most of the time and once I saw a huge *Ringelnatter* snake slithering by my foot. It gave me a scare. Another time, I was chased by three aggressive hornets. I was told two of those hornets could kill a child, and three a horse. I was running to get away from them, when suddenly they disappeared and I breathed a sigh of relief. I thought I had lost them. Five minutes later, they gave chase again. I heard them from afar as the sound of their wings resonated through the still air. I was frightened. What a relief when they finally stopped following me. In Germany, there weren't many dangerous animals. All I had to worry about were the poisonous *Kreuzotter*, hornets, wild dogs, and boars.

23

THE NAKED ORPHAN

Out in the woods, I found a small naked bird on the ground, and shaking from the cold. It was obviously frightened and cold after falling out of its nest. Not one feather covered the body. I was more than willing to rescue it from its plight when I decided to pick it up, placed it in the cup of my hand and took it home. I built a little cage for the bird and attended the baby bird day and night.

I caught all kinds of insects which consisted of rain worms and bugs. The bird grew feathers, became stronger, and began to chirp. By the looks of things, it could possibly grow to be a pretty big bird.

I figured it was a magpie, and these birds are by nature very smart. It took two months for it to be clothed in beautiful black feathers, with white stripes on each side of the wing. Its beak was black and it had a long black tail which gave off a dark blue shine in the sun

It came time to teach him to fly. It would be quite a trick to accomplish the feat. What gender was the bird? God only knew. I thought it was a male and called him *Vogel*. It didn't take long for him to get used to his name. At last, now came the time for the bird to try out his wings. The balcony was the perfect place so I tossed him from our balcony, hoping and praying he would stay aloft, and not get splattered on the ground below. Oh, what a thrill to see him take to the air, and fly he did. As time went on, the bird became more and more independent. I didn't have to feed it anymore and things were getting lots easier.

I wasn't aware, but these birds are little thieves and are prone to getting into trouble. Our neighbor planted lettuce in her garden, when from far off, Vogel observed her. After she completed the job of planting the lettuce he proceeded to pull out the plants one by one. Now that didn't go down overly well. When I called him, he came to me hoping I would have food for him. Every now and then I treated him with a juicy bug for which he thanked me by giving me a loud chirp. Without fail, he flew off early in the morning, and came back before dark the same day.

We had a bad storm, with hurricane-force winds. My bird failed to show up that evening. I thought something terrible had happened to him while he was out in the tempest. I kept looking for him, but to no avail. After I had lived in the U.S. for thirty-two years I went back to Germany to visit with my old friend Michael, when by chance, our conversation turned to Vogel. I asked him if he knew what happened to the magpie. He revealed the secret.

He told me my bird made it a habit of raiding one of the farmer's pigeon nests. The farmer didn't appreciate that, so he blew him out of the sky with his twelve gauge shotgun. Nobody knew for certain it was my bird; it could have been one of many magpies that made this area their home. It could be that Vogel grew to an old age. His offspring may still circle the ancient forests of Bavaria.

24

ALTAR BOY

My life in Lorenzenberg was briefly interrupted when I developed pain on the right side of my lower abdomen. Mama examined me and determined that I had an infected appendix. I don't know how she determined that, but she didn't take any chances of it bursting. She got hold of a doctor in Rosenheim who dispatched a car to pick me up and take me to the hospital. The trip was no more than thirty-five miles from my home. The car was elegant and furnished with leather upholstery. It wasn't an ambulance, but a luxury car by any standard. Within an hour we arrived at the hospital.

When we reached the *Krankenhaus*, "Hospital", the doctor determined it would be best to operate immediately. They readied me for surgery, changed my clothes, and put me in a hospital gown. I was taken to surgery by catholic nuns who placed me on a gurney. Once I was in the surgery room, a cup was placed over my nose and mouth. They asked me to repeat my name. I didn't get past Hans when I went under.

After surgery, I woke up in a dorm-like setting, with beds on both sides of the room. They didn't have a critical care ward. All patients were in one ward, and that made things difficult for patients just out of surgery. I woke up drowsy, and for a moment, I didn't know how I got to that place, or what I was doing here. The anesthesia made me sick and caused me to throw up. I was at the hospital for twelve full days, and that was tough. They made me do homework, and that was okay. At least it gave me something to do. I never really felt bad, except for throwing up.

The nuns discovered I had a gift for singing, and I became part of the hospital children's choir, it was fun. We sang mostly to elderly patients who liked hearing the old songs. It reminded them of when they were young and it gave us an opportunity to make them happy.

Way before the twelve days were up, I was ready to check myself out had they not kept an eye on me. Out of the blue, Papa came to visit me, and that was special. I didn't want him to leave without me, but after an hour, Papa left for home and I cried my eyes out.

There were lots of people around, but just the same, it was a lonely place. I missed my family. Mama never made it to the hospital. Why she didn't come, I will never know.

One morning, they transported a guy and placed him next to my bunk. I was told that he had been in a serious motorcycle accident. His head was swollen, and as big as a watermelon. I heard he wasn't wearing a helmet. He never regained consciousness while I was there. I hope he pulled through.

The county fairgrounds were next to the hospital. I heard the cars glide along the rails of the roller coasters with kids laughing and screaming from the bottom of their lungs. It was awful being cooped up.

I couldn't wait to get out of the hospital. On the twelfth day, Papa rescued me. We got on the train, and in about thirty minutes we were in Assling. When the train rolled into town it was already dark. The long walk home was tiring and the wound began to ache. I made it home with Papa's help as he took me by the arm and lifted me up. When I came home, Mama was waiting for me and happy to have me around. It was great to be home, and it didn't take me long to continue where I left off. Things hadn't changed any and I continued planning my days playing in the woods or spending time with my friend Michael.

At times, Mama sent me to buy groceries from a store in Assling and by the time I walked back, it was dark. The lonely road was spooky, giant trees of the forest embraced me with their dark branches almost touching the ground. To give me courage, I whistled as loud as I could, blocking out noises which might emerge from the forest. One night, as I was walking the deserted road, a pair of glowing eyes followed me in the darkness. They made me pick up my pace. It probably was just a housecat, but my imagination was running wild, thinking maybe it was a big wolf stalking me.

When I wasn't whistling, I was singing. My neighbors told me when they heard me coming home I sang a lyric no Bavarian farmer likes to hear. It goes like this: "Every farmer's son has his money in his bag but us poor suckers have none." Something is always lost in the translation, but you get the point. It didn't go over well because we were surrounded by farms.

The summer bid us goodbye and the autumn was at the door with golden leaves covering our yard. It was a wonderful vacation, and I dreaded going back to school. One thing I didn't know was who my teacher was going to be. I was still plagued with flashbacks from school back in Staudach.

Michael was in the same classroom, easing my anxiety considerably. My sister Helga was two years ahead of me and it was her last year in school. She was fourteen and I was twelve. In Germany everybody attended *Volksschule,* "Public School". When we reached eighth grade, we graduated. It was my misfortune that my sister Helga was sitting a few rows behind me and watched my every move. I couldn't wait until she graduated.

Life was getting easier for me in many ways, but I was shunned by the kids. I couldn't figure out what the problem was. As far as I know, none of my sisters ran into this problem. I knew I didn't have a hygiene problem. Getting to the bottom of this wasn't easy. One of the kids told me the problem was, I was Lutheran, and they were Catholics. Why would religion make people dislike each other? I learned why Catholics didn't care for Lutherans, and vice versa. It originated with Martin Luther during the Reformation.

I had a discussion with Mama who had no love for Catholics. I told Mama "I didn't care if I became Catholic, if that's what it takes for them to accept me." I wasn't sure how my suggestion would be received. Mama didn't object. I became a Catholic, and an altar boy to boot. I am not quite sure how I worked myself into that position. *Herr Expositus* "priest" encouraged me to give it a try.

I had to memorize lots of Latin, and that was tough. Thank God, I made the grade. I had to memorize a set of tablets in Latin which I had to recite at each mass. Over time, it became easy.

I can't remember much of it except, *feli de spiriti sankti* "the Father, the Son and the Holy Ghost". For each service, I was paid a quarter; I was rich! When I volunteered to ring the big church bell at six in the morning I received another quarter.

My sister and I were horsing around at home, which wasn't unusual, when we heard a knock on the door. Who could it be? Helga thought I was playing games when she yelled, "Okay you idiot, come on in," at which time the priest stepped in. Mama and Papa couldn't help but laugh which turned into a smirk when the priest came into the room. Helga apologized for the informal greeting and the priest forgave her. It was his second time to visit us. He conveyed to Mama and Papa I did a great job being an altar boy. What a surprise that was!

"I am going to kill you both, and if I don't, God will."

I got up no later than five in the morning to get to church on time. At home, there was no hot water in the morning, or any other time. It certainly woke me up when I splashed my face with ice cold water. To dry off was another issue. The wash cloth was frozen stiff from the night before. I grabbed me a piece of bread from the cupboard, dunked it in the malt coffee which I brewed earlier, and off to church I went. Had I not showed up to perform my altar boy duties, there would have been other boys who would have loved my job.

It was a must to have quality shoes to walk to church and school, especially in the winter. My old shoes were getting too small, and my toes were frostbitten. In the evening, I loved sitting by our little stove to warm my feet. It felt so good to warm up after a cold day out in the snow. After a couple of hours at the hot stove, my frostbitten toes had recovered and turned into a nice pink color.

It was surprising how much heat the little stove produced, more than enough to heat our apartment. The place was cozy despite the cold and snowy conditions outside. One Christmas, my parents bought me a pair of ski boots; it was the best present ever.

After skiing all day, the new boots got wet, and that in itself was not unusual. Instead of drying them the traditional way, I had the great idea of placing the boots inside the warm oven. In the morning, I would have had nice warm boots. Mama lit the stove in the morning to heat up the room without knowing that my boots were inside the stove. The boots were history. It was pitiful to see the new boots burn into a black, crisp ball of leather.

I couldn't ski for quite a while, and was on the lookout for another pair. I lucked out. One of my friends gave me his when he outgrew them. In my days, shoes and other clothing articles were never thrown away. The clothes were mended; the shoes or boots were taken to the shoe shop to get them fixed. Nothing was ever wasted.

To keep warm, we burned coal most of the time, but it was much more expensive than peat moss. If one wanted a hot fire, peat moss was the ticket. "Torf" is harvested in the marsh where they cut it in oven-size pieces during summer, and dry it.

During the winter, Bavaria was very cold, and in the morning, I found the inner walls of our home covered to an eighth of an inch in ice. We slept in featherbeds which kept us unbelievably warm. There was a coat of ice on the pillow next to my mouth. My warm breath turned into ice.

The featherbed gave me a sense of security, nothing could have harmed me. To add to my comfort and security, I took one of my cats and laid it around my neck. What a difference it made. I didn't need an electric blanket. The cats kept me nice and warm with their soft fur rubbing against my face.

At Christmas, we had plenty of spiked eggnog around, and I loved it. It was smooth, and warmed up my inners. The cats loved the eggnog as well.

It amused us, watching the cats stumble all over themselves, and falling down the stairs after they had their share. They looked like a bunch of drunken sailors on a night out. With the consumption of the eggnog, along with the cats, we were also getting a bit tipsy.

One Christmas after the conclusion of the Christmas Mass which ended at midnight, Mama allowed me to stay up until two in the morning. Christmas Eve was different. I normally had to be in bed by eight in the evening.

After Mass, I walked across the white frozen meadows; each step produced an unforgettable crunch when my feet sank through the frozen blanket of snow. I thought I was dreaming when I heard glorious Christmas music coming from the high church tower, it sounded angelic. Did I just ascend to heaven?

At first, I wasn't quite sure where the music came from. The sound seemed to originate just a stone's throw away. The cold air carried the music across the land. It was a special gift from above. I later learned that the trumpet players climbed into the church tower and played old Bavarian Christmas songs. It transformed the cold air into a glorious Christmas present.

We didn't go to church to get warm, on the contrary, our church was ice cold inside, and it penetrated clear to my bones. It was as cold as a meat locker. After sitting on the bench for a while, I became stiff and had a hard time getting up performing my duties as an altar boy. The Dorfen and Lorenzenberg churches were built around 1200 AD with walls four feet thick and kept the church cool clear into summer. The reason for the thick walls was, the churches served as a safe haven during political and religious persecution.

The doors were heavy, with strong iron locks, and the keys weighed almost a pound each. I attended church of my own accord. Mama and Papa never made me go to church. There were times when I questioned my sanity. Why did I get up early in the morning to sit in an ice cold church? I could have stayed home in a warm bed and been comfortable. I was drawn to church, and wouldn't have missed it for anything.

At six o'clock each morning, I rang the giant bell. When I pulled the rope, it lifted me clear to the ceiling. Each time the bell swung from one side to the other, it lifted me higher and higher. We had three bells in the tower, and when they rang in unison it was a marvelous symphony heard far and wide.

In the winter, the walls were covered up to a quarter of an inch on the inside of the church. My breath produced what looked like smoke coming out of my mouth. It took months for the walls to unthaw. On the other hand, in the hot summer months, there was nothing better than to be in church to cool off, and by the time winter came, the walls froze again.

One summer, the town replaced the high wall surrounding the cemetery, right off the main thoroughfare of town. While they were in the middle of the project, the badly deteriorated coffins were visible from the street. That was one morbid sight, but how else could they have done the work? I remember seeing skulls, and other bones sticking out of the dirt that caused the people to cringe as they walked by the cemetery.

The priest asked me to move some of the bones to a spot in the back of the church to give the skeletons a special place of rest. It was an awful job piling bone after bone on the mound which by now was a foot high. To finish the project, I placed a couple of skulls on top. No one knew whose remains they were. I treated the remains with respect and reverence.

Working with the priest, I made sure the chores I was responsible for, were done properly, although, at times, trouble followed me. Our priest understood that boys are prone to pull a few pranks now and then, and most of the time he didn't share our sense of humor. I worked with Manfred, another altar boy who lived in the next town. He was the son of a well-to-do farmer. He came up with an idea I would have never thought of.

Why not drink the wine the priest uses for communion? We gave it a try, and it was putrid! We made sure the priest had enough wine in the cup for the communion. How people drank the stuff, even for communion is beyond me.

One particular morning as we were getting ready for the service, we gave it another shot, hoping it would be better this time around, but it tasted as bad as before. We forced the wine down, just to see what would happen. Before we could say schnapps, the service was over. It sped up the mass considerably. I couldn't remember anything of what happened. Surprisingly, our priest didn't say anything after the service. He figured boys will be boys. To kill the taste and the breath of wine, we ate communion wafers. They were delicious!

During mass, we faced each other, Manfred on one side, and I on the other. That was a big mistake. We giggled and couldn't turn it off, the harder we tried to stop, the worse it got. Some people in the congregation smirked a little, but as a whole, it was clear, they weren't amused. After the service, we received a reprimand from our priest. After all, we were happy kids, and happy kids giggle. But in church? My sisters told me people came to church services just to watch me. I can imagine how my priest felt; never knowing what I had up my sleeves. With God's help, we both survived.

Our priest "Expositus" Huber never caught us helping ourselves to wine. We were good at concealing our drinking. One day, we slipped up, and poured water into the priest's cup instead of wine. During communion, we saw the priest clearly irritated when he took the first sip. We both got a look from the priest as if to say, "I am going to kill you both, and if I don't, God will."

I enjoyed holy processions. Our congregation visited neighboring towns where our priest conducted mass. We visited the most beautiful churches. The architecture was out of this world. Most were of baroque or rococo style, and I wished we could have stayed longer to appreciate these architectural marvels. It placed me into the mood to worship, and to top it off, the organ filled the entire church with angelic music. These churches were called *Wohlfartskirchen*. People traveled from far and wide to receive healing.

Being an altar boy had its privileges. During procession, walking with the priest and carrying the holy sensor. On a cool morning, it was delightful to feel the hot coals close to my body. I never associated these things as having anything to do with worship. The Catholic Church dates back centuries and there must be a reason for these rituals. There were times we covered a full ten kilometers to the next town. The walk took all morning, and we generally arrived around noon for service. After worship, we walked home.

There were no cars to give us a ride home. Along the way we enjoyed discovering things to explore. Our priest gave us boys a little money to buy lunch after the long walk. In those days, we ordered a bottle of beer with our meal, and nobody thought anything of it. After one of these processions, my friend Ernst and I crisscrossed through the green fields when we came upon a little creek. To our surprise, it was bristling with trout.

Ernst taught me a technique of how to catch trout, and it worked like a charm. I reached under the bank of the creek where the trout were hiding, and once I discovered one, I gently stroked it by the gills. They enjoyed getting tickled. All I had to do was grab it by the gills, and lift it out of the water. Oh, were they slippery! It was quite a struggle to keep the fish from jumping out of my hands. After admiring the beauty of these fish, we threw them back into the creek, and allowed the fish to live another day. What we didn't know was that this activity was illegal. We had no intention of breaking the law.

While Ernst and I were busy catching fish, and relishing the adventure, we paid no attention to our surroundings. I had just caught a good size trout, and was in the process of showing it to Ernst when an officer approached. I quickly threw the trout back into the water, but it was too late, the officer caught us red-handed.

We were so afraid the officer would arrest both of us, and throw us in jail. I was squirming, and wished I could disappear. He asked us where we lived, and with trembling voices we gave him our correct home address. He told us not to ever try this again. He didn't have to worry about that. In a matter of a week, our parents were notified. They had to pay a fine. I was grounded for some time, and the few privileges I had, were taken away.

I couldn't go out to play with my friends like I normally did, and Mama enlisted me to do housework. Had I been quick, I could have given the officer a fictitious address, but that would have been wrong. Two wrongs don't make a right.

When I told my friends how we caught fish, they didn't believe it. We also caught crawdads and they were a challenge. I had to be careful not to get pinched. I took a wooden stick, held the stick against their claw, and it didn't take long, they grabbed onto the branch and I lifted them out of the creek.

One evening, Mama locked me out of the house for the night. I had no idea what wrong deed I had committed. . Where was I going to sleep? I could have slept on the banks of the river, but it would have been way too cold. The next best thing was to sleep with the rabbits. They had a large cage, big enough for the rabbits and me. I gathered straw, which became my pillow, and slept the whole night through. When I woke up, a few rabbits curled up next to me and gave me extra warmth. Their fur was so soft and I liked lying next to them. It was better than what I had in the house.

After I left the rabbits, I snuck back into the house, careful not to disturb Mama who was still asleep. Later that day, she asked me where I slept during the night, and I told her I slept out in the cold under a big tree. I was looking for sympathy, but I didn't get it. Our discussion was over and I dropped the subject. She was one tough lady, nothing got her unraveled.

One night, we heard a commotion. The chicken in the barn were making all kinds of racket. Our landlord Marie took a broom and proceeded to the chicken coop. She discovered that a weasel had entered the coop and was about to take a chicken for dinner. That wasn't going to happen without a fight. She was going to attack the weasel with the broom, but the animal was much too fast.

She took a chance when she cornered a weasel. It defended itself displaying its razor sharp teeth. This time, it ended well, and everybody was safe, but one chicken lost its life. But not all was lost, as the chicken ended up in the pot for dinner. I was sure this was not going to be the last time the weasel would try its luck.

In the winter, the fur of the weasel changed from brown to pure white, a perfect camouflage. I watched them play in the snow. They were chasing each other, and would quickly disappear into their den, and then reappear just as fast. The weasels had to share the field with moles which provided a ready meal for these animals. Their slender bodies and agility allowed them to hunt in burrows which consisted of small mammals as well as chicken. The moles were one big problem, relatives of the gopher. They produced mounds after mounds of dirt across the field. That made mowing difficult. The farmers still mowed by hand with their scythe, and it was almost impossible to get around the dirt mounds.

When I was thirteen years old, I was looking for part time work and perhaps find a job that I would like. I was hired by the carpenter across from our school to help him clean up the shop on weekends, and do other small jobs.

I enjoyed the work, and marveled at all the neat things they were building. The carpenters were making tables, chairs, and entire kitchens. It was like magic how they were able to make these pieces of furniture. I got very little pay, if any at all, but they fed me lunch.

The shop was equipped with all types of electric saws. There were few safety features installed, and I didn't receive any training to speak of. I could very easily have hurt myself, but thank God I didn't. At the end of the day, my job was to clean up the dusty shop. It caused me to sneeze like crazy. After working there a few weeks, I changed my mind about becoming a carpenter. The sawdust didn't taste good.

When I wasn't with Michael, I spent time with Ernst who lived in the next town over. We shared altar duties in the town of Dorfen. Manfred the other altar boy and I performed our duties in the Lorenzenberg church. Herr Wanger adopted Ernst after the war. Our favorite place to play was in the barn with all kinds of neat equipment, like tractors and other farm implements. That was dangerous.

Ernst and I were playing on top of one of the haystacks when I decided to crawl down. There was a hay wagon parked next to the hayloft I failed to recognize. I didn't see the separation between the two, and I fell to the concrete floor below. The fall must have been ten feet or more. It was incredible that I landed on my feet. I knew God was watching over me that day. Herr Wanger heard when I fell to the floor and he came running, afraid I was hurt. When I saw him run towards me, I quickly ran out of the barn door, too embarrassed to face him. He couldn't believe that I walked away from the incident that could have severely injured, or even killed me.

As an altar boy, I was involved in weddings and funerals. A wedding was a grand occasion, and to see the bride and groom with a big smile was wonderful, ready to begin their life together. The groom had good reason to smile. He was elated to have found his wife, hidden from him for days. It is the custom in Bavaria to kidnap the bride and hide her until the groom finds her which sometimes took a day or two. After the ceremony, there was plenty to eat and drink. Most everybody from town came, invited or not. It didn't make any difference. The whole village wished the couple a happy and prosperous life together.

I loved weddings for another reason: I received two Marks for my service, and that was serious money.

My first funeral was a somber experience. First, there was a procession, winding through the narrow town streets at a very slow pace. The coffin was placed on a cart and pulled by a couple of Belgian horses. Musicians in Bavarian funeral clothing followed the coffin playing slow, morbid funeral songs.

When somebody passed away, a high-pitched bell from the church tower was rung, it was known as the death bell, announcing that somebody had passed away. It was a certainty I would be called to participate in the funeral service. I hoped it wasn't anybody I knew.

Seeing a dead person brought back memories of when I viewed a couple of close friends in the mortuary. It gave me chills. I had a difficult time when the coffin was lowered into the ground. Most caskets were simple pine boxes, nothing fancy. Family and friends bid their loved ones a last farewell. The priest read: "We came from dust and to dust we return." At that moment, dirt was tossed on the coffin, producing a hollow, eerie sound, which reverberated throughout the otherwise quiet cemetery.

Someone sang a favorite song of the deceased, with the musicians playing music, befitting the occasion. All I could hear was crying, and women wiping their tears. Other than being a somber occasion, there was a plus side to it all. Funerals were lucrative. I received two Marks for my altar boy services. After the internment, I was invited to partake in a marvelous feast which lasted well into the afternoon.

Families took time to visit, and people got reacquainted with those who they hadn't seen for a long time. It is much like in the United States with one exception. People consumed beer, the national drink in Bavaria. It was served until every guest had their fill. My teacher also played the old organ in church and was fond of beer. He had a beer or two, or three, and became visibly drunk, which meant no school for us in the afternoon and no playing the organ. We encouraged our teacher to drink. That way, we didn't have to go back to class.

We had special events in town, and one of them took place in the fall at a local farmhouse. The farmer constructed a rather large swing, unlike any other. The name of the swing was *Kirterhutschen* "chain swing". It was the biggest event in town for the children, and the kids were itching to give it a ride. It consisted of a long, slick wooden board. Two large chains were fastened to the girders of the barn, and the chains were then attached to each end of the wooden board. The boards were approximately ten feet in length, and approximately one foot in width. The surface was shiny, and very slick, which caused the riders to slide back and forth.

Two sturdy youngsters stood at the end, thrusting their bodies into the board. They were holding on to the chains with all their might. If for one reason or other, they had lost their grip, they would have fallen to the concrete floor below.

Once the board reached its full momentum, the swing almost touched the high girders of the barn, and in turn caused the kids to slide back and forth, making the kids hold onto each other for dear life.

The screaming kids were heard for kilometers around. On occasions, a child did fall off and was injured. I was one of those kids. I hit my head on the ground causing it to bleed profusely. The farmer came out, wiped off the blood, and I went back to having fun. Nobody called for the paramedics, and in minutes, it was forgotten. My sisters always made fun of me saying, I hit my head one too many times.

On a particular afternoon, I visited Michael. We were up to no good as we visited the local grocer and bought a bottle of wine. When I was a child, anybody could buy spirits, and they didn't care what you did with it.

On the way home, we sat down by a shady tree, which by the way is still standing. We finished off the entire bottle. We became sick as a dog, and threw up. From that point on, we had no desire to ever drink the nasty stuff again. It wasn't much better than the wine at church. Our parents never knew what we had done, and we weren't about to tell them.

One day, Walter, who lived next door, invited me to ride with him on our bicycles to buy rabbits. Before we took off, I checked with Mama who allowed me to go with him. We rode to the next town about ten kilometers away. What could possibly go wrong with buying cute little, furry rabbits?

The ride took us only thirty minutes. We stopped at a Gasthaus, got off our bikes and walked through the main entrance. Apparently they knew Walter was coming and had lunch ready for us with a bottle of dark beer. I had no problem downing one bottle when Walter ordered another. It tasted good, and I enjoyed being out of town where nobody was watching me.

After the first bottle I felt great, and by the time I finished the second, I became violently ill, and threw up. I was embarrassed. The waitress ended up cleaning up the mess I made. After this unfortunate event, I had no problem riding my bike home. I had sobered up and Mama and Papa never knew I had been drunk.

Sadly, the summer bid us goodbye and I had to think about going to school. Mama made sure I had clean clothes and good shoes for the long walk to school. School in Lorenzenberg had its pluses and minuses, similar to Staudach. I liked my teacher, Herrmann Schmidt, who was strict like all the other German teachers.

At times, he allowed us to have a little fun. Our school was a small country school, with a total of thirty-five kids. The building had two rooms, with four grades in each room, and that made it difficult for the teacher. As I mentioned previously, my sister Helga was in the same room as I was, and she was a pain. Helga sat in the back of the room, and I sat in the front, that way our teacher could keep his eye on me. One day, without warning, my sister rushed to the front of the class and proceeded to slap me in the face in front of my teacher and the kids. I didn't have any idea what caused the sudden outburst of anger. What disturbed me was the teacher thanked my sister for the deed. I was embarrassed, and under my breath, I swore I'd be getting even with her sooner or later.

I hadn't learned my lesson as yet when it came to completing my homework. My teacher wasn't amused at my excuses when I didn't do my homework. It was one of the times when I didn't turn in my homework when Herr Schmidt lost it. He backhanded me so hard that it caused me to bounce off the blackboard with a bloody lip. That was the second time I experienced that kind of brutality.

25

ESCAPE FROM SIBERIA

Whenever the opportunity presented itself, our teacher talked about WWII. It meant there wouldn't be anymore school work the rest of the day. The following is the story of his war experience when taken prisoner by the Russians.

Herrmann Schmidt was imprisoned by the Russians from 1942 until 1947.

He spoke fluent Russian after years in captivity, which came in handy when having to speak to his captors. He was drafted by Hitler in 1941, and forced to the front lines at the border of Prussia. His assignment was to stop the Red Army at all costs. His job was to hunt down Russian tanks, a *Panzerjäger,* and immobilize them firing the *Panzerfaust* "antitank weapon".

He relayed to us: once close to the tank, it was easy to put the monster out of commission. The big challenge was to get near it without getting shot or run over. Once within close proximity, the main gun couldn't shoot at a sharp angle, and all he had to do was to aim the weapon towards its belly and fire.

The German army marched through Mother Russia with impunity. The tanks, heavy duty army trucks and the *Luftwaffe* decimated the land.

Herrmann and fellow soldiers were walking beside their tanks for cover, always ready to take cover should the enemy unleash their Stalinorgel, "anti-tank weapon".

The Germans were deep inside the Soviet Union. It was remarkable how little resistance they encountered. They carried their army food rations around their waist along with a knife, a luger pistol, grenades, rifle and the Panzerfaust, "anti-tank weapon". They slept whenever they could, sometimes only minutes at a time when they were woken by artillery shells from one of the T34 Russian tanks or howitzers.

The Germans relied on their half-track supply trucks which carried most of the food and other supplies. Beer was always available, however it wasn't cool in the summer heat and Herrmann hated the warm brew. In the winter, it was a solid chunk of ice, provided it survived all the action.

Herrmann Schmidt was captured not far from Stalingrad and transported to a prisoner of war camp in Siberia in the dead of winter in 1941. After a grueling trip on an open truck where temperatures sank far below zero, he arrived at the camp. The journey lasted two weeks, and for food, the prisoners had to settle for thin soup laced with scraps of meat.

They slept on the truck most of time. Now and then, they were forced to get off the truck and sleep on the frozen ground which was even worse. The cold penetrated his clothes and before long, the whole body became stiff. The convoy of trucks with German prisoners stretched for miles. If a prisoner entertained the idea trying to escape, The Red Army had no problem shooting him. By the time they arrived at their destination, the soldiers were sick due to the lack of food and the arctic cold. The camp was surrounded with tall barbed wire, and no barracks to house the prisoners? There were none. All there was were snow covered field cods out in the open.

They weren't fed, and there were no doctors to treat the injured. The nights were bitter cold. The German prisoners tried to sleep, but were afraid, fearing they would never wake up. Many of them didn't survive the bitter cold nights. The fellow prisoners who survived wanted to give the dead a decent burial, but due to the frozen ground, they carried their comrades to the edge of the camp and stuck their stiff bodies upright in the deep snow.

It was an eerie feeling to see the dead soldiers standing at attention all around the compound. They presented no threat to the Russians. They were left there, until the spring, when the ground softened.

Only by a miracle did Herrmann survive three weeks. A Russian officer told Herrmann they were taking him to a carpenter shop, making furniture. He was transported to a different compound. A hard two day's drive by truck which took him from Kamenskoje to Magadan.

He became knowledgeable in making furniture when he was a young boy, and that may have saved his life.

He worked at the factory every day from early morning until late in the evening with little food and no way of gaining freedom. This went on for five years and he figured this was the end of the road for him. He'd never get out of there alive. He was among hundreds of German prisoners who accepted their fate.

Herrmann became acquainted with his guards on a personal basis. They trusted him and gave him more freedom than some of the other prisoners. One night, however, the opportunity presented itself to escape his captors. While everybody was asleep, he noticed a window within easy reach. He quietly slipped into his lined prisoner uniform he wore when working outside of the compound. It was a bitter cold night when he worked his way through the unlocked opening and down the twelve foot wall. He used his bed sheets for a rope, which almost reached to the bottom. To get to the ground, he had to jump two to three feet.

He felt bad leaving his countrymen behind, but the chances of survival was better to be alone. There was no time to waste as he approached a ten foot tall barbed wire fence surrounding the compound. The fence presented a challenge, and he wasn't sure if he was up to climbing the barbed wired fence. His body was weakened by the lack of food but he reached the point of no return. Panic mode set in when he started to make his way to the top. With adrenalin flowing, he reached the barbed wire on top of the fence. It was indeed a formidable obstacle to overcome.

He had to act quickly. He took off his heavy jacket to avoid cutting himself to shreds. The arctic air penetrated his body. He began to shiver, his teeth raddled. With a great deal of effort he climbed down by placing his shoes in each of the openings of the wire one at a time and made it to the bottom.

As he reached the ground, he was exhausted. Unable to go any farther due to cramps in his legs, he rested a few minutes to catch his breath. He was certain; The Russians noticed the open window and the empty bed.

They were looking for him alright. They lit up the night with powerful searchlights. He crouched down in order not to be spotted by the powerful lights. While searching for a place to hide, he found a grove of trees where he hid for the time being. Approximately one hundred feet from where he was, he noticed a building which might offer a refuge.

With the full moon lighting the landscape he was easy to spot. He had to get rid of his prison issued garb if his escape was going to succeed.

He only had a hunting knife he hid while at the camp. Making his way to the building, he crawled most of the way on his stomach to conceal himself. The snow on the ground was powder like and it saved him from getting saturated with moisture, but the bitter Siberian cold surged through his body.

His hands were frozen stiff which made it difficult bending his fingers. He was paralyzed. It was difficult just getting up from the ground. He had reached the perimeter of the building, when he noticed a Russian guard making his rounds. He found a side door which was partially open and slid inside. When he moved, pain shot through his body like a lightning rod.

Herrmann found a couple of tractors and other heavy equipment inside the building. It was a maintenance shop, and fortunately, he noticed an industrial type natural gas heater. He managed to turn it on, and hoping the guard wouldn't hear the commotion. The heater emitted a dull humming sound and with the door closed, the guard would have had a hard time picking up the sound. It produced precious heat, and in a few minutes his hands came back to life. Within minutes, his body slowly recovered.

Maintaining his stealth mode was critical, it was imperative not to make any sounds that could be picked up by the guard. He picked himself up, and checked the location of the Russian. He was still by the corner of the building smoking a cigarette. Herrmann strategized how best to sneak up to the security guard without being detected. He had the advantage of being in the shade of the building created by the moonlight.

He had to be out of the area before daylight, and by now it was five in the morning. To bring his escape to fruition he inched his way out of the door, carefully stepping into the deep snow without making a sound.

Lucky for him, it was fine powder which absorbed the noise coming from his army boots. He managed to conceal his approach by staying in the shadows and downwind as he came ever so close to the guard. The element of surprise was in his favor, and he was confident of his mission to succeed. The guard had a rifle draped over his shoulder. If Herrmann made a mistake, the end result would be a quick death. On the other hand, if he succeeded, it would mean he could live another day.

He quietly moved forward, one step at a time. He crept towards the Russian, his knees almost touching the ground, hoping the guard wouldn't detect his presence. Now was not the time to cough or sneeze and if he did, that would be his last sneeze. He crouched cautiously behind the guard, and it was now, or never, to make his move. Ten feet from the guard, he still had the benefit of the shade produced by the overhang of the roof. With the stealth of a leopard, he jumped the Russian from behind, and drove his hunting knife deep into the man's back. The Russian was fatally wounded.

The white snow turned blood red. Herr Schmidt quickly stripped him of his uniform, and pulled him under a dense pine tree that hid his body from view, but one thing he couldn't erase was the blood stained snow. He urinated, which caused some of the snow to melt, causing the blood to soak into the soil. He quickly made his way back inside the warm building to change his clothes. The uniform was a perfect fit.

After getting dressed, he burned the prisoner issued clothing, leaving no trace behind. With the powerful rifle and the Russian uniform, nobody would recognize him as a German prisoner of war. So far, so good, but time was his biggest enemy. He had to move from the location fast.

To travel to his home in Germany he has to navigate a distance of some 4585 miles, or 7379 kilometers. The big problem was to get enough food, and wheels to cover the distance. He eliminated a few Russian soldiers along the way when he commandeered a truck or two. Whenever possible, he rode a train pretending to be a Russian soldier on his way to the war zone.

His trip took almost a year before he was close to the German border. He traveled nights whenever possible to avoid traffic. Out in the country, there were tractors by the farms waiting for the spring planting. Other than that, it was quiet as he crisscrossed the Russian steppes. He entertained the idea of taking one of the tractors, but they were too slow and noisy.

He had no idea the war had ended on May 8th of 1945. He thought he heard heavy artillery fire in the distance; perhaps what he heard were Russian soldiers on patrol. If that wasn't bad enough, the deep snow presented his biggest challenge other than running into more Russians. He became trapped in the deep snow and being alone, it was a big problem. To escape from the snow drift, he placed wooden branches under the rear wheels of the truck, stepped on the accelerator and was able to free himself.

At one point during his trek, he became very sick. He had difficulty breathing and even coughed up blood. It was fortunate for him he found a place under the big trees which provided cover during the cold nights. He felt he may not survive, and prepared himself mentally for his last breath. He hadn't eaten now for over a week and grew weaker by the minute.

In the early evening hours, he noticed a deer nearby. It was God sent, so he reached for his gun. He gathered all his strength to pick up the rifle to fire and he scored a direct hit, the deer collapsed. This gave him renewed strength, knowing the deer would provide precious food. He made his way toward the animal and dragged it over to his hideout. He had a few dry matches and plenty of wood on the ground to build a hot fire.

His body was still weak, but the coughing had stopped by now, and his lungs didn't burn anymore. He cut up the meat, and prepared to lay it on top of the fire when he noticed a pair of glowing eyes at about a hundred feet away. There was no doubt in his mind that a wolf had got a whiff of the deer.

The carnivore remained at the spot for around thirty minutes when another wolf appeared. He knew he was in trouble as the masters of the wild watched his every move. They were preparing to join him for dinner. Just in case, he kept his gun at the ready. Fortunately, the powdery snow kept the weapon dry. He didn't want to shoot the animals - they were just as hungry as he was.

The wolves were getting too close! With caution, he reached for his gun and shot into the cold, arctic air. The pair ran across the white forest meadow and disappeared into the dark, green, undergrowth.

The bright moon transformed the landscape into a winter wonderland. It was beautiful observing everything around him. He heard owls screeching from nearby trees and an occasional wolf in the distance. He didn't let down his guard however, and kept the powder dry. The aroma of the meat was killing him and he couldn't wait to cut off a piece of the deer carcass. When he finally did, it tasted delicious and melted in his mouth.

After he had his fill, he attempted to relax and get some sleep. It didn't take long before he drifted off, but kept waking up during the night, hoping he wouldn't be surprised by more visitors. The cold air licked his face, but the fire kept the rest of his body warm. Before long, the bright morning sun woke him and he was lucky to have survived the night. The meal strengthened his body enough to make his way out of his hide-out where he had been holed up for over a week.

There were times he felt like giving up. But not now when he finally reached the Czech border after a very long trip through the cold, dark, Russian wilderness. As he approached the border, the guards waved him through when they saw his Russian uniform and military truck he had commandeered earlier, and within a hundred feet of the border, he gunned the truck and plowed through the brick fence at a great speed, punching his way to freedom. At the same time, he heard bullets bouncing off the cab of the truck. Shards of glass sliced through the still morning dawn resembling daggers. It was a miracle he wasn't injured or killed. Bullets were lodged in the back window; fortunately they didn't penetrate the glass.

We didn't want him to quit. There had to be more. We were fascinated and wanted for him to keep going. It was like a dream, but we had to face reality and read our assignment.

26

GREET THEE GOD

Each week, we had one hour of religious study. Being an altar boy was to my advantage. It was custom to greet the priest, *gelobt sei Jesus Christus* "honor be to Jesus Christ." When I met other people, I greeted them saying, *grüss Dich Gott, and "Greet thee God."* When saying goodbye, one said, *behüht Dich Gott* "God protect you," and it is still the custom today. It was a wonderful way to greet each other.

One morning, I met up with the priest on the way to school. He looked at me and asked me if everything was okay, and I answered, "I had no breakfast or lunch, and I am hungry." He invited me to his residence, and fed me a bowl of soup with a slice of bread. What a wonderful gift. I never forgot his act of kindness.

I had difficulties in math and I was distraught. The priest told me, God didn't care what kind of grade I got, as long as I did my best. He told me, God loved me. I felt exonerated. The heavy load was lifted from my shoulders. He made my day.

On Easter, prior to planting their crops, the farmers formed a parade down Main Street. They cleaned and polished their tractors, dressed the horses, and showed off their shiny farm implements. If the tractors needed painting, they gave it a quality paint job. The green and red tractors looked like new with their black tires glistening in the morning sun. The farmers showed off their farm equipment pulled by huge Belgian draft-horses. It was obvious who had the best looking team of horses.

Bells attached to the collars of the horses, emitted marvelous sounds resonating though the old cobble stone streets. Each horse was uniquely dressed with gorgeous collars interwoven with colorful flowers. The whole purpose, other than showing off their best tractors and equipment was to receive a blessing from the priest, and to petition God for a successful growing season.

Before I became a Catholic, I was Lutheran, like my parents and their parents before them. It was standard for the school to offer religious studies. Catholicism was the only religion taught in Bavaria. If one was Lutheran, you had to find a pastor, and in Bavaria, that was a challenge. We didn't have a Lutheran Pastor within a hundred kilometers. The school located a nun who was to teach me about the Bible. She rode her bike in good or bad weather to instruct me. She was amazing. Children can be cruel, and I was no exception. I couldn't care less if she showed up or not.

The lady, God bless her, went out of her way just for me and rode her bike ten kilometers one way, just to see me. One day, she arrived to see if I had done my homework which I had failed to do. She became very upset over my uncaring attitude. She got up, threw the Bible at me and abruptly left the school. I never saw her again. I felt bad, and later in life I prayed that God would forgive me.

During Sunday Church Service, I performed my duties as I always had. This time, I was in charge of the sensor, which was full of hot coals. I swung the device with much enthusiasm, but aimed it a little too high. I was shocked when the hot glowing charcoal fell out of the sensor and on the rug. It left a couple of black spots in the ancient red rug.

The fire department wasn't called. We were well prepared for these sorts of things. I got a bucket of water and the fire was extinguished. Perhaps I should have picked a career as a fireman. What amazed me was, the priest didn't reprimand me and life went on.

At one of the Christmas Eve Services, I was performing my altar boy function when the priest requested I bring him the wafers for the communion. With wafers in hand, I cut the corner too sharp around the altar and ran into the Christmas tree, almost knocking it over. Lucky for me, just a few bulbs fell off the tree. I was embarrassed and afraid to show my face. The congregation found it amusing and clapped when they discovered all ended well without anybody hurt and the Christmas tree still standing.

In May the same year, my teacher chose me to be one of the performers in a play at the local Gasthaus. We had a few rehearsals, and sometime in early May, we were to perform. My part in the play was building a wooden box, or perhaps a bird house. I discovered the whole town came to see the play. The place was packed. I was nervous and wished I could have escaped out the back door, but that wouldn't have been proper, and with much angst, I waited for the performance to begin.

I had sweaty palms, my heart was racing. The town's people enjoyed seeing the kids on stage perform and gave us generous applause. While the play was in full swing, the beer was flowing freely, and that was my salvation. The audience didn't notice any errors, and to my delight, the play came off without a hitch. One big disappointment, my parents nor my sisters were attending the event.

On a particular Sunday afternoon I accompanied *Herrn Expositus* "the priest" to a neighboring town. He had a small motor scooter, just big enough for both of us. After we got back in the late afternoon, I told Mama three of us were riding on the scooter at which point she asked, "How could the three of you fit on that little motor scooter?" My answer, "There was the priest, myself and the Holy Ghost."

With sorrow, I heard later that my beloved priest, committed suicide. He fell in love with a woman, and that is a no, no in the Catholic Church. He felt he betrayed the congregation. What a loss. He left this earth so early in life. He had so many great qualities and made everybody feel special.

Our neighbor, Marie, lived in a small wooden house nestled in a grove of oak trees. She owned four or five goats. They bucked, and ran over us as we played. The animals amused us. It was as though the goats were part of us and to our delight they were always ready for a skirmish.

It was hilarious to see the goats being milked. While she milked the goats, they tried to buck her and were less than cooperative. But that didn't deter Marie. She talked to her goats like she would to her grandkids and had her bucket full of milk in no time.

At one point, Marie talked me into tasting the milk; it tasted weird, just goatee. I enjoyed playing with the animals, but left the milk for others to enjoy, but left the milk for others to enjoy.

Cleanliness was not her forte, unlike most Germans. Never judge a book by its cover, and that was the case with her. She loved to visit, and we talked for hours upon hours. She smoked all day, and knew it wasn't good for her health, but she kept on smoking.

She always had her grandkids around; one was Vera, the other Renate, we called her Bubba, they were fun. We tried our high jump, long jump, and mimicked the goats. The goats had no problem jumping four feet high, standing still. I was never good at jumping and left that one to the goats. There wasn't anybody who could beat them.

One of her sons was Walter, quite a character. He loved his beer. When he was drunk, most people avoided him with good reason. He became angry and started a fight without much provocation, other than that he had a heart of gold. He was known to have beaten up a few guys in his day. He was strong and nobody dared to confront him. He and I got along great. But then I was just a kid.

One day, Walter asked me if I wanted to go on a hike with him in the Alps, and without hesitation, I said I would love to do that. I remember we took a bus ride out of town and into the Alps, only a couple of hours' drive.

We scrambled off the bus and began our ascent. It was so much fun as we climbed up the steep mountain. During our climb, we ran into heavy fog, and it was difficult for us to find our way. It was way too dangerous to keep on climbing, not seeing where we were going. We decided to stay put for the night.

Lucky for us, we found a hay barn and bedded down. As we were about to go to sleep, it thundered, and lightning struck close by. I had never heard thunder like that in my life. I loved it, and for some unknown reason, I wasn't scared. We were awestricken at the performance. It was spectacular to see the lightning, followed by the loudest crackle and boom.

After the storm passed, we fell asleep in the middle of the hay and straw. We gathered hay and placed it under our heads to form a pillow. It was fairly comfortable. In the morning when we got up, we both smelled like a silo. Straw was imbedded in our hair and hay was attached to our pants and shirt. We merely brushed ourselves off, but the aroma of the hay was still with us.

We gathered our strength and climbed the hills looking for berries. We thought it would give us a little strength in order for us to move on. We were pleased to find a patch of wild raspberries. They were so sweet. In the distance we observed a red fox picking berries as well. The fox kept a keen eye on us and was ready to flee should the animal perceive we were a threat.

We hadn't ventured far when we came across an *Alm* "cottage" where we had lunch. Walter paid for everything. He knew I had no money.

We sat down and ordered sausage and sauerkraut, the standard fare. We both had a dark bottle of Auer Bräu beer. It was a marvelous experience to find peace and quiet in an otherwise noisy world.

We stayed one more day and spent the last night in the same barn as the previous night. It was pitch dark, and we didn't have the luxury of the lightning strikes which helped us in the *finsterniss,* the "darkness". The next morning, we climbed down the mountain. Walter asked me if I was hungry. He didn't have to ask, I was always hungry. He knew of a restaurant at the bottom of the mountain where we stopped to have a nice breakfast. Now he was talking my language. Our descent went much quicker. We discovered a trail which led us straight down without having to climb over boulders as we had to do whilst climbing up. We stopped at the *Adler Gasthaus,* settled down, and waited for the waitress to take our order.

In Germany, you'd never find eggs and bacon on the menu. A typical breakfast consisted of hard rolls, slices of cheese, fruit and juice. Coffee was very expensive and we settled on beer instead, but this time we selected Flötzinger Bier. The food gave us strength for our trip home. That was the last time he and I spent time together. Walter moved from home to work in the Ruhr Valley as a coal miner and I found me a job in Rosenheim. It's a much larger town 30 kilometers south.

Before leaving for the U.S., Walter and I made a pact. We agreed that if we should ever have a war again between the U.S. and Germany, we wouldn't fight, but rather have a beer or two to celebrate our life.

Late in the summer was potato harvest time. I was pleased when the farmer I had worked for the previous year, asked me to work for him again. It was hard work, continuously having to bend down, dropping the spuds into the burlap sacks. I must have done a fair job the year before, but working for minimum wages was economical for the farmers. I did this every year and enjoyed seeing familiar faces again, it was special.

At noon, we were invited to a fabulous lunch. The food was out of this world. We were served pork, sauerkraut and *apfel strudel* "apple strudel". Beer was always on the menu which was served at all the Bavarian functions. We got a full hour's break for lunch. To get back to the field, we jumped on the wagon drawn by a couple of tired, old plow horses.

During work, I told the women who gathered around me, all the secrets I swore my sisters I would never tell. The women loved to see me, just to hear what was happening at the Berbers'.

I didn't think it was a secret when I told them, "I wanted my sisters married off so they would leave home." To get rid of them I employed a strategy. I made use of an interesting marketing technique. I told as many people as I could, "I had the most beautiful sisters anybody could find," and that wasn't a lie. I further told them, "They love to cook and keep a tidy house."

Many young men arrived from far and wide to meet my sisters and when my parents were gone, it multiplied. It was obvious, my plan worked. My sisters got married alright, but it took much longer than I had anticipated. Eventually I did get my wish, as one by one they moved away.

In the summer, my sisters and I loved chasing fireflies at dusk. The fireflies came out at dusk, and there were lots of them. We wanted to investigate to see what made them light up. It was strange, once we had them in our hands, the light went out. To me, it was nothing but magic how these creatures had their own headlights. We have an amazing God who created all these creatures for our enjoyment.

I graduated from eighth grade and realized my life was going to change. I didn't know to what extent, but I figured Mama had something planned for me. My parents weren't influential in the community, and that disqualified me to go on to higher learning. Growing up in a small village, I wasn't taught a foreign language or other courses required to go on to high school. We were shortchanged going to school in a small country school.

27

THE APPRENTICE

On a bright sunny morning, Papa suggested that he and I take a train ride to Rosenheim, thirty kilometers south from Lorenzenberg. He didn't have to twist my arm. I liked the town with all the shops and beautiful parks. The River Inn from Innsbruck snaked its way through the middle of town. It was a marvelous attraction.

The ride didn't take long, and within thirty minutes, we had arrived. But this particular trip would be a life changer for me. All along, I pondered in my mind what wonderful things Papa had planned for me.

First we stopped at a *Gasthaus* 'guesthouse' for a little snack and to cool off in the shade on a warm day, sipping a glass of beer. We proceeded to walk down Main Street, looking at the shops and the beautiful displays in the windows. I enjoyed myself, and we bonded. I didn't have the opportunity to be with Papa a lot, so we enjoyed our moments together.

As we continued walking into town on the sidewalk, we came across a bakery, and Papa knew how I loved baked goods, like pretzels and rolls. When we arrived at the main entrance of the store, a sign read: 'Apprentice Wanted, Inquire Within'. Papa didn't waste time and walked into the store ready to buy some treats I thought.

How wrong could I have been? Without consulting with me, he inquired of the owner of the store. I thought why do we have to talk to the owner? All we wanted was to buy some rolls or Danish pastries. The owner, Herr Birnbaum, came at once and Papa introduced himself. He and Papa exchanged niceties about the weather, and where we came from. Herr Birnbaum asked Papa who I was, and I introduced myself to him as Günter. Herr Birnbaum asked Papa if I was his son. Papa answered him and said, "He indeed is my son."

I couldn't believe my ears when Papa told the man he would leave me with him if he could use me as an apprentice. Papa had a marvelous marketing approach when he spoke to Herr Birnbaum, building me up and actually bragging about me.

I thought I would never hear those words coming out of Papa's mouth. It actually made me feel proud. Usually people don't say these things about someone until after they had gone into eternity. I was numb, still in shock and lost for words.

Herr Birnbaum looked me over and said, "You will make a great apprentice and I would love to have you," as he patted me on the shoulder with his big, muscular hand. I thought the slave trade had been abolished by now, but I was wrong. The proprietor of the business told Papa it would be fine to leave me with him - I would be in good hands. How could he be doing this to me, not knowing the man from Adam? Neither one asked me what I thought of the move. Young kids were not allowed voice their opinions.

I was a strong boy weighing in at about 100 pounds and almost fourteen years old.

I had to come to grips, my playing days were over and the reality of life was about to set in. Papa left me at the store, and this man was now my legal guardian, replacing Mama and Papa, so to speak. He had the responsibility to clothe me, feed me, and look after my wellbeing. Papa carried out Mama's wish. He wasn't going to come back with me.

Was this for real? Did I just have a bad dream? I was waiting to wake up from this horrible nightmare, but I never did. I could not believe Papa pulled a stunt like this, and left me high and dry on this beautiful day that had turned it into a 'tragedy' for me. People are not much different than animals, especially birds. At a certain age, the little ones have to learn to fly, and now it was my turn to spread my wings.

The bald eagles will throw their little ones out of the big nest, and the chicks have no alternative but to fly. The father bird will circle under the juvenile, and will catch it in midair if it has difficulty staying aloft. For me, there was no safety net; I had no choice but to fly.

Herr Birnbaum appeared to be nice and introduced me to the help in the store. I liked the girls working there. They were about my age and beautiful. I thought this might work out after all. He showed me where I would sleep the first night, and I was impressed with the accommodations. What a gorgeous bedroom, it even had pictures hung on the wall. The bed had a fancy comforter with the softest pillows.

If that was going to be my bedroom, it would probably work out just fine. I had a sneaky suspicion however; this was just a set up. He knew I probably had never been away from home, and this would make the transition easier. I didn't let it drive me crazy not knowing what lay ahead. I thought I'd just go with the flow. What will be, will be.

Papa just left me with a complete stranger, and I had no idea how things were going to work out for me. I knew one thing for sure. Things were about to change, and that was a certainty, no doubt about it.

Mama always told me, *"Boys need to play."* My playing days had come to a screeching halt. I knew full well, sooner or later all the fun and games would end. She told me, *"You will have a long, hard life ahead,"* and her words came crashing down on me now.

I hardly slept a wink the first night and sobbed like a baby torn from its mother. The morning couldn't come quick enough. I was anxious to find out what my first day would be like. When my boss woke me, he showed me where the bathroom was. I took a shower and brushed my teeth. Never in my life had I taken a shower. That was a new experience, I liked it.

He introduced me to the crew of ten bakers; the shop was huge and noisy with the many sounds of machines. The ovens were humongous; I felt the intense heat coming from the bread just taken out of the oven. It was unbearable standing by the ovens as the heat penetrated my clothes and it felt like I was on fire.

Herr Birnbaum took me to a store to buy me work clothes and toiletry items. The work clothes resembled a white chef's uniform to be worn when visiting customers. A couple of other sets were for working in the shop. Those consisted of a light T- shirt, and grey checkered pants. I was fascinated by all the hustle and bustle in the streets. I saw street cars, other vehicles, and lots of beautiful buildings on both sides of the street. All this was fascinating for a country boy.

The first day was a breeze, but nonetheless, I was leery what the rest of the week would be like. The first night, I slept in his guest room. Later, I was shown where my permanent home was going to be. I had to climb six flights of stairs, which led to a huge hall. All the bakers who lived out of town, and only went home on weekends, stayed there. I had zero privacy!

My bed consisted of a simple cot, with a thin mattress, and that was about all the comfort I would have. There were no nightstands and very little storage room for my personal belongings. This was going to be my home for the next three years until graduating from the apprentice course, on the way to becoming a journeyman baker. I accepted the fact that this was going to be as good as it would get. Miracles do happen. After about a year, I was moved to another building which had better beds and a thicker mattress.

I went to sleep that night without a problem. I was worn out by all the new things I saw. They expected me down at the shop at five o'clock ready to go to work. It was nothing short of a miracle, I woke up before five o'clock.

The foreman showed me around, and all the bakers welcomed me, shook my hand, telling me what my chores would be that morning. I liked the smell of the fresh bread and all the activity around me.

Every baker had his chore to do. One prepared the dough in a huge machine which mixed it into a big ball; another machine cut the ball into smaller, workable pieces for the bakers to make it into a loaf of bread, or any other baked product. Other men were working with other machinery, preparing a variety of baked goods for the store.

A couple of bakers ran the ovens, inserting the loaves, rolls, or pretzels. I walked around to observe all the activities, and how things were conducted. After I had been at the place for a while, I discovered the bakeshop was run with precision, and putting the bread into the oven was a special art. Most of the time, it was the master baker working the ovens.

You had to pull rank before getting that job. We had two master bakers, one was around seventy years old with much experience, and the other was much younger, around twenty-five years old. The younger one was a cool guy named Siegfried, and he was very good at what he did. He helped me, showing me how to make certain types of products, like the pretzels. He took it upon himself to take me under his wing. I learned fast how to make pretzels and all types of rolls. He was a strong amateur boxer, and for that reason, I respected him an awful lot. I had good reason to stay on his good side.

When we spoke, the subject of smoking entered into our conversation. He told me that if he ever caught me smoking, he'd beat the tar out of me, and I knew he wasn't kidding. I subsequently never got hooked on cigars or cigarettes, not that I didn't try.

One night, another apprentice and I had a great idea smoking a cigar while in bed. The only problem was, our boss made a bed check at 10 o'clock sharp each night. Even with his stiff leg, Herr Birnbaum climbed up all six stories to check on us, and we had better be in bed sound asleep.

We observed Herr Birnbaum smoking 'White Owl' cigars, and we figured he would only smoke the best. From all appearances, it appeared he enjoyed them. We went to a cigar store near the bakery and told the lady at the counter our boss sent us to pick up a couple of cigars.

She knew our boss, and believed us, or maybe she didn't, the latter was probably the case. The total cost of two cigars was a couple of Marks. We emptied our pockets and came up with the correct change. I don't think we fooled her one bit, and she knew what we were up to. She placed both cigars into a small bag, and with sheepish grins, out of the door we went.

We each had a cigar to enjoy before going to sleep that night. Hopefully, our boss wouldn't catch us. Up the flight of stairs we raced, and couldn't wait to light the brown, leafy sticks. We had our matches ready, and in no time, the cigars were lit. Our experiment began.

All this time, we were afraid Herr Birnbaum might walk in on us. We listened for footsteps we normally heard resonating through the stairwell, but none could be heard that night. We were taking a big chance of getting caught as the smoke filled the room and beyond. I was waiting for a euphoric experience, and anxiously waiting for the tobacco to kick in. We inhaled to achieve maximum pleasure.

We did this a couple of times, thinking the more often we did this, the better the result. It didn't take long. I became sick to my stomach, and threw up most of the night. That took care of our yearning to smoke cigars. They were way overrated.

We flushed the killer sticks down the toilet. For some unexplained reason, that night, Herr Birnbaum never made the trip up to our dorm. We played with fire, but weren't caught.

The next morning, I had a hard time waking up. It was a long day, and I had no appetite. I skipped breakfast. I was sick for sure! That same morning, I was learning to make pretzels; but now, my stomach had already turned into one. I caught myself falling asleep, standing up. One of the bakers woke me up when he threw a ball of dough at me, and that woke me up. Later that morning, I finally started feeling better.

Learning how to make pretzels was actually fun. It was an art to have a perfectly finished product, ready for the oven. It took several tries to get it just right. The bakers kept a sharp eye on me. It was all about production, and they demanded results with perfection.

At times, I helped take the bread out of the hot ovens, lined the loaves up on a long board, and stacked them on a rack. The loaves were very hot and caused my hands to blister.

I had to be fast if I didn't want to have blisters all over my forearms and hands. I couldn't hang onto the hot bread long, and accidentally I dropped some on the hard floor. I was punished for allowing the bread to fall and crack on the tile floor. The punishment consisted of being hit over the head with the *Schüssel,* 'long board' used to remove, or insert the baked goods.

I was working with a master baker Herr Egger, who was one tough cookie, who never cracked a smile, and was all business. I was scared to death of the man and afraid he would let his anger out on me.

At times, my job was to load the furnace with coal. It was a dirty job that turned my white uniform black in a hurry. Breathing all the coal dust couldn't have been healthy. On the other hand, I liked it. There was nobody watching over my shoulder to see if I did the job correctly. As long as I kept the fire burning, everything was okay. Later on, the bakery switched to gas, which gave me a break from the nasty job.

I liked my morning breaks where I had access to the wonderful pastries I had seen on display in the store windows. I was able to eat all I wanted, and that was pure pleasure. The only problem was I had only thirty minutes to enjoy this. Oh, how I wished my stomach had been bigger. At lunch, I got an hour's break when I was treated to the most wonderful meals. We had a full time cook, and she cooked the most *wunderbare Speisen,* 'scrumptious meals'.

It was great to eat the best food in town. At lunchtime, everybody was provided with a bottle of beer to wash down the food. At this time, I couldn't stand the smell of beer from previous times when I drank too much.

It didn't take long for me to gain weight. Before I knew it, my pants were getting a little tight around my waist. I asked my boss for a larger size pants to fit me. He thought that I was a little too skinny anyway, and he didn't object to buying me a couple of pairs of trousers.

When I inquired about my pay however, my boss was reluctant to discuss this with me. I found out I was getting a Mark per week. I worked sixty hours Monday through Sunday. He told me that my pay was non-negotiable since he furnished me with everything I needed. However, I wouldn't have turned him down, had he offered me more money.

It wasn't a lot of money, but he fed me, clothed me, and took care of my needs. He gave me room and board, and all in all, I didn't complain, and if I had, nobody would have listened to me. Actually, it worked out well. I was taught about the art of baking without having to invest anything.

I was spanked regularly and accepted it as part of being an apprentice. One morning, the lead baker woke me up at around two in the morning and told me to come down to the shop. I got dressed, stumbled down the six stories, still asleep. As soon as I entered the shop, I saw the bakers lined up, and one by one, they slapped me. When they were done, they sent me to go back to bed.

I labored climbing the six stories back up to my bunk. I only had a couple of hours until I had to get up and I wished I could have slept longer. It gave me lots of time to ponder what my life was going to be like working in that place where spanking was a routine exercise. I believe the bakers were just having fun. What a cruel joke! I never found out why I was punished, but it must have been serious enough. They thought they'd teach me a lesson, and to never forget the chores before going to bed. Shouldn't they at least have told me why I was spanked?

Every Saturday afternoon, I got on my bike and rode home, but only on a nice day. If it was rainy, or snowing, I rode the train. At times, I didn't have the money for the train fare, and I was stuck in Rosenheim over the weekend. Staying in town, I had to wash my own clothes which Mama washed when I went home. Lucky for me, there was a laundromat provided. I had enough money. I bought an iron for my clothes, and I did an okay job, but nothing like Mama did.

My job on Saturday afternoon was to wash down the shop, clean the machines, and get everything ready for Monday morning. I scrubbed the wooden barrels for the sour dough, and that was a tough job. The dough had dried; it was as hard as a rock, and impossible to get them totally clean. I constantly pulled wood slivers out from under my infected fingernails, and that hurt.

I completed my work by two in the afternoon on Saturday and got on my bike before dark and commenced the long ride home. The bicycle ride was 40 kilometers, taking me through charming towns along the bank of a beautiful river that reminded me of the Ache River in the Bavarian Alps. It took me about three to four hours to get home, and thank God I never had an accident. I upgraded my bike by adding lights, a rear view mirror and flaps on the back fender that kept the rain from *spritzing* 'squirting' my back. By the time I was done, I had the best looking bike in town.

162

My job required me to go to the backyard of the bakery where I'd find buckets and cleaning utensils. There, I found the largest rats, almost as big as cats. My boss set traps and caught a few of them. They were huge due to the abundance of food. They had no problems chewing through the flour sacks or the wooden boards.

On Christmas in 1956, I went home via train. We had much snow on the roads, and riding the train was my only option. At our bakery I bought a *stollen* to take home. A *stollen* is a braided loaf baked with nuts, raisins, and citrus. It is a Bavarian and Austrian tradition, a must for Christmas.

On that cold Christmas Eve on the way to the train station, I bought a bottle of wine. I thought it would add to the holiday spirit. I was walking on the snow covered sidewalk, and black ice. I had to get to the *Bahnhof* 'train station' quickly because I didn't want to miss the last train home. Under one arm I carried the *Stollen,* 'Christmas loaf' and under the other, I carried the bottle of wine.

I slipped on the ice, and the wine bottle broke into a thousand pieces. I was okay, but the wine was now an integral part of the sidewalk. I picked myself up, and literally skated all the way to the train station. I just caught the train in the nick of time. Had I missed it, I wouldn't have been able to leave until the next morning.

We had a wonderful Christmas, and it was great seeing my sisters who came home from work to celebrate with us. My parents were delighted with the *Stollen* for *Weihnachten,* 'Christmas', and by morning, it was guaranteed, it would be gone. It reminded me of the good old days. Helga came from Munich where she was an apprentice learning the photography business. She hated the job and was looking to get fired.

A couple of days earlier, I was busy baking a thousand loaves of *stollen.* It was very hard work, and my body was aching from standing on my feet ten hours at a time. I braided the dough, placed the stollen in the oven, and after they were brown I removed them from the oven. The job was normally handled by one of the master bakers, but they had left earlier in the day.

After a week's work, I came home Saturday afternoon and brought my dirty uniform with me so Mama could wash and starch it over the weekend. She did a marvelous job and all of it without having a washing machine, or hot water. By early Sunday afternoon, I either rode my bike, or caught the train back to Rosenheim. When I arrived, I had to get everything ready for Monday morning. Before quitting on Sunday evening, I prepared the sour dough for the next morning, and made sure the ovens were ready. But before I started my chores, I was treated to all kinds of scrumptious Danish pastry left from Saturday. What a feast!

During the week I got a break. I attended bake school which taught the theory of baking that included chemistry as well as practical applications. I found the classes interesting and besides, it got me out of the bake shop, even though my work was still waiting for me at the end of the day.

My boss, Herr Birnbaum was a short man, but quick on his feet in spite of his stiff leg caused by an injury during the war. I liked him, and many times he stuck up for me when I was accused by one of the bakers of not doing my job. I enjoyed riding along with Mr. Birnbaum to deliver bread to our customers.

Since his one leg was stiff, and the delivery van had a stick shift, it was difficult for him to operate the vehicle by himself. He steered, and I gave it the gas, which created a problem at times. I either gave it too much gas, or not enough. It was a comedy on four wheels, but we got the job done nonetheless.

One weekend, when I came back to work, I received disturbing news. One of our bakers was entrusted the care of the building which included the bakery and our living quarters. In retrospect, it was a huge mistake. He was from Italy on a work visa, a hard worker who loved to party and have a good time. It was a cold weekend, and for the room to be warm when he got back from partying, he filled the potbelly stove full with coal.

That was great reasoning, but he failed to realize the stove could get too hot. The result was the whole building burned to the ground. I got back on Sunday evening to see everything burned, except the bakery and the store. My meager possessions were consumed by the fire.

My boss arranged a temporary place for us to stay, about a mile away from the shop. We had to get up even earlier in the morning, more like four o'clock. Many times, it was raining when we walked to the shop, it was awful.

I roomed with Herbert, another apprentice; he was the quickest when it came to getting dressed. Before I had time to get my feet on the ground, he was out of the door. Herbert was easy to get along with. He was learning to become a *Konditor* 'cake decorator'. I envied him, and would have loved his job. The people he worked with were not as crude, and more cultured. I realized right then, I had the wrong job. One thing was for certain, I would have received fewer spankings.

I performed all kinds of duties, and one of them was to deliver bread to our customers early in the morning on a bicycle. The front wheel was small and low to the ground. It had a rack up front to carry the large basket that contained all the baked goods I was delivering.

I looked forward to going on my routes with the wonderful fresh air filling the bottom of my lungs and besides, it got me out of the noisy, hot bake shop. The doves welcomed me with cooing, as I rode along the alee. I made six to seven deliveries a day, depending on the weather. I managed to have a smile on my face, which at times was difficult, especially when visiting the military. Not, that I didn't like the military.

I had a bad morning when I delivered five-hundred breakfast rolls to the German border patrol. Before I left the bakery, Hilde counted the rolls by hand and dropped them into the big basket. Sometimes I counted them, and if I was off a few, that wasn't a big problem. I brought them back, and they were sold in the store.

On the way to the border patrol, I encountered a steep hill, and with that heavy of a load, it presented a problem. I weighed less than the basket up front. Due to the disproportioned weight, the bike tipped forward, and the basket fell off the bike causing the rolls to careen down the steep hill.

Not only was I late getting to my customers, but the rolls were laced with gravel. I was chasing the *Semmeln* 'rolls' down the hill as fast as I could. I lost the race, and the rolls won. Cars were backing up and honking their horns. I was gripped with angst, afraid of losing my load to the cars.

When picking up the rolls, I failed to heed my own safety as cars were flying by me left and right. To my delight, some of the drivers stopped and waited until I picked up every single roll.

It all panned out, and I felt like hugging them for being so kind. With my basket full, it was a challenge to lift the basket back on the bike. One of the drivers saw me struggle and helped me to get the basket on my bike. For his reward, I gave him one of the hot rolls which he accepted with gratitude. That was one roll the border police didn't get!

It was amazing; none were run over by the vehicles, not one. Some of the rolls were bruised, like my ego, and embedded with gravel, but other than that, they survived a near tragedy.

I finally arrived at the base, an hour late, and that was bad. The troops were already having breakfast, and without the rolls, it was a bad situation. In Germany, people always have rolls served with meat and cheese. The gentleman who accepted the rolls, and counted them for accuracy, was not amused when he saw the bruised rolls. If he had experienced what the rolls encountered, he'd be bruised as well.

He had the nerve to ask me why I was so late, and I told him that I had an accident. He didn't have any pity and continued his count as if he hadn't heard me. Finally, he asked me why there was so much gravel mixed in with the rolls, and I told him that I didn't have time to remove the gravel. He accepted the rolls, and as far as I know, nothing was ever said to my boss.

The border patrol had not yet removed the swastika on the building which was clearly seen on the main entrance, along with the German eagle. It took a while to erase the Hitler symbol, but the eagle remained which is Germany's symbol. The swastika was removed after the people complained to the *City's Bürgermeister* 'mayor'.

Bread and rolls weren't the only products I delivered. Pastries were in the mix of things, and God knows how much I loved them. My boss should have never asked me to deliver these goodies to our customers. At times, I did things I should never have done, and this was one of the times.

My stomach got the best of me when I was on my way to deliver the delicacies. The girls in the store did a beautiful job packaging them, to make sure that none of them would be damaged during transit to the customers. One of the pastries was called *Bienenstich* 'beesting'. They were utterly delicious, but fragile. When I rode the bike, I had to be careful to avoid chuckholes.

Making a delivery one morning, the aroma of the pastry got the best of me. I purposely decided to drive into a couple of chuckholes, knowing full well that it was the death of the *Bienenstich*. I knew the customer would not accept them, and I was 'heartbroken'. I had no choice but to eat a few of the broken pieces before heading back to the bakery. I found a nice shady spot, sat on a manicured lawn, and I had myself a feast.

I didn't eat them all, but since they were destroyed, there was no telling how many were left from the original count. My boss was not amused by my antics. I received a deserved whipping. From that point forward, I avoided anything remotely looking like a chuckhole.

I made deliveries during the summer, as well as the winter months, when it was a cold and nasty. After I made a delivery one morning, I found myself trapped behind a big rig. I couldn't move out of the way fast enough with my heavy load.

I noticed the truck backing up. The driver did not see me. The huge wheels were getting taller by the second as they came ever so close, and I figured the end was near. Out of nowhere, a bystander saw me, hollered at the driver to stop the truck, and again I was saved in the nick of time. Could it have been my guardian angel?

On a snowy day, my boss sent me to a nearby town to pick up a sack of flour that weighed as much as I did. The employees placed the sack on the front of the bike, where normally my big bread basket would be, and off I went. The trip took me down a steep hill, iced over with a covering of snow.

I knew I was in big trouble! I tried very hard not to lose the bike, but the sack of flour began to slide sideways as the bike, the sack of flour, and I careened down the hill. I came to a stop just short of running into the back of a truck. Lucky me, I was not injured. The bike and the sack of flour were not heavily damaged, except for a puncture hole on the side of the sack. By the time I got back to the bakery, I had lost a considerable amount of the contents, lighting my load considerably.

It was a beautiful, sunny day, when I went on a delivery run to the outskirts of town. I walked into the store, and I greeted the customer with a happy *Guten Morgen,* 'good morning'. The customer returned the greeting, and got busy counting the rolls he had ordered. For some reason, the store owner went to the back of the store. I noticed a shiny one Mark piece sitting on the wooden shelf used by the lady customers to set down their shopping bags.

Mark was the German currency before the conversion to the Euro, used today. I assumed Herr Pschorr never noticed the money lying there. How wrong could I have been? I dropped it into my deep pants pocket. When he came back into the store, he bent over the counter to see if the coin was still on the shelf. He looked straight at me, and asked me where the coin was that was lying on the shelf.

I didn't say anything. My face turned many shades of red, and my heart sank when he reached into my pocket, and lo and behold, he pulled out the shiny coin. He knew I didn't have that kind of money. It wasn't mine. He gave me an option, calling my boss, telling him what I had done, or he could give me a whipping, so I opted for the latter.

Boy, did he let me have it. I was black and blue, but very relieved knowing that this was the end of this episode. I never tried to talk my way out of it, knowing full well, lying was a sin, and so was stealing. I had been caught red-handed. If I had lied about taking the money, I would have committed two sins, and the punishment would have been much worse.

The moral of the story was, stealing is a sin, and I would never, ever, take anything from then on that wasn't mine. I thank God the man had the courage to carry out the punishment which changed my future for the good.

I was still abused, especially by one young baker, Werner. He loved to see me squirm and threw heavy weights at me, used to weigh the raw dough. At times, the weights landed on my head, and blood was running down my face, and bumps covered my head.

After this, I had my fill, and decided to get on the train and head for home. Mama was surprised to see me, and inquired why I decided to come home. She was not happy at my arrival and put me on the next train back to the bakery and even paid for the one way ticket. She told me to stand up for myself. It was time I became a man.

When I came back, they were overjoyed to see me. In my absence, they had to do all the dirty work themselves. I had a hunch, Mama and Herr Birnbaum had a talk, and she most likely told him that this had to stop. Of course she wouldn't tell me that. I ran away three times, and each time, Mama sent me back.

Had I been in her shoes, I wouldn't have had the courage to do what she did. In retrospect, it helped me and made me stronger when facing adversities. We had another apprentice who decided to run off, and never came back. I was left with twice the workload as before. I suppose his parents didn't have the guts to send him back, perhaps their decision was the right one.

For a change in scenery, I went to visit my sister Gerlinde. She was working in Rosenheim at a department store called Juhatz, dishing out ice cream, what a delightful job. I would have given anything for a cool job like hers. Every so often, she gave a small sample. It was so good!

One night, my sister was late coming back to her apartment, and curfew was at 10 pm. She was locked out, and had no place to go that night. Gerlinde knew where I was staying, and decided to pay me a visit in the middle of the night. I was shocked when she crawled into my bed. She told me what happened, and that she had no place to spend the night.

With a stern warning, I made it clear to her that at five in the morning she was to leave. It was at that time, the midnight shift arrived for a break. Just imagine if she had been found in my bed! Rumors would have gone wild for sure. At five o'clock sharp, she was on her way out, but only after I dropped a couple of breakfast rolls into her skirt pocket.

One night when my boss made a bed check, I was not in my bed at curfew. I went to visit my sister Gerlinde and the time just got away from me. It was after ten before I got back to my place. I reported to work the next morning at five o'clock. Herr Birnbaum approached me, and without warning, gave me a whipping.

I told him I went to see my sister, and he didn't believe a word of it. He accused me of seeing a girl in town. I wished I had done what I was accused of, and then my punishment would have made it worth my while.

I didn't have to go far to find girls. We had very nice young ladies working in our store. I don't know where they went after work. I never did find out, but that may have been a good thing in retrospect. I only saw them in the store serving the customers except for one, her name was Herta. We liked each other, but we were only friends.

We respected each other, and it felt good to have a friend to talk to and share our Birnbaum experience. We were kids at the time, only fifteen years old, and had grown up in a sheltered environment. We were away from home and exposed to all kinds of temptations. Up to this point, the worst things I had done was drinking beer, and smoking a cigar which made me deathly ill.

Each year, we had the *Herbstfest* 'fall parade in town'; I entered the festivities, representing my bakery, wearing my baker's white dress attire. It was wonderful to represent a great and well respected company. It gave me a sense of pride and the opportunity to see all kinds of floats, antique cars and other interesting things.

At the end of the parade, we went to the beer tent. A big mistake. It was located in the middle of the county fair grounds, and not unlike like any other county fair in the U.S. with its scary, fun rides.

My fellow bakers ordered all the beer I wanted, and stupid me, I drank everything they pushed in front of me. They were amused watching me get drunk. I couldn't recall how I found my way back to my bed. I had difficulty breathing, and that could have been a sign of alcohol poisoning. It was awful! I couldn't understand why people drank just to get drunk. For a long time, I couldn't stand the smell of beer.

It was a hot sunny day, around 85 degrees Fahrenheit when Herta and I decided to go on a ride to a nearby lake to cool off. She sat on the bar of the bike and I pedaled. I was hoping to at least get a friendly kiss. After we arrived, she slipped into her bathing suit. While she was changing her clothes, she told me to turn around and not look. It was a tough call, but I abided by her wish and I never peeked once. I could have kicked myself.

We shared things that were going on at the bakery since she had more access to information than I did, being around the other girls. I learned my boss was a sexual deviant. He occasionally took one of the girls on a bread delivery run, and took the liberty of groping them. He went to trial, and was sentenced to six months in jail. Whenever my customers asked me where my boss was, I was to tell them he was on vacation in Italy. The question was did my customers believe my story?

These are the things I found out when talking to Herta. I was disappointed when I heard this. I respected my boss, and in a way, I wish I had never been part of that conversation.

One Saturday afternoon while cleaning the shop, I washed down the huge mixing machines that processed around a thousand pounds of dough each; I hurried so I could be on my way home and be with my family. The floor, the walls, everything was wet, including me. The rest of the bakers had already left for home long ago and I was alone in the huge shop. I always made sure I disconnected the power to the machines before cleaning them. I knew water and electricity didn't mix.

I immediately passed out. I felt the electricity surging through my body. Suddenly it all stopped, and everything was very quiet. I felt myself going through the roof of the building, cutting through the clouds.

The huge plastic electric plugs were located in such a way, whereby I could only see the top cover. The power supply was of high voltage to drive the huge machines. I pulled out the plug, unbeknownst to me, the bottom plate had broken off, and I reached directly into the electric plug. I immediately passed out, and felt the electricity surging.

Suddenly it all stopped, and everything was very quiet. I felt myself going through the roof of the building and cutting through the clouds.

It was an amazing experience and it felt wonderful as my spirit left my body. I was flying like a bird without limitations. I didn't want to come back;

I felt free at last. The strange thing was I didn't think it was unusual for me to be in this state.

While I had this out of body experience, it was marvelously peaceful as I went skyward, heaven was waiting for me, but God had other ideas, and sent me back.

I don't know how long I was lying on the concrete floor unconscious. It could have been two minutes, five minutes, or twenty minutes. When I came to, I found myself lying on the wet floor and disconnected from the electric plug. Perhaps my heart had actually stopped beating for a few seconds or minutes. With that kind of power, I should have been fried.

After I came to, my heart was beating very heavy. In spite of it all, I finished the job, and rode my trusty bike home that afternoon. It was a miracle I was alive and thanked God all the way to my parents' home that I was still here.

When I arrived home, I told Mama about the incident, and she called my boss and told him what had happened to me. When I got back the next day, Herr Birnbaum didn't waste time and took me to a doctor to check my heart. As far as he could tell, the accident didn't cause any damage. I heard him say, "This was a miracle," and he had never seen anybody walk away from being electrocuted with that much power and live to tell about it.

I had worked at the bakery for 1½ years when Papa received a job offer at the Colorado University Medical Center in Denver. Papa accepted the offer. They had read about him in medical journals and the research he conducted on human brains. The doctors at the hospital were impressed. They wanted him. It took us another 1½ years to complete all the necessary documents in order to immigrate to the United States.

Papa became acquainted with a Jewish doctor by the name of *Herr* Neubürger who read about Papa's medical research. He became our sponsor. He immigrated to the United States prior to Hitler's reign. He made it possible for us to make the United States our new home. Herr Neubürger was a generous human being and went the extra mile to ensure we were taken care of during this iconic transition.

He offered Papa a lucrative position, and still allowed him to continue his research which led to an earth shaking medical discovery. It took lots of courage to invest in a family he didn't know, and to top it off, none of us spoke English.

Still in Germany, I made the mistake of leaking the news to my fellow workers that I was immigrating to the United States. They thought I was crazy, and accused me of making up this story. *Herr* Egger, the master baker, was very much anti American, and made my life a literal hell. He said to me he wished New York and Chicago had been bombed out of existence.

28

WANDERLUST

Had I been smart, I should have kept my mouth shut, but I was so excited about our epic journey, I couldn't keep quiet. It was difficult for me to wait until getting out of the bake shop. Every minute seemed like an hour. My mind was fantasizing about sailing across the stormy Atlantic to the New World.

I was hoping the United States would become my new home, provided we passed all the background checks. Papa left from Amsterdam, Holland, with a ship by the name of Rotterdam. I was envious, and wished I had gone with him on the big, exciting journey.

I was working in Rosenheim, but I bid Papa farewell on one of the weekends previously when I was home. He wrote to me on occasions, and sent me pictures of Denver, Colorado. I was at awe how deep blue the sky was.

I was getting excited, and couldn't wait to get the word, the final okay to emigrate. I was under the impression there were still Indians with bows and arrows and cowboys walking around with their guns hanging from the holsters.

It made the prospect even more adventuresome, thinking that I might get into a situation where I would have to use a gun to defend myself.

Before leaving Germany, we made the trip to Munich a couple of times to visit the U.S. consulate, and that is when I realized things were moving rapidly, but it still wasn't quick enough for me. The American consulate arranged an appointment with a physician for a thorough physical. He wanted to make sure we were healthy. We had a temporary delay when the doctor discovered spots on Helga's lung. They checked again, and discovered it was a problem with the X-ray machine. At last, we had passed all the requirements, and the process began in earnest.

A tall, distinguished U.S. Marine at the consulate with his blue, brisk uniform stood guard. I thought, maybe I could be a Marine instead of a sailor, but the Navy won out. I was fantasizing all these things in my mind, and knew it wouldn't be long before I would be saying goodbye to my friends and relatives.

Mama sold everything we had accumulated, and how she did it, I will never know. I wish I could ask her now how she accomplished it all. Before long, our place was empty with nothing left which wasn't nailed down.

I was too young, and didn't realize how much Mama and Papa sacrificed to make the change so late in their life. She was fifty-two and Papa was fifty. It was an unselfish act, and the reason they did this, was to give us kids a better life and a brighter future.

I never had any hesitation about leaving my homeland, but the problem was, I didn't know one word of English. My school offered no foreign languages as did the larger schools. My parents didn't know English either. How scary was that?

The night before we left, my buddy Michael took me in, and I slept in luxury that night. I don't know where the rest of the family spent the night, but I suppose we spread ourselves around town, staying with friends.

Our cat Putzi was with me that night, but in the morning there was no sign of him anywhere. We saw him jump from the third floor of Michael's house, about fifty feet in height. He survived without a scratch. He was one tough cat and we knew then, he didn't want to go on the journey with us.

Translation of two letters I wrote to Papa while in America.

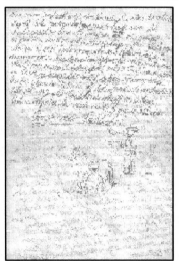

Letter written to Papa in 6/26/57

Dear Papa,

I want to thank you for the books of animals you sent me. I really liked going through them. I was fascinated by the birds and snakes. Are there snakes like that in Colorado?

Colorado must have beautiful birds as well.

How are you doing, Papa? By now, you are probably a trapper. I am doing great at the Birnbaum bakery. I love their food and I am well taken care of. They are working me very hard however.

The other apprentice took off, and never returned. I guess he got tired of all the work. We are all very excited about our upcoming trip, and we can hardly wait.

The people I work with are jealous, and tell me it is very bad over there, and everything is so expensive.

But the way you write, they are making up all these stories about America. Recently one of our neighbors ran over our cat, and didn't even bother to stop. The cat dragged its way home, its back was broken.

Walter put it out of its misery and killed it. A man from Grafing came by and brought a dead red fox for you to stuff. He was sorry when I told him that you were no longer living with us. I just saw a movie in Rosenheim about Colorado.

The picture was absolutely wonderful, and seeing the Rockies was awesome. It showed trappers riding their horses through the Rockies and trapping animals. It showed Indians like the Black Feet Indians and the Apaches. Papa, have you seen cowboys and Indians yet? I would be very interested in seeing them. It showed a father and son smoking the peace pipe with the Indian chief.

I have to end now, many greetings from Your Ponne.

Letter written to Papa 9/17/57
Dear Papa,

How are you? I hope you are doing well. I am also doing well. At Birnbaum's I have already gained thirty pounds, and come in at 130 pounds total.

I am already wearing your shirts, and the blue jacket you let me have. Mama has already sold most of the stuff in our home. Now it isn't that comfortable anymore, all the walls are bare and all we have left are a few odds and ends.

I am glad that most of the stuff is gone, and in less than two months we are going to be on our way to America. I am excited to see you again after all these months.

The house you bought in Denver has to be beautiful. You wrote that I have to attend high school. I will have to take instructions in English.

Perhaps, when on the big ship, I can learn a little English. I converse with people. In Rosenheim we just concluded our Herbs fest "fall festival". We had lots of work, and I am glad it ended today.

Helga works at Siemens in Munich, and she is earning a lot more now. Papa, are rattlesnakes as dangerous as people tell me? My hope is I will never come across any of them. You told me that you have already seen one in the wild, and heard its rattle.

That has to be very frightening.

Dear Papa I can't think of anything else to write, and I must close.

Many greetings from my heart!

Your Ponne

29

OUR DEPARTURE

Dr. Neubürger contacted Papa after he read the medical journals about Papa's research as a scientist in Germany, working at the Max Planck Institute. He was eager to speak to Papa about employment in Denver at the University Medical Center. Papa would be a valuable asset. Dr. Neubürger offered Papa a lucrative position and sponsored us to immigrate to America.

After talking it over with Mama, they accepted the offer. Mama had not been happy living in Germany with the memory of the wars, and immigrating to the United States would lift the heavy burden from her heart. She was at a point where she mistrusted the German people. The primary reason Mama and Papa entertained the idea of coming to the United States was to give us kids a better life without having to worry about the mighty Russian Bear next door, or the resurgence of a powerful Germany.

Papa left a year before we did, to test the waters. While in Denver, he acclimated himself to the Amkerican culture and familiarized himself with the two hospitals, Denver General and Rose hospital. He purchased a house for us we called home. We left Lorenzenberg in the early morning hours November 12th, 1957, boarding the train, and heading out of Assling. We pulled our little green wagon to the train station we still had from our odyssey 'Fleeing Hitler'.

The green cart helped us through the hellish times, and it served us well to reach a new land, known for its freedom and liberty. After we boarded the train, we left the cart at the station. I hope some soul found good use for it.

With joy, we boarded a huge train, belching smoke like a dragon. We were sad leaving my oldest sister Herta, behind. She was married and had a family which made it impossible for her to come with us. She had always been there for me, but she wouldn't be there in the future to guide me.

Herta was a great comfort during the bad times, as well as the good times, taking care of me, her little brother. It was like a funeral leaving her behind; I wouldn't see her for a long time.

Mama had a fall out with her, and we couldn't even say goodbye. It broke my heart. I was fifteen at the time, and saw my sister not until nine years later, in 1966 when she came for a visit. We had a wonderful time. I wished she didn't have to go back to Germany. It would be another eleven years before I saw her again when she came for another visit.

The train which took us to Bremen, had all the conveniences one could imagine. It was even equipped with a sleeper and dining car. This was the life I could have gotten used to, and perhaps it was our future. The locomotive was huge, and blew billows of black smoke as we raced northward.

I was fascinated at the landscape. Mama pointed out many historic sites along the way. Mama knew much about history. She was my history teacher. It took us two full days to reach our destination. To contain my joy was difficult, knowing we were getting closer to our departure. This event was bigger than big. I had never in my life experienced what was transpiring in front of my eyes.

The train took us through the Fulda Valley, with its rich history. It was the primary invasion route for invaders. Its flat terrain was a perfect thoroughfare with few obstacles. As we continued, there were many more points of interest along the way. One huge statue was Barbarossa, the king of Germany who was king of the Holy Roman Empire. As we traveled through Aachen we arrived at the huge statue of *Karl Der Grosse* 'Charlemagne'. He was the first Emperor after the fall of Rome.

What added to our enjoyment was the food we were served in the dining car. It was first class. The best part was there was no additional charge. The people on the train were relaxed and sociable. Many were traveling on business and others were on their way to their vacation destination.

The mountains had long ago disappeared, and the green rolling hills came into view. As I remember, we didn't stop at a lot of places. We were on the *S Bahn* express which stopped only at major cities on the way to Bremen.

We disembarked in Bielefeld, close to Bremen, where Mama and Papa studied, Papa a Lutheran pastor, and Mama a Lutheran nun. Many years prior, my uncle Karl talked Papa into taking his sister out for a date. They hit it off, and it wasn't long until they were married.

I regretted not asking my parents why their plans were derailed. Maybe, it had something to do with the war. Bethel was a city within a city. It even had a bakery and butcher shop. Bethel was self-sufficient in every way.

We arrived there by street car, and were welcomed like royalty. Mama was acquainted with most of the nuns, and they had a joyous reunion.

We stayed two nights and were housed in their welcoming center. The amenities were terrific. We were served a fabulous breakfast, lunch and dinner. They were very hospitable people and made our stay wonderful. Bethel had, and still has, a world-renowned sanitarium for mentally disabled people.

During Hitler's reign, the asylums were emptied, and the patients were sent to the concentration camps throughout Europe, where they met a horrible fate.

The bakery intrigued me. I was shown the huge ovens and was invited to spend time in the shop to view the operation. It seemed to be more modern than the bakery in

Rosenheim I left just a week earlier. The ovens were shiny and everything was very clean. It was so immaculate; I could have eaten off the floor. It was wonderful not having to work in a bakery anymore. I was now a visitor!

Papa's major at the university was pathology, his minor was theology. He worked as an intern in the psyche ward, and witnessed horrible deeds carried out by Hitler. During Hitler's reign, the asylums were emptied, and the patients were sent to the concentration camps throughout Europe where they met a horrible fate. This troubled him forever. Papa did not visit Bethel on the way to America. It would have brought back the memories of brutality and inhumanity.

After the third day, it was time for our departure. When we arrived at the train station, we noticed our cat was missing. Putzi had eluded us again, and that was a sure sign he didn't want to be part of this trip.

Everybody was now searching for our cat and by luck we found him hiding in some bushes. We wasted no time, placing him in his cage and he let us know how he felt about the situation, hissing at us.

Mama's departure from Bethel was emotional. She knew it would perhaps be the last time she would ever see the nurses. She visited twenty years later, but by then, some of her friends had passed on.

We boarded the train, final destination Bremen. One of the passengers on the train had quite a few stories, telling me he lived in upper New York. He owned a successful business, manufacturing auto parts. By what he told me, he had worked hard to achieve a life of luxury. He owned two cars, and by the way he described it, his house was a mansion. In Germany, you were lucky to own a bicycle, let alone a car. After what he told me, I became even more eager to get to America.

My imagination was running wild. What kind of life would we have? Would we live in luxury like the people I met along the way? What would I be doing in the U.S. without knowing English? It was all so very frightening. At the same time, I felt an overpowering excitement, but angst gripped me and wouldn't let go.

Arriving in northern Germany, I noticed distinct differences between people of northern and southern Germany. For the most part, they were taller with square faces and had a fairer complexion.

I learned later, Bremen was one of the Hansa League cities, established many centuries ago. It was part of an economic alliance between cities in the Baltic and the North Atlantic. Other cities belonging to the league were *Hamburg, Lübeck, Danzig*' 'Dansk' in Polish, and *Königsberg* 'Kaliningrad' in former Prussia.

After a joyful trip, finally we arrived in Bremen, the beautiful, romantic port city on the Atlantic. Bremen is a picturesque town with much history and the birth place of the Brothers Grimm who wrote many children's stories.

The Grimm Brother's stories for the children are harsh. Each story ends in tragedy for the kids who do bad things. The message is, if the kids are bad, there are consequences.

In the town square stood a sculpture of the Bremer *Stadt Musikanten* 'city musicians', which consisted of a donkey, dog, cat, and a rooster, welcoming the visitors to the city. The story went like this: the donkey outlived his usefulness to his master and trotted off into town where he met three other companions who found themselves in the same predicament. They played music, and were a great hit with the town's people who embraced them. I am sad to report, I missed the famous statue.

We arrived in Bremen, too early to board the ship, so we were given time to mill around town. At noon, we sat down to have lunch at a restaurant. Afterwards, we treated ourselves to window shopping.

Looking at the merchandise displayed in the windows, I didn't realize Helga had left my side checking out other sites, and I grabbed a girl standing next to me, thinking it was Helga, only to be shocked when I realized, it wasn't my sister. It embarrassed me no end. I was lucky she didn't slap me.

The time had arrived for us to venture to the pier where our massive ship was waiting. We *flagged* down a taxi, and within minutes the taxi driver dropped us off at the pier. We unloaded our luggage with the help of a porter, who took them to our state-room. The name of the ship was the SS America. It was the sister ship of the SS United States, which held the record crossing the Atlantic in the fastest time.

At three in the afternoon, we were allowed to board. We stood in line for about an hour to present our documents to the port authorities. All was in order and we were given the okay to board. Many passengers were traveling to countries, like Britain, France and on to New York.

Observing the huge ship, I wondered how many people it accommodated, and how much freight it could carry in its belly. I heard from reliable sources, it could hold two thousand passengers and a crew of seven hundred.

Upon entering the ship, we were escorted to our stateroom, large enough to accommodate the four of us.

I ventured topside to investigate; looking over the pier were cranes, still busy loading freight and lifting it into the belly of the ship. I believe I saw one of our crates lifted onto the ship, and I was relieved it made it in one piece to the pier. One of the crates contained our feather beds which were the most valuable item we brought along. They came in handy in Colorado during the cold winter months.

The time came to say goodbye to my homeland. We pushed off the pier and the ship was nudged by a couple of tugboats. I didn't feel all that sad leaving; I was busy thinking what adventures lay ahead in the days to come.

My sisters, on the other hand, especially Gerlinde, had a much tougher time as we heard the German band playing, Muss *ich Denn, muss ich den, zum Städtele hinaus* which was sung by Elvis Presley long ago. It touched me too, but soon the playing was over, and we were out to sea. I bid my homeland goodbye, hopefully not for the last time.

It hadn't sunk in yet what was transpiring before my young, adventurous eyes, and little did I realize it would be another thirty-two years before coming back to my beloved Bavaria.

When the ship left the pier, my sister Gerlinde wiped her tears. I knew she had remorse leaving Germany, leaving the country we all grew up in.

We freshened up for dinner. We entered the dining hall, and how elegant it was. One of the crew members escorted us to our dining table. Even our name was written on a card, and placed on the table. The tables were adorned with beautiful tablecloths and fresh flowers. Where were the flowers grown? On the ship?

The waiter handed us menus, but we couldn't read what was offered. We wished there would have been pictures of the cuisine, then all we would have had to do was point. My sisters looked at each other perplexed, not having any idea what to order. We had no idea what we were getting ourselves into. Not knowing a word of English became a huge obstacle.

We were lost, and what made matters worse, the waiter didn't know German. We just pointed at something, hoping we made the right selection. Mama usually knew what to do, but even she was at a loss. In a short time, our meal arrived. It consisted of nothing, but broccoli on small plates. We had never been introduced to the vegetable, and didn't know how to eat it, or what to eat it with.

Hungry as wolves, we were looking for a wonderful meal. We were disappointed. This meal didn't at all look like something that would still our hunger. I took a bite, and wanted to spit it out. The waiter knew we weren't happy with our selection, and since he spoke no German, he summoned a waiter who was fluent in our language. Now we were in business and ordered what we appealed to us. I ordered pork, Mama and my sisters ordered fish. Things were definitely looking up, and we enjoyed our first meal aboard the ship. I made sure my dish didn't get close to my sister's. I didn't want my meal contaminated.

While on our epic journey, we got to know people who had emigrated to the U.S. many years before us. They described to us where they lived and how they lived. To us, it was pure luxury, judging by our standards. We lived a simple life in post-war Germany, and there was no luxury.

I couldn't wait to get to New York and experience the affluence I heard people talk about. I knew we were coming to a country that was blessed. I became anxious to see a city I had only read about in school and not in a favorable way. We were still a few days away. It seemed as though time stood still. Couldn't the ship speed up a little?

30

BRIDGE TO AMERICA

Throughout our journey, my desire to become a sailor became ever so strong. Being out on the open sea was exhilarating, and not getting sea sick, confirmed that a sailor's life was in my future. There was nothing like it. Smelling the seawater, and hearing the waves crash against the bow of the ship was spectacular. Watching the various sea birds and observing their elegant maneuvers as they danced above the huge ocean waves was spectacular.

The night sky was filled with millions of stars, turning the sky into a sea of lights. The bright stars were our companions throughout the journey, guiding us to our final destination. I loved being on the deck of the ship and to watch the firmament unfurl.

Hundreds of seagulls continued to accompany us out in the open sea looking for food we tossed overboard. I took a loaf of dry bread and by the time lunch was served, the bread was gone. After lunch, I went below decks to get more to feed the scavengers. In my absence, more birds arrived. There must have been over a hundred or more. It wasn't long before I had thrown all the bread I had into the air for these hungry, aggressive sea gulls fighting for every small morsel.

We still had three days of sailing to do, and my sister Gerlinde cried her eyes out over the boyfriend she had left behind. Before the tears landed on the deck, she met this handsome Italian man. Gerlinde didn't speak Italian, and he didn't speak German, but they hit it off. Love had no boundaries. It was the love boat in the truest sense of the word and it turned into a fascinating future. In the meantime, Mama kept vigilant, knowing Gerlinde had befriended this Italian man. One evening, Gerlinde was going to meet this fellow, but Mama wouldn't have any of it. She slapped Gerlinde and forced her to stay in the cabin that night.

Mama was stern, there was only one way, and that was her way, or the highway, and in this case, it was the ocean. The Italian, Victor, was on his way to Chicago where his relatives were waiting for him. This was the beginning of an adventurous life for both. Gerlinde and Victor met a few more times when Mama wasn't looking. Not even the stormy Atlantic kept them apart.

The journey progressed as the ship cut through the Atlantic with ease until we encountered a severe storm on November 16th and 17th, 1957. The Atlantic is known for its heavy seas. As time went on, the sea grew even more boisterous.

The monster waves reached clear to the bridge of the ship that caused the big ship to rock up and down, and from side to side. I had a great time. Most people were getting seasick, and wished they were dead. My sisters were seasick as well. It was miserable for most people, who were cooped up in their cabins with frequent trips to the bathroom.

That took the wind out of their joyous adventure interrupted by the ferocious storm. They were stuck in their cabins, and not enjoying the trip very much. The powerful waves with their white crowns intrigued me. In spite of it all, the seagulls still followed us. They were such elegant fliers, and at times, it seemed as though the gigantic waves would swallow them, but not a chance. At the same time it appeared the angry ocean could have swallowed our ship in one gulp. The vessel shuddered each time it dove into the deep ocean. The four powerful screws lifted out of the water, producing a loud, deafening roar.

The dining hall was empty, giving the waiters and cooks a break, unless they were also seasick, I believe the latter. I wondered why the tables had aluminum edges, now I knew why. It kept the food from falling onto the deck or into the people's laps.

We finally outran the storm, the calm returned, and at last, everybody continued having a good time traveling on the magnificent ship. One by one, passengers ventured onto the decks, and tested their sea legs, still weak and a little wobbly. From then on, we had smooth sailing. The mighty S.S. America was a cruise ship with all the amenities one can imagine. It even had a swimming pool with a slide and other fun things for the younger guests, like us.

After seven days cruising, the city of New York was visible in the far distance. Finally, we were getting closer to our destination. We were reminded of the Italian luxury liner Andrea Doria which sank in 1956. The luxury ship collided with a Swedish freighter off Nantucket Island and sank eleven hours later. Some forty passengers lost their lives in this tragedy.

As our ship came into the harbor, we were welcomed by the hearty aroma from the Hills Brothers coffee plant which filled our lungs. The smell of coffee permeated the entire harbor.

As our ship steamed towards our pier, tug boats on either side of our ship performed a spectacle, shooting red and blue streams of water into the air, high above the surface of the harbor.

The Statue of Liberty towered above the city. What a sight! She was elegant, and an inspiration to the new arrivals. Millions found freedom and liberty from tyranny. Millions of immigrants before us came ashore at Ellis

Island who built the nation we see today. The Germans who had gone before us said, "The United States is the land of unlimited opportunities." Observing the riches of the land, it was true. New cars everywhere, people were well dressed, restaurants were on every corner, the streets were clean and everything was in order.

Many years later, I had the opportunity to climb up into the Statue, and clear to the crown. It was an exhausting climb in the narrow stair case. There was no way to turn around during the climb until you reached the top. It was prior to 9/11. I was awestruck at what unfolded before my eyes. All around were the *Wolkenkratzer* 'skyscrapers' reaching into the heavens.

After disembarking, we met our guide at the pier. She guided us towards La Guardia airport. She was patient, pointing out the things we were going to encounter. I observed the S.S. America, and for the last time, I saw the gigantic bow of the majestic vessel towering above the harbor. She made it possible for us to reach this blessed land.

Along the way to the airport, we crossed busy intersections, and I couldn't help but notice the huge cars with their fins protruding from the rear of the vehicles. It was truly fascinating. It gave us the impression the cars were designed to fly with their elegant wings.

We walked another long block, and climbed into a yellow cab, taking us to the airport. In a short time, the airport was within sight. I was amazed at the many planes which were parked on the tarmac, ready to take the passengers to their destinations. "I can't believe I'm getting to fly on this huge four propeller machine". I had always dreamed about flying, but the probability was remote. Now it became a reality.

31

OUR NEW HOME

Our luggage was checked through customs, and off we went to the boarding area. I was busy watching planes take off and land. Oh, what a sight! We were awestruck at what was unfolding. People going to and fro, and hurried from one gate to the next. We had never seen so many people in one place. Where were they all going? God only knows.

We were sitting in the boarding area for two hours, which gave us lots of time to check things out. Next to the boarding area, I walked to a store selling everything from coffee to books. I picked up a magazine, but I couldn't read it. I was frustrated. I was getting thirsty; Mama gave me change to buy a Coke which only cost fifteen cents. I wanted to tell the lady I wanted a Coke, but I couldn't. Nobody knew German. It was maddening! I pointed to the Coke sign, and then she knew. I had only once before tasted Coke and loved the flavor. It tasted the same as in Germany.

At last, the attendant at the gate announced we were about to board. Thank God for our guide, she stayed with us until we boarded the plane. One by one, the passengers boarded the big plane to their assigned seat. I was shocked when we were directed to the first class section. Was there a mistake? No it wasn't, Mama did a superb job selecting our seats. After all, this was our first flight and we were going to fly half way through the American skies.

The attendants made certain we had pillows and blankets. After the plane climbed and reached cruising altitude, the stewardess brought us cloth napkins and the choicest food. We were offered delicacies which included ham, chicken and an assortment of other dishes. It was up to us to select the many varieties of dishes which were on the menu. I selected ham, which was close to what I was used to. The seats had plenty of leg room, but wouldn't you know it, my sister Helga sat by the window where she had a panoramic view of the sky and its puffy clouds. My sisters squeezed me into the middle, and I had to strain to get a view from the window.

I offered Helga some of my food if she'd change seats with me, but there was no way. The stewardesses were fantastic, waiting on us hand and foot, to make sure we had a pleasant time flying. Indeed we did! In those days, flying was an extraordinary event! The passengers were treated special. A big bonus, the stewardess spoke fluent German.

After a long four hour flight, we arrived above the Denver skyline; the view was breathtaking with beautiful bright red, blue, and green lights sparkling in the dark clear night. The air was so crisp and clean, one could see for a hundred miles in each direction. We buckle up as the plane slowed down and banked steeply to line up for landing. The captain did a magnificent job with a smooth landing.

I was anxious to get off the plane to see Papa who was waiting for us on the tarmac with his colleagues and Mr. Neubürger, our sponsor. When we climbed down the plane's staircase, I saw Papa, and almost jumped into his arms. Mama gave him a huge hug which lasted for a couple of minutes. My sisters embraced Papa, and stayed close by his side, not letting go, all the way to the parking lot. Tears streamed down our cheeks for joy, which soon turned to ice from the frigid air. At last, we were together again. His friends introduced themselves, but we didn't waste time getting out of the frigid cold.

We proceeded to the parking lot, where we were met by the most beautiful cars I had ever seen. Many were driving Cadillacs with their unmistakable tail fins, and bright red rear lights. To me, the whole scene was like a fairy tale. The land we only dreamed of, and read about in school came alive. It reminded me of Karl Mai's books depicting life in the Wild West. He did fabulous job writing about the cowboys, and the Native American Indians. It was amazing; he himself had never set foot in America, and only knew about the way of life in the America via books.

Gerlinde and Victor got married a year later and were blessed with six children. Victor passed away four years ago, and my sister Gerlinde misses him very much. They were married fifty-one years, and built a successful life together.

I searched for the SS America to see what happened to the ship over time. I discovered the ship ran aground in 1969 during a treacherous storm by the Canary Islands. Tug boats were pulling the ship towards Spain when the ropes snapped.

They attempted to reconnect the ship, but it was impossible. The huge waves battered the tug boats and the ship on all sides. It would have placed the crew at great risk, and the rescue effort was scuttled. Over the years, the S.S. America was demolished by the force of the ocean. The Atlantic reclaimed the vessel. First the stern broke off as it listed to port, the back funnel was next, and at the end, the ship fell to port side. Today, all there is visible is the rusty bow protruding out of the churning water.

> I am sad for her demise, rusted out, rendered to become one with the sea, and never to sail again.

Prior to this tragedy, the ship was sold to several nations. It is sad to have seen this happen to such a majestic vessel that brought us to the United States of America. I felt sad for her demise, rusted out, rendered to become one with the sea, and never to sail again.

I made a point to watch movies about America when I lived in Rosenheim, Germany. One movie, I forgot the name of it, depicted an American Indian talking to a cowboy in German saying *guten morgen Herr Chief* "good morning chief." That struck me kind of funny, hearing an Indian talking German.

It was close to Christmas when we arrived in Denver, and for the first time, I saw beautiful, decorated homes and the colorful lights as they reflected off of the snow. It was magic. In Germany, it wasn't the custom to decorate the exterior of the houses. Only businesses had Christmas displays, but it was nothing like in the U.S.

I was anxious to see our new home; I imagined it to be special and beautiful. Indeed it was. I was proud of Papa! He made a great choice by picking the home of our dreams, and he did it without Mama's input.

Walking into the home, it revealed beautiful oak crown moldings in the family and dining rooms with gorgeous hand carved oak doors. I loved the enclosed front porch.

Papa gave me a tour of the home It was magnificent. The house was furnished with three bedrooms, two baths and a huge basement. The splendor of this home blew me away. Up to this point, the most we ever had were two bedrooms and an out house.

The house was totally furnished with beds, cabinets, and a dining table with chairs. I was puzzled where the furniture came from because we left everything in Germany. Finding out, the furnishings were donated by people from the neighborhood Lutheran church. How generous they were. They wanted us to feel at home in this beautiful land.

It was incredible how generous people were; everybody shared with us what they had. I had never seen such love in my life from people we never met. What better way to show Christianity than by helping people in need.

Exhausted from the long trip, we slept well the first night in our fresh beds. When morning came, Papa had already brewed coffee; the aroma filled the home.

Denver is the mile high city with thin air. It took a while to acclimate, but we had this issue settled in a short time. Papa had to be at work at the Denver General and Rose hospitals by eight in the morning. The trip was two miles. It was a two mile walk but for him it was it was an easy stroll.

Curiosity got the best of me when I asked Papa if I could go with him to see what he did in the lab. We climbed the stairs to the fifth floor. He did it with ease, but it was tough for me to keep up with him. I am certain, there were elevators we could have used, but Papa wouldn't have it any other way.

It was interesting in his independent scientific medical studies at the Medical University of Denver. Once in the lab, various human organs stored in large glass jars greeted me, and the smell of formaldehyde was overwhelming. He had brains, lungs and other human organs sitting on shelves. Would Papa introduce me to Frankenstein next?

When I touched one of the brains, it felt rubbery, like when petting a porpoise. I asked him what he would be doing with them in the jars. We walked over to his powerful microscopes, and he showed me the structures of the brain cells. He was able to identify healthy cells versus abnormal cells by various colors. Papa perfected the color variations in cell formations. I should have asked him if he could spare one of the brains on the shelf in case I ever needed a transplant.

I couldn't wait to investigate our neighborhood. Soon we were introduced to an open mall at the fabulous Cherry Creek shopping center. We had never seen shopping centers with beautiful stores and restaurants that were begging us to come in to get something delicious to eat. The temptation was great. So many things to purchase, but my parents were just window shopping. Our favorite stores were Sears and Woolworth where I was introduced to root beer floats. Everything was new to me, even the famous American hamburgers.

I ordered a hamburger with French fries, but I didn't know how to eat it. Observing other people preparing the hamburger revealed to me what to do. I learned quickly how to properly consume the American dish. Ketchup was running through my fingers and down my arms. It was messy alright. I passed the American food initiation with flying colors. The old saying, 'Monkey see, monkey do'.

I had never seen hamburger buns either, or hot dogs. I could never figure out why the Americans call a sausage hot dog and a piece of meat between two buns a hamburger. I thought a hot dog was a grilled dog. I wasn't about to eat dog meat but I was relieved when I learned that a hot dog was a sausage, and had nothing to do with a canine.

Why do Americans call a hamburger roll a bun, or for that matter, why do they call it a hamburger? The hamburger originated in Hamburg, Germany, and strange as it sounds, I had never heard of a hamburger growing up.

To integrate into the American culture was frustrating, but at the same time, it was lots of fun learning the American way of life. I wouldn't trade it for anything. Going to downtown Denver was fun. Stopping in at the Woolworth store was special. I spent a considerable amount of time and money there, but only after I had secured a job cleaning houses.

The Woolworth store catered to German immigrants, where one could buy

German records, as well as ethnic clothing. I was attracted to the soda fountain, and it goes without saying, I tasted their delicious root beer float.

I loved going downtown, but I could only get there by bus before I learned to drive. I thought about owning a car, but there were a couple of problems, and one was, I had no money and no driver's license. Taking a driver's test would present a challenge because of my lack of English.

Mama and Papa never learned to drive, so they were of no help when it came to driving. They took the bus, or walked wherever they went. I figured there must be an easier way, besides riding the bus, or walking. A car was a must.

Mama and Papa though thrifty, had barely enough money to get by. My desire was to be Americanized, and what better way was there, than spending money and buying things I didn't need. In order for me to buy the goodies offered in the stores, I had to get a job. To be employed, I had to learn English. My first job was cleaning houses for friends where I earned a little spending money.

I was told that I did a better job than their previous cleaning lady. I appreciated the compliment, but my aspirations were not to clean houses, but to get a real job, a man's job, and that was bussing dishes at the German Heidelberg restaurant.

By this time, my sisters both acquired jobs as waitresses at the Heidelberg. Gerlinde put in a good word for me, and the restaurant hired me as a bus boy. My sisters had the same problem, not being able to communicate. To take the customers' orders, the guests simply pointed at the selection of dishes they wished to order. That way, they didn't have to be proficient in English. What better way was there to learn English?

Riding the city buses was an adventure until we familiarized ourselves with the routes. For just a nickel the buses took me all over town. What a bargain! To get to my destination was a challenge.

Understanding the driver was difficult, and missing a word here and there, often added a few miles to the trip. Paying close attention to street signs was a must. At times, the limbs of the trees hid the street name, or the bus went too fast and caused me to miss where I should have got off. It was stressful, but we made it, learning the custom of the land, and eventually the language.

Walking was great! I enjoyed the fresh air, and observing the plants and the animals around me was wonderful. The blue sky was the bluest, much more so than in Germany where the sky was pale blue in comparison.

Whenever anyone approached me, I hid. I was afraid to talk. I did everything to avoid people. I was self-conscious, and didn't want to sound like a dummy when I attempted to speak. The first thing on my agenda was to learn English, and to learn it quickly. I resigned myself to attend public school, but the question was where?

My memories of the German schools and their military style of operation haunted me. I had flashbacks from the carpal punishments I received. The idea of going back to school didn't appeal to me, but submerging myself in English would be the best, and the fastest way to learn.

I discussed it with my parents, and they thought it would be best. I was fortunate; a junior high school not far from my home accepted me. One of our new friends took me to the school and arranged a meeting with the principal. Oh, God was I scared!

Age didn't seem to matter, even though I was a couple of years older than my peers. Fortunately, the school accepted me despite the age difference. Was I jumping from the pan into the fire? I could not understand one word of English. It was frightening. I realized it would present the biggest challenge of my life. The teachers would have to be patient with me.

The name of the school was Gove Junior High in Denver. It was close to my home, and an easy walk through the neighborhood. The first day in school was different alright. Not knowing what to expect, and not being able to talk to the teachers or the kids scared me to death. I planned on leaving the school and never returning. I was like a fish out of water, and literally gasping for air. Each class had about thirty kids. I was the center of attention. I didn't need this. I was shy to begin with;. It was a huge problem for me.

I was dressed in a suit and tie and carried my books in a briefcase which made me look like a typical nerd. The kids looked me up and down, and giggled. I looked for the closest exit door, but I stuck around, hoping things would improve. Looking around, I saw guys wearing blue jeans, t-shirts with sleeves turned up where they hid a cigarette pack. I liked the informality. The girls were cute in their petticoats and bobby socks, and meeting one, was an attractive thought.

I had a plan and put it into action the next school day. I intended to dress just like them, minus the cigarette pack. My objective was to show them a thing or two about being properly attired. That evening, I walked to Sears, bought a pair of blue jeans, cowboy denim shirts, and a pair of penny loafers.

I reasoned, if I dressed like them, they wouldn't even notice me. After all, this was cowboy country! Why not dress like one? The next day, I sat down at my desk and proceeded to listen to Mr. Barnes, but couldn't understand a word he was saying. I pretended to understand, but I didn't fool anyone!

Kids stared at me and laughed out loud. Were they complimenting me on my new outfit? Maybe so! I was at the end of my rope; I hid my anger, and at times, it drove me right up the wall. I wanted to know what they were saying. I figured, if I endured this, I could survive anything. I had one more bridge to cross.

Mr. Barnes was a great disciplinarian; kids didn't dare play games with him. When he became angry, he turned red in his face, and neck. I saw the arteries in his neck get bigger. Things were not going well for the students. I couldn't understand anything he said, but I had an inkling what was up.

One snowy morning as I walked to school, Mr. Barnes stopped and asked if I wanted a ride which I accepted with gladness. He was driving a 1956 Lincoln, the most beautiful car I had ever laid my eyes on. I liked it even better than the Cadillacs.

I thought that would be a fine car to own. If I worked hard, and saved my money, maybe I'd be able to buy one just like it. But for the time being, I set my sights a little lower. My wish was to get a car like the parents who dropped off their kids at school drove. I noticed many Fords, Chevrolets, a few Buicks and Cadillacs, but no foreign cars. They came later.

The third day, I noticed Mr. Barnes with a German / English dictionary lying on his desk. He went to great lengths to teach me words, but it was of no use.

In math class, the teacher got upset with one of the students. He slammed the kid against the wall. I had flashbacks from the German schools, seemingly a perfectly normal way to correct a misbehaving child. That was the way teachers handled it. Other than that, Mr. Holland was a great teacher. He took his time teaching me math. If it hadn't been for my language handicap, it would have produced results much quicker. I was never scared of him, and made sure, not to give him any reasons to get upset.

In German, the number one has a hook attached to the top, but in the United States, it's just a vertical line. He asked how I wrote the number eleven, and I drew him two vertical lines with a hook which made it appear as two sevens. Afterwards, he showed me the American way. We were both confused. In the meantime, I proceeded to work on my math problems. In Germany, we used different methods to work out problems, like multiplications, divisions and subtractions. Mr. Holland couldn't figure out how I arrived at the correct answers, but gave me a passing grade anyway.

To my amazement, I pulled a B. Math was not my strong point. In the past, math classes didn't excite me in the least. In his class, it made sense. It showed me, a good teacher made all the difference.

I needed all the help I could get with my English handicap. The school assigned Al, to help me, who spoke Yiddish, close to Low German. He was a short, thin kid, but bright. At last, I was able to communicate with someone. Since nobody else spoke German, he became my lifeboat.

I stuck to him like glue. He escorted me from one class to the next and took me to my locker. Once I learned the combination of the lock, I gained confidence, and became more independent. Soon, I navigated around the school on my own, but I still needed his help when talking to a teacher.

As time went on, things became easier. I started to grasp the English language. Each day, I studied late into the night until I fell asleep at the kitchen table. In the morning I discovered I had scribbled all over my papers.

I was sleeping and dreaming while doing my homework. From then on, I went to bed.

I was forever thankful for Al. The Junior High School was heavily Jewish, and me being German, it presented a problem. I had no knowledge of the holocaust. He told me of the horrible things that happened to the Jewish people. I admired him for staying with me. Any other Jewish boy would've run the other way. I was proud of him. Later, I learned he became a successful attorney.

The German schools, never talked about it, and it wasn't in any of the books. I was shocked when I heard about these things. This could not be, "My countrymen couldn't have committed such a hideous crime." No, this couldn't be true! I raced home and asked my parents about it, and their reply was, "Sadly it was." I was ashamed of my nationality! How could this have ever happened?

Now I understood why some Jews didn't want to have anything to do with me. One Jewish kid wanted to fight me, and I never knew why! This was heartbreaking! I wanted so much to be friends with him, but there was a divide I couldn't conquer.

It almost took a year for the school to grade me; the teachers were wonderful and patient. I worked hard, trying to fit in, and not be the odd ball.

In Germany, I was the class clown and I paid dearly for it. Why should that change in America? I became very frustrated, which got me into trouble. One day, I got carried away. I made a paper plane, and I let it glide through the classroom.

Did I ever get into trouble! The teacher screamed at me, and her face turned a bright red. I couldn't understand a word she said and I could well imagine what came out of her mouth, and it wasn't complimentary. She may, or may not have known I couldn't understand her. It was frustrating for both.

In gym, I played American sports like baseball, football and basketball, but the problem was I had no idea what these games were about. I couldn't figure out why one would want to hit a little ball with the big stick, throw a ball into a basket, and chase a guy with a weird shaped ball under his arm.

I was good size, and the kids thought I would be an asset when they included me playing football; A big mistake! I didn't know what direction to run when I was handed the ball. I ended up running the opposite way, and everybody hollered at me. I was ready for the nut house. When I came home from school that day, I told Mama, I will never, ever go back.

Mama had other ideas, and sent me back the next day to face the same music. She always told me, never give up. There were no problems in life, only challenges. It was one big challenge; more than I bargained for.

When playing baseball, it was confusing, never knowing when to come back to the dugout or go back out into the field. They placed me in the outfield. I was so bored that it almost put me to sleep. They couldn't have placed me anywhere else. I didn't have a clue what was going on, and how the game was played. When a ball came my way, I couldn't catch it, and if I was lucky enough to grab it, I didn't know what to do with it.

I tried basketball, but I didn't like that either. For one thing, I was way too short, and the game was played too fast for me to keep up. It was a disaster playing any of the American sports. As far as sports were concerned, I liked wrestling best. I didn't have to be fluent in English, and could do my own thing as long as I pinned my opponent. I was pretty good at this event, and enjoyed it. One day during practice, a big guy fell on my head with all his weight and I thought I was going to die. It hurt so much!

I survived the episode, but my ear was black and blue for the longest time. I believe it is referred to as a cauliflower ear. I did well in wrestling and won a few matches. My opponents told me they couldn't get a hold of me because of my slippery skin and speed. I had something going for a change. I worked out each day, running up and down the stairs many times to condition my legs. I rode my bike many miles each day which helped me to get into shape.

I went out for track, it was tough, until I got used to the high altitude.

One day, we ran around the oval track, and to my surprise, I performed better than I could have imagined. I developed a big lead, but I had a big problem: I couldn't ask anybody how far I had to run, and where the finish line was.

I stopped somewhere during the race, and asked the coach, *"Where to stop."* I was getting tired, and it would have been nice to know when and where the race was going to end. Lucky me, at this particular juncture, I had almost reached the finish line. The coach pointed to the finish line, and by a miracle I still came in first.

Things weren't going well with Mama and Papa. Mama and Papa never argued much. Papa would give into her ninety percent of the time and for good reasons. That afternoon, Papa had had his fill with her.

He walked outside of the house and made sure the windows were wide open. This was preplanned. Not taking any chances, he was outside of the house; in case Mama threw something at him then he'd be able to duck. With a loud voice he cussed her out, and called her names I had never heard him use before.

I was shocked. It was a good thing it was in German. That way, the neighbors didn't know they weren't having a friendly argument. When he came back into the house, the atmosphere was tense. She didn't throw him out, but made him sleep in a different room from then on. He paid dearly for his bravery. I believe there was more to the story than I knew.

Had I come to the United States by myself, I would have gone back to Germany. Learning the language was tough but in retrospect it was well worth it. I am very happy living in the U.S. and I am forever grateful to have had the privilege to share my life with so many wonderful people.

Oh, if only I would have had a personal interpreter. We had a couple of Korean boys come to school and they didn't know English, and they were confronted with the same problems. Their challenge was much greater than mine since the Korean language is much different. English is a Germanic language, and many words are similar.

Pretty girls were all around, but I couldn't talk to them, it was maddening. Apparently a girl had a crush on me. She handed me a card, inviting me to something. I tried to make out what it said, but I couldn't. I summoned a friend to explain to me what the letter was all about. It was for the eighth grade graduation, and she wanted me to be her date, and dance partner at the prom. I was much honored that she chose me. It was a memorable occasion alright. I was too scared to go by myself, so I asked my sister to come along. Big mistake!

Mary's parents came to our home to pick me up. She probably thought it was strange to have my sister come along. After we arrived at the ballroom, we were each handed a glass with Coke. I was sitting next to Mary when I accidentally spilled my glass of Coke on her beautiful formal dress. That changed the whole tempo for the evening. I felt terribly bad. I could have crawled into a corner and stayed there all night.

I ended up dancing with my sister the rest of the night, and what fun was that! On our way home, nobody talked. Mary seemed to ignore me and it felt like an eternity until we arrived at our home. We were fortunate she offered us a ride home after the prom. By the way, the girl never gave me the time of day after that incident. Had I only not been so clumsy.

I worked almost fulltime and going to school. It was a bit much and it didn't help me academically, but I had money to spend. I should have saved what I earned, instead of blowing it on other things, like my new, used car.

I never had anybody to counsel me on finances nor a male mentor to guide me. I probably wouldn't have made so many mistakes. I thought I knew everything like many teenagers. It took a few more years to figure out I wasn't all that smart.

In the fall, I was transferred to East High to start 10th grade. While attending school, I worked fulltime at the local Pizza Oven, washing dishes. I did my best, and made the plates and silver wear sparkle like champagne glasses. The English language was not a problem

The manager told me, I was the fastest dishwasher they ever had, and offered me a raise to sixty cents an hour from fifty-five. I don't know what I was thinking, but I told him I didn't deserve the raise. I had not yet reached perfection.

My boss's name was Sam, and he was stunned at my comment. Nobody ever rejected a raise. It was a first for him and me. I was raised humble, and never made demands. In Germany, I earned very little, and what I was earning now was unbelievable. I was rolling in the dough. Who needs a raise! From that moment forward, I never refused a raise.

A week later, Sam handed me my check, it reflected the increase, which made me happy. Before I got the job at the Pizza Oven, I bought a new bike, and that way, I avoided the stops going through town with the bus.

The Raleigh bike had eight speeds and cut through the air like a dove. In anticipation of getting the bike, I was so excited, I couldn't sleep. I dreamed about the bike, it was like falling in love. I saved enough money to pay cash for it, and that made it even more special.

After washing dishes a few months, I was promoted to place toppings on pizza. I was fast, and did a good job I suppose. I liked the job, but whenever somebody ordered anchovy topping, it almost made me throw up. Picking up the little slimy, stinky fish was sickening.

Six months went by, and I was promoted to run the ovens and cut the pizza on the bench with a big knife. I developed a rhythm; it was music to my ears. I wish they had paid me by piece work because I was fast. I was on top of the ladder, and couldn't go any higher unless I became the manager, but that position was locked up by Sam, the boss.

While employed at the Pizza Oven, the guys played tricks on me. They asked me to tell the girls naughty things. That only worked for a short while until I figured out what they were up to. I was thankful the girls didn't slap me. Working there had its benefits. Whenever customers failed to pick up their order, I got to take the pizzas home.

My family ate pizza almost everyday, but after a while, they got sick of the fare and I ended up giving them away to our neighbors. The Pizza Oven went by the way of the S.S. America. The building was torn down when the city widened the road.

Mr. Vollmer, a German, owned a number of bakeries in town. I visited him, and asked him if I couldn't work for him. I was shocked; he hired me on the spot. I started the next day working from midnight until eight in the morning.

I was baking all kinds of breads, pastries and cookies of all types. I enjoyed the job and it paid me more than the Pizza Oven. I worked with a bunch of great guys who knew how much I enjoyed having coffee during the night. Without fail, coffee was waiting for me when I got there. It was a great way to start my shift with full steam ahead.

For breakfast, I ate a whole loaf of bread, straight out of the oven. It was delicious. I worked many hours, and it didn't leave me time for anything else. I came to the realization, money wasn't everything. To top it off, it was difficult for me to stay awake in class.

After I had gone to East High for a year, I was transferred to George

Washington High, a brand new school. On my first day, I was greeted with a Swastika painted on the front door. Was it meant for me? Could it have been a coincidence? I didn't know what to make of it, but I felt uneasy about this event. I tried to ignore it but it brought back memories of the past which I would have rather forgotten. I didn't tell Mama and Papa of the incident, afraid it would have revived the horrible events of the past.

I loved the new school, which still had the smell of fresh paint, and the walls were without marks. It had an Olympic size swimming pool, where I spent lots of my time. In the dead of winter, the pool was marvelous. Through the giant glass windows, I observed the snow on the ground while I was swimming in a heated pool. That was the life. You would find me in the pool most afternoons.

I counted it as a privilege to attend a school that was rated tops academically. The library was fantastic, stocked with just about any book of my choosing, one of which was 'For Whom the Bells Toll'. It was the first book I read in English and was actually able to understand what I was reading.

During the summer, I visited the local pool, not far from home. I loved going there to develop a tan, but it wasn't without pain. First, I burned to a crisp, later on, my skin turned nice and brown. The pool wasn't heated like at school. The nights were cool and this caused the pool to be frosty in the morning.

When I stepped into the pool, it was so cold, it almost stopped my heart. To avoid the shock, jumping in was the best way to overcome the shock. That way, my entire body became numb. The pool was equipped with a diving board, and I loved it. I prayed I wouldn't land on my belly. I was never a fancy diver, but just diving into the water head first was a success.

School started in the fall, the studies became easier, and things were finally falling into place. I made friends who contributed to my contentment. I worked hard, and by the time I reached twelfth grade, I had enough credits to graduate.

I had all the difficult classes behind me which allowed me to enroll in classes like art, choir, wood shop and German. Twelfth grade was a breeze, and I enjoyed life to the fullest. Outside of school, I still had a heavy work load, and finding free time for recreation was a challenge.

Living with Mama and Papa wasn't without stress. Mama for some reason wasn't happy about me living with them and I understood that. To help out a little I offered to assist them with money, but it was mostly a free ride. Papa had enough income to support a household. By the time the bills were paid, there wasn't much left.

Riding my bike to school on a fair day was enjoyable, however when it was cold and rainy, it wasn't so much fun. I wore my raincoat, and covered my books so that nothing got wet. The tough part was that my hands froze in the winter. I don't know why I didn't wear gloves; it would have taken care of some of the problem. I wanted my hands and fingers free just in case I needed to get something out of my saddle bag, mounted on both sides of my bike.

When it was cold and snowy, even wearing gloves didn't ward off the cold on my fingers. It was not recommended riding a bike on ice. One morning as I was riding my bike to school, the bicycle chains froze. I ended up pushing the bike, slipping and sliding all the way. I was ecstatic, when kids from school saw my plight, and gave me a lift. I never forgot their act of kindness.

By the time I arrived at school, not surprisingly, my bike was the only one in the huge snow covered parking lot. By the time the school ended, the snow was up to the chain. I dusted the snow off the seat, made sure the chain wasn't frozen, and I very carefully rode the bike home.

People thought I was crazy taking chances like that, exposing myself to all kinds of danger. Everywhere I went, I rode my bike, including to the Heidelberg restaurant where I worked as a bus boy.

The summer ended way too soon. I was back in school at George Washington High in Denver, Colorado. The second year, one of my choice classes was wood shop. It allowed me to make all kinds of furniture. I was very happy that the class was still available. The first day, when I stepped into the shop, I was greeted with machines humming, hammers pounding, and getting instructions from the shop teacher. I couldn't wait to get going, but what was I going to build? The teacher said I could build anything, as long as it fits through the door.

I was searching for an item I could make. The teacher gave me a book with lots of furniture pieces I could build. Out of so many, I couldn't make up my mind. Everybody built bird houses, lamps, and many other things. I decided to build a cedar chest. Ask me why? I didn't know, but it seemed like a challenge.

It took me the whole semester to finish it. At the start, it looked like I was building a coffin. Guys teased me, "Who is going to be buried in your casket?" I replied, "If you don't lay off of me, it might be you." I learned to work with various woodworking tools, and thank God, I never hurt myself on the band saw or any of the other tools.

I couldn't wait for the class to begin. The smell of the wood, and the sound of the machines, got me into the mood. I cut out the pieces, and made sure I had the proper sizes. I glued the side boards, the cedar bottom and with the help of clamps, I was able to construct a well built cedar chest. I cut the trim for the lid and bottom, glued them into place, and the next day, everything was dry. I used fine sandpaper to give it a smooth finish, and followed it up with a coat of varnish. The project was completed before the semester ended, and I was delighted to receive an A. I was relieved that the cedar chest fit through the shop door, just barely.

I was proud of what I had accomplished. Mama and Papa thought I did an okay job and placed the chest in the family room. A friend of mine had a pick-up and hauled it to my home. It almost looked like a TV set with the doors shut. I still have the chest in our guest room.

After school, I had to be at work at five in the afternoon at the German restaurant *Heidelberg*. I rode my bike clear across town and I had better be on time. I finished up around midnight after lifting the chairs on top of the tables in order to mop the floor. I worked there as a bus boy, which required me to clean tables and take the dirty dishes into the kitchen. It was an okay job, but I kept my eyes open for something more challenging and better pay.

I wasn't afraid to ride my bike home in the middle of the night. We had little crime and I wasn't afraid.

When I wasn't on my way to work, or school, I rode through the country with my trusty Raleigh. It was special. I felt the morning breeze brush my hair, the birds singing, and I relished the beautiful flowers in bloom. I wrapped myself in the delightful fragrance of the colorful wild flowers by the side of the road.

Riding my bike was by far the most pleasant way to travel. I didn't need gas, not much maintenance, just a couple of strong legs and healthy lungs. Another benefit was, I got plenty of exercise, but at the same time, I received a bruising when I mixed it up with traffic. Riding my bike was getting a little dangerous. I had a few close calls. That's when I decided to save money to buy a car. If I kept riding the bike, it was just a matter of time until I got into a serious accident.

It didn't take long! I was involved in a collision that could have been fatal. All told, I had three accidents, and one almost killed me when I ran a red light.

At midnight, after I was done working, I rode my bike home from the Heidelberg restaurant. It was a hard day at work and I was tired. I looked down for only a second. I ran a red light and drove into a pick-up at full speed. The estimated speed of the truck was 35 mph. I bounced off of the hood of the truck, and was hurled fifteen feet through thin air onto the concrete sidewalk, missing a row of trees along the way.

> I bounced off of the hood of the truck, and hurled fifteen feet through thin air.

I landed on my feet in an upright position. Had I hit one of the trees, or the concrete sidewalk with my head, I wouldn't be here today. The good Lord was with me that night. I was in shock! Pain was shooting up and down my spine. I was worried about my injuries when

I felt my blood-soaked shirt. I had skinned my back, and could barely stand up.

The driver of the pick-up walked up to me, and to his surprise, saw me standing up and breathing. He apologized for hitting me and said, "I don't like to hit boys on bicycles." That is all I could understand him say as he continued talking to me. I could tell he felt very bad for me, but happy that I wasn't 'seriously' injured. It wasn't long. I heard sirens blaring and red lights flashing and elated that a police officer was coming to my aid. I couldn't understand what the officer told me as he surveyed the accident scene. After the police officer took the truck driver's statement, the truck driver was on his way. It wasn't his fault. I ran the red light.

I wanted to notify my parents. Searching for a phone at midnight wasn't a small feat. Nobody carried a phone, not even the cops. The shock was wearing off and the pain in my back was unbearable. I couldn't see the severity of the injury, but I saw blood dripping down my pants. I had to call my parents. I walked to a house not far from the intersection, knocked on the door, and an elderly gentleman opened the door.

I spoke very little English, and was unable to tell him what had just happened. The old man had no clue why I went knocking on his door at midnight. I said telephone please, and the gentleman directed me to the phone in the corner of the kitchen. With all the excitement, I had difficulty remembering my phone number. It finally came to me and I started dialing on the rotary phone.

Mama answered, and I told her that I had been in an accident with my bicycle. She didn't ask me how I was, or how badly I was injured, and wasn't overly concerned how I would get home. She reasoned I got myself into this mess, and I had better figure out how to get myself out of it. While I was talking to Mama, the elderly gentleman sat on an old wooden chair close by, and told me to speak English. I told him the best I knew how, I could not speak English and neither could my parents.

He told me again to speak English, and repeated it over and over. My reply remained the same. I couldn't speak English I told him. I was German and just immigrated to the United States. He became even more agitated at this stage. I was gripped with angst as I saw him point a big gun at my head. He held the gun with both hands and his twitching finger on the trigger. I was praying, "Dear God help me, please get me out of this mess." I survived a wreck, and now this was happening. I didn't want to die.

I was terrified, hung up the phone and ran towards the front door. All the while, the old man followed me, still pointing the gun at my back. I scrambled from the kitchen, through the hallway and literally flew out of the house and down the steps to the sidewalk. I had to get out of this situation fast.

At this point, the pain had subsided somewhat, but I was fearing for my life. I returned to the scene of the accident; the cops placed my bike into their trunk, ready to take me home. I was shocked, the bike was in fairly good shape, and with a little TLC I'd be able to ride it again.

The pain returned. I shook uncontrollably now. I heard my teeth rattle. The police officers took me home without going to the hospital for a checkup. They may have offered to take me, but I couldn't understand what they were saying. The officers didn't know the extent of my injuries. They couldn't see my torn up back which was covered with my blood soaked shirt.

It was a short ride home and Papa was anxiously waiting for me at the door, glad to see me in one piece. I peeled off my shirt, causing me excruciating pain. The blood dried and the shirt clung to my back. My throbbing pain felt like a thousand arrows were imbedded in my back. Mama comforted me by saying nonchalantly, if I survive the night, I will be okay in the morning. I was worried. I said to her: *das macht mich aber froh,* "Oh, that makes me feel terrific." Angst gripped me, afraid I would not wake up in the morning due to possible internal injuries.

In case I succumbed, my sister Helga laid next to me. I eventually fell asleep and thank God I woke up the next morning. I rejoiced to still be alive. It took four to five weeks for me to get back to my normal self. Pain took me captive, but ignored the problem. I had to get back on my bike.

In another instance, on the way home from school, a lady cut in front of me with her car, making a left turn which caused me to be thrown into the ditch. I received minor scratches, and my bike survived yet another accident.

One night, riding home from work, a drunk driver heading the wrong way at low speed, hit me head on. It threw me off my bike and I ended up on the shoulder of the road. What a miracle, I walked away with a few scratches. One thing is for sure, my guardian angel was working overtime.

Locating a car was on the top of my list. I loved riding my bike, but this had to end, I couldn't take another skirmish. I began searching for a car and there weren't many I didn't like. All I expected out of a car was to get me to work, and occasionally drive into the Rockies to go skiing. I didn't care what the car looked like, as long as it got me around. Due to my budget constraints, I gave up on the Lincolns and Cadillacs. I knew next to nothing about mechanical things.

I was even less informed about the various makes, and models. The size of motors didn't matter. The gas was very inexpensive, cheaper than a cup of coffee. Without having any knowledge of motors, any car would have been okay. My sister Helga bought a new, blue, DKW from Germany, oh, what a poor excuse for a car. Hopefully, I wouldn't end up like she did. The car looked beautiful, but it was a dog, it howled going down a road.

Checking the newspaper ads, one caught my eye. A 1952 Buick Dynaflow for $220. I worked like crazy, and saved every penny, enough to buy the car. I had $300 in the bank. I couldn't get my mind off of the car. I called the seller and made an appointment to look the car over. I rode my bike to the seller's address which wasn't far from home. I saw the car in his drive-way and fell in love with it. It was love at first sight. The car appeared to have been well maintained. It had a huge V8 engine, plenty of power, and then some. Cash in hand, I paid the seller the agreed upon price, and he drove me home.. The seller placed my bike in the trunk and gave me a ride home. Not far behind us was his wife driving the Buick I had just purchased.

The possibilities were immense where I might travel with this limousine. I dreamed of going skiing in Winter Park or Arapaho Basin for a start. For that to happen, the car had to be the best looking vehicle in our neighborhood! The first thing I did was, wash and wax the car, not that it was dirty. She was now ready for the highway, but I wasn't.

I overlooked one very important part of this American dream. In order for me to drive legally, I had to get a driver's license. I couldn't drive the beast, and knew no one could show me how to operate the car. I was frustrated. To gain a little practice, I drove the car back and forth in our driveway. That would hardly qualify me as an experienced driver.

Our neighbors probably thought there was something wrong with me when they observed me driving back and forth on a one-hundred foot concrete drive-way. They probably thought I was afraid to drive on the street, or I had some kind of phobia. I was itching to leave our home and drive this jewel all over Denver and beyond, but I couldn't.

My friend Art, volunteered his mother to go with me to get my license, and I am sure she was rather nervous about the whole experience. My driving left something to be desired, and with luck, we made it to the DMV office. I was handed a small book, reading the questions very carefully, just to make sure I passed the test.

Oh, what a pleasant surprise. They told me I aced the test. My heart jumped for joy, but was I ready for the driving test? Now came the hard part! This was where the rubber met the road. I was nervous! The instructor slid into my car, a calm man. I acted with confidence! After all, I drove around a thousand feet on concrete. I let the instructor know I knew my stuff as I slid into the driver seat with confidence. We proceeded to drive out of the parking lot, when he asked me to drive through a residential neighborhood. I was relieved he didn't ask me to drive onto the freeway.

The instructor knew I wasn't ready for freeway traffic yet, as a matter of fact, I was not ready for any kind of driving. I felt deflated! I failed to come to a complete stop at the appropriate distance in relationship of the intersection when I approached the stop sign.

He asked me to Parallel Park. What a disaster. The car was the size of a tank, and it would have been a challenge for any driver to park the monster between two cars. I failed to accomplish the task, but with luck, I didn't damage any cars. Now this calm, cool instructor wasn't calm and cool any longer. He asked me to drive him back to the DMV parking lot. He kept rubbing his hands, scratching his face and the color of his face rose to a morbid white color.

He figured the best way for him to stay alive was to take the quickest route back to the DMV office. Needless to say, I flunked the driving test, and that bruised my ego big time. I was ashamed to come home and tell Mama that I didn't make it. She must have had a premonition when she told me, I wouldn't pass the test.

My next door neighbor's granddaughter came on a visit from Missouri, and I wanted to get to know her. I knew she had a driver's license, and besides, spending time with her might be fun. I walked over to my neighbor's house and introduced myself to her. She was a nice girl and I was certain she was qualified to teach me to drive.

I asked her if she wouldn't mind teaching me a thing or two about driving my car. She replied with an affirmative yes, and told me she would be delighted. The same afternoon, she suggested, "Why don't we take a little drive out of town and I will teach you to drive." We were driving east to a secluded part of town. She knew it might be best to avoid heavy traffic to begin with. I told her I needed some traffic, but this road has none. I reckoned she had something else in mind other than teaching me to drive.

My mind was on driving, and I didn't volunteer for anything else. What she wanted could wait until we got back into town. She cut the training short, and we drove back to her grandma's home. She said goodbye and I never saw her again. I couldn't believe it. She could have said, "It would be nice to get together again", but it didn't happen. In one hour's time, a potential relationship went down the drain. All was not lost, however. The second time at the DMV, my driving was a success. Yes, I received my license at last.

Now that I learned to drive, I was looking for a different job. Night work was getting to me. I searched for a job in the Rocky Mountain News and ran across an ad which stated someone was looking for a young man to help in a lumberyard. I called the number listed, and lined up an interview.

I had no idea the job entailed driving a huge Mack truck. I met the foreman; we chatted a little, and walked over to the truck. He asked me to get into the cab and back-up. I climbed into the truck and attempted to back up to hook it to a trailer.

I had a big problem, how do I drive a stick shift? I had no experience. My car was equipped with an automatic transmission, and I was not at all prepared to drive a semi. When I shifted the truck into one of ten gears, the vehicle died every time, and lurched like an angry Brahma bull.

Needless to say, I didn't get off of first base. He told me it would be best if I looked for work someplace else and escorted me out of the yard. He wished me the best of luck. I couldn't help but notice the foreman scratching his head. He couldn't understand why I didn't know anything about trucks.

My dad was a pathologist, not a truck driver. Coming to find out, when I took the written test, it was for commercial trucks. It was very strange that I wasn't required to drive a truck during my test at the DMV.

When I took the test, I remembered it dealt with things like running lights and other truck terms. I was puzzled. I thought it was standard procedure; everybody had to be knowledgeable about trucks.

My car served me well and got me wherever I wanted to go. I continued to ride my bike whenever I had an empty tank and wallet. The Buick got 10 miles to a gallon on a good day, but mileage was not a great concern, the gas was only 18 to 20 cents a gallon. Keeping my job was a must, and to pay for this baby, I'd have to find a second job. I *was* responsible for the insurance, gas, and maintenance.

32

THE STORY OF A GERMAN SOLDIER

I belonged to the German Edelweiss Club in Denver, where I'd go dancing on weekends. It was fun getting together with other Germans and talking about the past. I had a marvelous time, although my dancing needed much improvement.

My sister and I were sitting at a table by the window and sipping on our drinks, when we noticed a gentleman walking by us and taking a seat two tables down from us. He wasn't a bad looking guy; I figured he was probably German. My sister pretended she didn't notice him, but I knew better. He was around six feet tall, with blond hair and a square face.

My sister Helga didn't mind keeping me company. Was she watching out for me? She always thought of me as her little brother. I didn't need to be chaperoned any more. The last time, it turned out to be a disaster. Another reason she came along was she might find her prince charming.

I paid for the gas, but drinks were on her. In a way, I wished I hadn't brought her along. I had the desire to get acquainted with young ladies sitting by themselves on the next table. Something went wrong. I ended up dancing with Helga all night. I stepped on her toes and caused her pain throughout the evening. The following Monday she went to see the doctor and discovered no bones were broken. That was the last time she accompanied me.

The gentleman we noticed earlier came over to our table and he introduced himself as Siegfried. Helga was glad to have someone else to talk to. We discovered, he was one of the very few German soldiers who escaped Stalingrad. I was intrigued and decided to meet again the following week. He promised me he would tell me of his escape fro Stalingrad.

It was on a Saturday, a week later, when we met up again at the Edelweiss Club. This time, I bought him a dark beer, just the way I like mine. He loosened up after a couple of beers and began to tell me about his war experience. Every word that came out of his mouth was carefully selected. He didn't want to frighten me I suppose. He wasn't happy to talk about his experiences and would have rather not recall the hellish time.

He was very fortunate to be alive and didn't understand why God spared him. Hitler ordered his generals to attack Stalingrad, *Volgagrad* today. The generals advised Hitler, such a move was a strategic error; it would give the Russians the upper hand.

Stalingrad was the turning point of the war. The Russians obliterated the German defenses one by one. The gentleman's name was Siegfried Schulz and fought in the infantry. He knew things didn't go well for Germany. At the start of WWII the Russians couldn't stop the Germans who were better equipped and conquered town after town.

The battle for Stalingrad took place August the 23rd of 1942 and lasted until February the 2nd of 1943. The Red Army had no choice but to counter attack. It was now a matter of survival for the Russian people. Massive amounts of troops and military vehicles were moved to the outskirts of town. It was reported, hundreds of thousands of troops and tanks gathered to attack the Germans. The Red Army assembled their forces in November 1942, and attacked in mass, cutting off the German supply lines. The Germans ran out of food and water, and slowly succumbed to the severe cold and hunger.

> Siegfried Schulz related to me, they ate the corpses of their comrades. They ate the bark off the trees and ate the shoe leather after they cooked it.

Siegfried Schulz related to me they ate the corpses of their dead comrades. For water, they drank their urine. They ate the bark off the trees and ate shoe leather after they cooked it.

The Germans lost hundreds of thousands during this campaign, and most, if not all died a horrible death. Siegfried escaped the Russians while they were loading the German prisoners onto trucks to transport them to the interior of Russia. He slipped away unnoticed during the dark of night and fought his way out of town with a Kalashnikov rifle he obtained from a dead Russian.

He had to get rid of his German uniform quickly, or his escape would be short lived. He only moved at night, and commandeered a number of Russian vehicles for his escape to Germany. He fired his rifle and shot a Russian soldier who was guarding the perimeter of the war camp. The Russian succumbed to his injuries, and Siegfried changed into the Russian uniform to conceal his identity. Food was difficult to find in the dead of winter. To find nutrition, he accessed homes while the people had gone to work on their farm equipment, getting it ready for the spring. He lived off of wild game at times whenever he could. The fields were covered with deep snow, and there was nothing but frozen ground. If he was lucky, he settled for a wild rabbit as it hopped across the empty tundra looking for blades of grass.

He had been walking for many miles in the subzero temperature. With the lack of nutrition, and warmth, he had to find transportation. It was early in the morning when he saw a Russian military truck a ways off. As he approached the vehicle, crouched into the ditch and remained there while moving slowly towards his target, the truck. He was now in a stealth mode as he closed in. He learned this strategy at the German *Barrass*, 'Boot Camp'.

It was an eighteen wheeler, belching smoke which turned the surrounding snow black. The Russian was hauling a long four axle trailer. Siegfried needed transportation to travel closer to the German border and the truck would provide his needs. A Russian soldier climbed out of the truck to smoke. Siegfried noticed he left his rifle in the cab and if he moved quickly, he might be able to subdue the driver. Siegfried was carrying his Russian rifle with sufficient ammunition to carry out the task.

It was now or never as he readied himself to get a good shot at the man. With one shot, the Russian fell mortally wounded into the white snow. Siegfried inched towards him with caution, making sure he was dead. After checking his pulse, he was certain the Russian had indeed expired.

He felt terrible at what he just did. He murdered an innocent man who wanted nothing more than to get to his destination and return to his family.

But now was not the time to get emotional, he had a job to do. Siegfried moved the body to the side of the road and covered the soldier in deep snow. There was not a trace of him. He was now deep in his frozen, white grave.

Siegfried moved with speed as he climbed into the truck, checking the gauges to make sure he had enough fuel to drive at least a hundred kilometers down the road. The German was in a precarious situation, knowing the Russians would be looking for him soon. There were no portable radios in those days, and no one could have known what transpired unless they located the dead Russian.

Siegfried was curious as to the contents of the trailer. He found a key to open the back and was shocked at what he saw. It was a car carrier, with cargo of at least five or six army staff cars inside the trailer. Siegfried closed the doors, jumped into the cab and drove off. He felt the constant crunch of ice and snow under the wheels of the truck as he drove on the lonely, snow covered highway.

There was little traffic coming from the opposite direction. The German monitored the highway traffic constantly, afraid he might be followed. He was checking the mirrors and erred on the side of caution. Now would not be the time slide off the road and lose the load. He held steady, traveling one hundred kilometers per hour which may have been a little too fast. He was nervous and knew the Soviets would be on his tail soon. One of the problems, the military truck could easily be spotted.

After traveling a couple of hundred kilometers, he pulled off the road, making sure he wasn't noticed by anyone. There was no traffic now. Siegfried walked to the back of the trailer, opened it, and checked the vehicles. Siegfried resembled a Soviet soldier with his Russian uniform. There was no reason for anyone to be suspicious. The cars were on a rack inside the trailer, and all he would have to do is drive the closest to the back door of the trailer and drive off. He checked the gas gauges and was happy to notice the car had plenty of gas to drive a couple of hundred kilometers.

He inserted the key into the ignition. The car purred like a kitten. After he drove off, he locked the doors of the trailer so as to not alert anyone. It was now midnight. The Soviet staff car would use much less fuel than the big truck, and would get him closer to his target, the German border. He had the headlights, a warm car and plenty of gas. With the adrenalin flowing, he was driving faster than it was safe. It started to snow and the highway began to accumulate several inches of snow. He had no snow chains and if the snow kept piling up, he would be stranded.

With apprehension, Siegfried made the decision to park the car by the highway and disappear into the thick woods nearby. It had now been at least ten hours since he commandeered the truck and no doubt, the Russians were on his trail. To distract his pursuers, he walked backwards into the woods making it appear as if someone walked out of the area instead of into the forest. The snow was about a foot deep and it made it difficult.

The forest would be his ally for the time being until he found a way to move on foot to the next town. Russia's immense distances made it impossible to cover the country on foot in the winter months. For the time being, he found a place under thick pine trees which provided concealment. He had nothing but the clothes on his back and the boots on his feet. He collected dry branches and began making a fire with the dry matches he had in his pocket.

He remained the entire night at the location. It was hard to sleep as he heard the howling of wolves and other strange sounds. He knew that if he stayed at this location long, the wolves would find his hideout due to their excellent hearing and keen noses.

With absolute horror he saw lights in the distance penetrating the thick forest. The deafening sounds of motorcycles reached his ears. This could not be, not now. Siegfried at once rushed to extinguish the fire he built earlier.

He piled mounds of snow on the flames until it snuffed out the fire. Close by, he found a snowdrift which might hide him from his pursuers. Searchlights lit up the night as trucks and other military vehicles drove past his place of concealment. He dodged another bullet. The search party never discovered him and kept going in a easterly direction.

The morning couldn't have come early enough. With no fire to keep him warm, his body was stiff from the arctic conditions. He rubbed his thighs to increase blood flow and got up to shake the snow off of his uniform. The military training prepared him for times like this, but nothing prepared him for the hunger pains.

He had no idea if there was a town nearby where he could grab a bite to eat. His Russian would have given him away had he asked for food. He knew a few words, but to form a complete sentence would have been a stretch.

The morning was beautiful with no clouds, and the sun warmed his back as he continued his journey. He labored as he walked, and it was difficult to lift his feet each time he took a step. Siegfried couldn't believe his eyes at the sight of a train. As he came closer, people got on and off. If he attempted to board the train, his appearance would not have caused any suspicion. His attire was like any other Russian soldier.

The train was about to roll out of the station with black smoke rising from the engine as it gained speed. Siegfried ran, and just in time, he jumped onto the platform of the last car, hanging on for dear life. This was no small feat in the condition he was in. If he crouched in the corner, thinking he'd be safe and no one would notice him. The conductor did come through and just nodded as he passed by. He dodged another bullet. For the time being, he was safe. His hunger pains became worse and worse and would have done anything for food, even at the chance of getting caught, which would have meant death.

After a two hour ride, the train pulled into a small town. Siegfried collected all his strength, got up and climbed off the car. Now what? People were going to and fro, paying no attention to him. How was he going to garner food? How long was the train going to stop? In the severe cold, with snow covering the street, he selected a spot where people would hopefully notice him as they walked by.

The few words he knew in Russian weren't going to help him much. He had to keep silent, or else it might reveal his identity. Siegfried reached out with his cold, frost bitten hands for food, but no luck. Would anyone help a deranged soldier, shell-shocked from the war? He mumbled to himself, as if mentally deranged, and continued to reach out to anyone who might toss him a morsel.

He looked like death warmed over, with frost bitten toes and hands. It was difficult to maintain his stance. At last, a Good Samaritan handed him a piece of sausage with a slice of rye bread. He held the food tight between his icy hands. He devoured the food with a couple of bites. What a blessing it was to have food in his stomach. He thanked God. He remained at the location until the train began to move. Just in time, another person offered him a roll with jam which he tucked under his coat just before he jumped back on the train.

Mile after mile, the train meandered through rolling hills and grain fields. With the clickity clack of the train it was difficult to sleep. The train came to a crawl after a long night he spent on the floor of one of the cars, hiding from the conductor. He gathered all the strength he had and jumped off the train after it came to a full stop. It was still dark when Siegfried decided to move on by foot.

The Soviets were probably closing in on him. Would they catch up to him before his escape to freedom? These thoughts shot through his mind and it began to take a toll. How much farther could it be as he walked for hours always listening for sounds and headlights of vehicles in the darkness? My God how much longer will I have to travel until I reach the border? Instinct of survival took over. The sun had just risen above the tree line and warmed his body, oh, it felt so good. With renewed hope, he moved westward. It had been a long time since the last bite of food. He drudged along at a slow pace and even with the warmer temperature, he began to fade. He had by now covered roughly ten kilometers when he entered the outskirts of another small town.

If he stayed healthy, he might make it to the border, if not he would be forever lost in a strange land where the days in the winter were short and the nights long and cold.

A long cold night, with only sounds of wild animals kept him company as he plowed through the deep snow. The last couple of hours he was way short of his intended goal of 10 kilometer. A small grocery store came into view. It was around seven in the morning with just a few people going about their business. He would have given anything for food. A truck was parked on the side of the road with the engine idling. It appeared the driver had just gone inside after he made a delivery. The opportunity presented itself to climb into the truck and drive off.

Siegfried had to make a fast decision. He looked left, he looked right, and with one swift move he climbed into the cab of the truck. It was warm and cozy inside and to his delight, he found a sandwich wrapped in newspaper lying on the seat providing him with sufficient energy to carry him through the day. He literally attacked the food and didn't linger as he devoured the ham and cheese sandwich while clinging to the big steering wheel. In case he needed more food, there was enough inventory to carry him through the rest of the journey.

The gas gauge indicated he had three quarter of a tank of fuel, probably enough to reach the border. He continuously checked the mirrors afraid the police were closing in on him. He had driven approximately two-hundred kilometers when he saw a sign written in Russian and Czech "One hundred kilometers to Prague."

If nothing unforeseen was going to happen, he would be at the border by early morning the next day. The last one hundred kilometers seemed to be the longest as he nervously screened the landscape. He reached the Czech border at approximately five o'clock in the morning. The Czech soldiers allowed him to proceed past their checkpoint, thinking he was making a food delivery.

Siegfried drove to the side of the road pretending he was checking his food supplies and where he was concealed, finding refuge behind a building. He proceeded to climb back into the truck and drove towards the checkpoint. The area was staffed with armed soldiers and several tanks. The darkness was his ally as he climbed out of the truck and crawled towards the fence. The area was lightly staffed and nobody noticed him. Poor lighting hid him during his daring escape attempt.

He scaled a ten foot fence and with one foot at a time he reached the top of the razor sharp barbed wire, extending along the entire length of the fence. He threw his heavy Russian army coat across the barbed wire. He suffered a small cut on his right thumb, but that couldn't keep him from climbing down the other side.

He drew the attention of Czech soldiers when they heard a loud thump on the west side of the fence. He jumped to freedom, but only after the soldiers fired short bursts with their Russian rifles, but by then, it was too late. A couple of bullets crazed his jacket. Oh, it was so close. He thanked God he wasn't injured or killed.

Siegfried immigrated to the United States shortly after the war and enlisted in the U.S. Air Force. The U.S. Air Force was his future and he made it a career.

The war was pure hell on both sides. The Russians suffered a combined total of 1,129,619 casualties recapturing Stalingrad. Many German soldiers died in captivity and the Russians eventually transported the remaining 91,000 German soldiers to their labor camps in Siberia. 40,000 Germans were buried in mass graves on the way to Siberia.

Only 5000 were released by the Russians when Chancellor Konrad Adenauer and Stalin reached an agreement to allow a few to go home.

After he revealed his war experiences, he bought me another round of beer. We talked a little longer, and discussed how fortunate we were living in the United States. Around midnight we got up from the table and headed for home, promising each other to meet again.

On the way home from the German club, I thanked God that Siegfried escaped the war and made it to the U.S. I am sorry to say, we never met up after our visit and I lost track of him while on active duty in the United States Navy.

33

THE SPLENDOR OF THE ROCKIES

In the late fifties, we never bothered locking the door although Mama and Papa had keys. Whenever I came home at my curfew time, I found Mama fast asleep in her rocker. She was waiting up for me, just to make sure I was safe. Curfew was still enforced, even at the age of twenty.

It was around Thanksgiving, when I came home late, and it was obvious I had a little too much to drink. Back then, the cops looked the other way unless you were involved in an accident. Many people drove drunk, and didn't realize how deadly it could have been. For whatever reason, a cop stopped me. Maybe I did a lousy job staying in my lane. He told me to leave my car by the curb, and gave me a lift home.

Another time, I came home past curfew. I thought I was in the clear after visiting friends. Time just flew, and I didn't realize it was so late. When I came home, the door was locked. I rang the door bell, but no one answered the door. I was left out in the cold.

It was end of October, or the beginning of November, the nights were cold. I had no blanket to cover up when I decided to climb into the back seat of my car to sleep, hoping it wouldn't be as cold. I was wrong. It was freezing cold, my teeth rattled, and my feet were cold to the touch.

I waited until the sun came up when I rang the door bell again. This time, Papa opened the door. It was a good thing, hypothermia was setting in. Papa and I had a special relationship. He could have allowed me to enter during the night, but was afraid to face Mama.

He felt bad and to ease my pain, he made me a delicious cup of hot chocolate to warm up my cold, stiff body. Mama hadn't got up as yet, and we made sure, we were out of the house before she got up.

On weekends, one of the places I went with Papa was the natural history museum in Denver. It was special seeing the beautiful animals displayed. After getting older, I went by myself. There were all types of animals from every part of the globe, and it was as if the animals were alive expecting them to move.

Whenever I visited, they had new displays of animals from all over the world. The museum was close to home, just a short walk. I made it a game, attempting to guess the animals' names, and where in the world they were from. It was cheap entertainment. I learned so much.

The Denver zoo was close to my home as well, and at the time, it rivaled the San Diego zoo, the best in the country. It was huge, and it took me hours to completely view the exhibits. I made sure to read all the information of each animal, remembering their names, and where they were found, much like I did at the museum.

Skiing in the Rockies was second to none. I enjoyed the times when I visited Winter Park. It had everything for the skiers. For the novice the slopes were easy to negotiate and for the expert were steep slopes, pushing the skiers to the limits. The runs were long, winding their way through thick forested areas. The trees were loaded with heavy snow, creating a winter wonder land. The lower branches touched the ground after a heavy snow fall. I found all kinds of animal tracks from squirrels to cougars.

I invited a foreign exchange student from Switzerland to accompany me skiing. It was wonderful speaking our mother tongue once again. She was an accomplished skier, better than I was. We had a great time, and had many things in common. We didn't live far apart in Europe, and shared the same culture.

After the school year, she went back to Switzerland. Had she not gone back, who knows what would have happened. I hated to see her leave, but we kept in touch via mail. As time went on, the writing stopped, and I didn't hear from her anymore.

Winter Park was a lovely place which had everything for a skier. All over the mountain, Austrian as well as Bavarian music resonated through the forests. It got me into the mood. It was the happiest place on earth.

There was a time when my school friends gave me a lift to Arapaho Basin. The ski area was for skiers looking for challenges. Did we ever have fun, schussing down the steep slopes at a great speed. It was dangerous and a foolish thing to do. The experience of a speed ride was exhilarating. The skis barely touched the ground as I schussed down the slope at speeds of sixty miles per hour. The trees were a blur, and my ears and nose turned into icicles.

My goggles fogged up, and I had a hard time seeing where I was going. I took them off, and before long, I became snow blind. All I could see now was a white blanket. I lost the topography of the slope it was an accident waiting to happen.

I failed to notice a sharp drop off that led down a cliff. Off the cliff I went, and ended up buried under a pile of the white stuff. It took me all afternoon to dig my way out of the trap. I regretted that the day was pretty much gone and by the time I was free, the ski lifts had stopped for the day. The important thing was that I wasn't injured.

Another time, I came half way down a slope, when I approached a ski jump. There wasn't much time to make my decision. Should I avoid the jump? It looked like it might be fun and unbeknownst to me; the jump was for ski acrobats, and not for a novice like me. I decided to go for it. Down the slope I went, preparing for the aerial flight. My heart was pumping, and I was ready for the thrill of my life. As I lifted off the ramp, it threw me straight up ten to fifteen feet into the air about, and on the way down, I landed on my back, instead on my skis. I could have broken my back, or landed on my face.

My friends had a good laugh. I made a fool out of myself. Here I was from Bavaria, and they expected me to be a top notch skier.

The love of skiing never left my system, no matter how old I became. I skied whenever I could, even when I worked all night long. Staying up all night, and skiing all day, was not a problem. I enjoyed the mountains so much and looked forward going back during summer vacation.

The following year, during summer break, my friend Art and I set out for Estes Park, a very picturesque spot in the Rockies, and to live and work there was a dream. To make this a reality, we had to search for jobs. Art found a part-time job working as a bus boy. I was still looking to get hired. In the middle of town, I spotted a bakery, walked into the store and asked for the owner. He met me in the store and asked me, "How can I help you?"

I told him in my heavy German accent, "I vant to get hired as a baker." He looked me up and down and asked how much I knew about baking. I said, "I vorked as a baker's apprentice in Germany." I guess he liked how I responded and said, "You can start work tomorrow morning at two o'clock." He was in baker's attire with flour on his apron and gray curly hair stuck out from under his cap. He didn't give me much time to think it over. With much enthusiasm, I said, "I vould be delighted to vork for you."

By this time, the money was running low, and I was very glad to have found a job to pay for my living expenses. I shared an apartment with another guy, but it was still expensive to live there. I wanted to come home every so often, but I didn't have the money for the bus ride. Mama and Papa never learned to drive, so I was on my own. It reinforced me to get a car and not rely on my friend Art's mom to haul me around.

I was so excited about the job; I forgot to ask the man how much I'd be paid. I found out the next day he was paying me $2.65 an hour. The pay wasn't the best, but it paid for my necessities. The downside was that I worked nights when most kids had fun gong to parties.

The job forced me to show up at work at around midnight. The first day, I walked into the shop, and the owner introduced me to the crew. Everybody shook my hand and my new boss didn't waste any time and showed me what my job entailed. I baked all types of breads, and pastries. I worked on the bench, another baker ran the ovens and still another mixed the dough.

I had been at that bakery for about two weeks, when one of the bakers gave me a hard time. I couldn't take it any longer. This harassment had to stop. I grabbed a big ball of dough and threw it in his face and walked out of the shop. I never looked back. It took me a long time to get worked up, but when I had my fill, I let him have it.

Some of my friends from school worked at the famous Stanley Hotel, and encouraged me to apply there for a job. I made a trip to the hotel to look the place over. The bakery was second to none. It had the finest equipment and everything was very clean. You could have eaten off of the floor.

I wasn't bashful, and asked to see the manager. The master baker came right away and interviewed me. He asked me about my background in the business. He asked me, "can you bake pastries and breads?' My reply was, "I vas a baker's apprentice in Germany and I learned to bake all types of breads, including pretzels." As far as pastries, I had very little experience. To my surprise, he hired me on the spot with a higher pay than the previous bakery.

Mike, the master baker, showed me around the shop and assured me he wouldn't cut me loose until I had full knowledge of my job. I started the next morning at around two o'clock. The first couple of days he showed me what the job entailed and observed my performance. After he was satisfied with what I did, he entrusted me with more responsibilities.

Working there was a joy, and I allowed me to work independently. He didn't have to hold my hand, and it freed him to do other things at the shop, like decorating cakes etc. It was a busy place, baking breads, pies and pastries by the dozen.

The hotel was world renowned and held a reputation as being the finest. Much was expected of me, which meant the pastries and the breads had to be the finest of quality, second to none. But as time went on, it turned out to be a stressful job.

Everything had to be perfect, making sure the rolls and other baked goods were flawless. I worked there until it was time to go back to school. All the people I met, and worked with, enriched my life and helped me to mature. It was great working at Estes Park with the beautiful mountain peaks in the background and the fresh mountain air. To work there, was a pleasure, but the thing I regretted was, I wasn't on vacation to enjoy the Park. Other folks were having a great time, going horseback riding, hiking or just enjoying the scenery.

After my experience in the Rockies, I went back to High School. One day, a Navy Recruiter enticed us to join the Navy. It didn't take much persuasion. I had already made up my mind of joining the Navy. He showed us slides and of course only depicted exciting scenes, working on a carrier and being a pilot.

I didn't set my sights that high! I wanted to join and travel the world, and I wasn't particular what kind of work I would be doing aboard ship. I loved the Navy uniform and couldn't wait until I wore one. One of my relatives on my mother's side was deployed on the light cruiser Emden, in Germany.

The ship steamed the Atlantic and the Baltic Sea, sinking a number of ships. They camouflaged the ship when out at sea and constantly changed the appearance, making it difficult to spot.

It was one of the few ships that made it back to the harbor in one piece. The ship continued to operate in the Atlantic and the Baltic until the war ended. This is only one account, but then I read another account which stated, the ship ran aground and was scuttled in 1945. The Emden was also used as a hospital ship transporting wounded soldiers as well as civilians from Eastern Germany to the west for medical care.

I joined the Naval Reserve in Denver, but before joining, I had to take the test. Taking tests wasn't my forte due to my English handicap. The Navy required a higher standard than the Army, and it was tougher to get in. I was determined, and one way or the other, nothing could keep me out.

Wherever you apply for a job, they make you take a test to evaluate you, just to make sure you are a good fit. The Navy was no exception. The written test took up most of the afternoon. I was forced to guess at half of the questions. I figured it would be a miracle if I passed the test.

It was frustrating not being able to comprehend what I just read. Guessing didn't cut it. I was asked to remain at the Naval Center until my test scores were announced. I was sweating it, and almost left. I knew I didn't make it. After waiting for an hour, the station Captain called me into his office, and told me I flunked the exam. No surprise there! I was at the lowest point in my short life and devastated to think I had failed what I was longing for. The captain told me I missed it only by two points. My guessing wasn't bad.

I was shocked when he said, "You are in." I came so close, and the captain saw in my eyes how bad I wanted to join the U.S. Navy. He didn't have the heart to flunk me. I was so excited, I could have hugged him, but I controlled myself. The captain gave me a huge break. I felt as if I had won a million dollars. I rejoiced all the way home. If anybody was looking for me, they would find me on cloud nine in the coming weeks.

Things were getting rough at home and I couldn't wait to leave. What better way than travel around the world, and Uncle Sam picking up the tab. I went active the following December. The same year I graduated from high school.

I had to come back down to the reality of life. I was forced to work if I wanted to keep my Buick running. That car cost me a fortune, similar to my sister's misfortune with her German car. In those days, cars weren't as reliable as they are today and you never knew when something would break. The brakes typically were replaced at thirty thousand miles; the tires lasted twenty to thirty thousand miles. The fan belts and the water hoses were the biggest problems, and it was a guarantee, when on a trip, anyone of these could break.

I wanted to know much punishment my car could take. One day after school, Art and me decided to drive to Colorado Springs, a seventy mile trip and we didn't tell our parents, not a smart thing to do! I floored the car all the way to Colorado Springs, maintaining a constant speed of 120 miles per hour, never letting up.

We thought, if we got there quick, our parents would never know, and all would be fine providing the cops didn't stop us. Ant traffic cop would have been excited seeing a car running that fast. We were lucky, or maybe unlucky. What I did was foolish. I could have had a blown tire or anything else could have gone wrong.

Young people did foolish things, and some got injured or even killed. The following week, my car's rear end went out, and it cost me an arm, and both legs. Was the trip worth it? It was a fast one, and I found out the capability of my Buick, although at a huge cost.

I first met my friend Art at school. We had classes together and knew I needed help in English. I found someone who was going out of his way to help me. He didn't live far from school, maybe a quarter of a mile. One day after school, we walked to his home where he introduced me to his parents. They seemed to be nice folks with high moral standards.

They were a religious family, and on Sunday they were at church no matter what. His dad was a university professor. Art was bright in just about any subject. We took German together. I helped him in his German, and he helped me with my English and math. Learning English was a chore. I had a difficult time speaking, and writing was even worse.

The following embarrassed me: in German, hell means a bright light or you could say the sun is hell. I heard kids using hell all the time, and I thought it wasn't a bad word. I was at Art's home, and attempted to speak proper English.

I wanted to impress them by using a word I learned around kids in school. His mother asked me, "Would you like Coke or a snack?" I wanted to show my appreciation and replied, "Hell, yes." I assumed it was a good choice of a word, and during the course of the afternoon, I used it many times.

Art took me aside, and told me what I had just said to his mother was inappropriate, and explained to me what the word 'hell' meant. I was very much embarrassed, and if I could have made myself invisible, I would have. Had I continued using the word, I wouldn't have been welcome at his house anymore.

I profusely apologized to her, and told her, "I didn't know what I was saying." She told me, "Don't worry about it." She forgave me and things were much better. I made sure that the next time; I wouldn't make the same mistake.

Art and I did lots of fun stuff together, including horseback riding. It was a cheap way to spend the afternoon. I didn't have to worry about the horse breaking down, and paying for repairs. We ran the horses hard which was *verboten*, and before we came back to the barn, we walked them, and allowed the perspiration to dry off.

We would have gotten in trouble had the people known what we were doing with the horses. It was no fun just to trot along; it was much more fun to gallop through the countryside with the wind blowing through our hair, and hearing the hoofs dig into the ground causing the dirt to fly into the air.

At times, the horses wouldn't cooperate with us. Art was riding a beautiful black horse. The animal tried to knock him off. The horse went into a gallop, and then suddenly stopped. I did something stupid! We traded horses, now I could have had a big problem. I was riding along without a problem, but before I knew it, the horse took off at a fast gallop with me hanging on like there was no tomorrow. I held the reins as tight as I could, but then all of a sudden, without warning, the horse came to an abrupt halt and almost threw me head first onto the ground.

I could have killed myself that day, but thankfully I stayed in the saddle. The horse knew exactly what it was doing, it wanted to knock me off any way it could. After that episode, there was no more trouble the rest of the time.

Art asked me if I wanted to go rock climbing with him and another friend. I had never done that before, but it sounded exciting. The following week on a Saturday we climbed into my car, and off we went into the Rockies, trying out our 'rock climbing skills'. We didn't use a safety rope, a big mistake. The only time we used ropes was to repel off the cliffs. We had so much excitement; It was more than Disneyland could offer.

Close to the University of Colorado at Boulder were three tall rocks, the Flatirons. The surfaces were smooth with not many things to hold onto. I was climbing with little foot and hand holds. During the course of my ascent, I became stuck. I couldn't move up, down, or sideways. I hung there, contemplating what to do. My options were zero to none. Two feet below me, I saw a small size ledge. If I jumped, and landed on

> I prayed to God, "Please come and rescue me."

it, I'd be able to work my way down the mountain. But that was a big if. I had no choice, but to go for it. I held my breath; sweat was running down my forehead as angst gripped me. I prayed to God, "Please come and rescue me."

With my eyes closed, I let go of my right foot and jumped down to the outcropping. It worked, and with much relief, I descended the big rock. When I reached the floor, I got on my knees and thanked God for saving me.

Art and his friend were elated that I made it down alive. They descended and we met at the bottom of the cliff, glad to be alive. We agreed, next time, we would be bringing our ropes.

I was blessed to live in a beautiful place like this, where the Rockies reached into the sky above the clouds. After the fear of climbing wore off, my friends and I were talking about making another trip into the deep Rockies. Art's grandparent's had a cabin deep inside the forest, off the beaten path.

Art's mom got her Volkswagen Bug ready, we threw everything into the small trunk, and off we went. She was a good driver and in about two hours we arrived at our destination. What a beautiful sight! The cabin was in a valley, with mountains all around and a creek flowing beside it. Art's mom didn't stay long and felt we were okay by ourselves in this wilderness.

We didn't load ourselves down with a lot of gear, and even left the clock and watches at home. In those days, there was no phone, and if anything should have happened, it was a long way to civilization. We never knew what time it was, and didn't care, we had fun.

We went to bed when it got dark, the owls were calling, and I swore we heard wolves howling in the distance. We lay in our beds telling each other scary stories. It was not the time for these conversations because we were told that Big Foot was in these parts of the country. The monsters were huge, standing seven to eight feet tall. We pretended we weren't scared, but down deep inside, something told us, it was dangerous to be by ourselves up there with no gun or lock on the door.

Later in the night, one by one, we fell asleep. Thank God we survived the night. We got up with the sun. We were hungry as wolves and the cereal we brought along was very inviting. We even had milk to pour into the bowl filled with cornflakes.

We had no clue where we were going to go the first day. It all looked so inviting. Wherever we turned, it looked like paradise. We packed our fishing gear, peanut butter sandwiches for lunch, and out the door we went. We found a good size creek, it was the Platte River. A small, inviting creek. We rigged our fishing poles, and with the bait on the hook, we commenced fly fishing.

To our surprise, the fish were biting like mad. It wasn't even noon, judging by the sun, we already reached our limit. We knew what we were going to have for lunch and supper. We hiked back to the cabin. Art cleaned the fish and fried the trout on an open fire. What a meal! We decided to take a little break from our exhausting day and sleep a little. We woke up when we heard a strange sound coming from the underbrush, not far from the cabin. Was it Big Foot? Was it a black bear? We stayed in the cabin, watching the movement of the leaves as the creature stirred.

We heard grunts, and snorting from a huge beast. My God, what could it be? Would we be devoured tonight? We saw brown fur through the opening of the bush. It was a moonlit night and we didn't need a flashlight to see what was out there. More grunts and snorting. At last, a big brown bear stepped out into the opening. We were much relieved, but we weren't out of the woods yet. Bears can be dangerous and unpredictable. We had heard, when in the presence of bears, it is a good idea to take pots and make loud, clanging noises. We collected the pots and produced all kinds of a racket. The bear apparently disliked all this commotion and wandered off into the thicket.

We had access to electricity in case we wanted to cook inside on the electric stove, but we never did. We used an open pit to fry the trout which was the best way, giving it a great outdoor flavor. The next day, we hiked all day, and caught more trout for dinner. The cold, blue Platte River, supplied us with lots of big fish.

The rest of the week, we had no more visitors. We never saw Big Foot, or the bear we had seen earlier. It was now time to depart

> The blue Platte River supplied us with plenty of trout.

this paradise when Art's mom drove into the driveway with her blue Volkswagen Bug to take us home. We had lots of stories to tell her on the way home. It was a hell of a vacation I told her.

One of the winters, I went cross country skiing with a bunch of guys from work. I had the time of my life. We were high in the Rockies, and it was so peaceful. There was nothing like gliding through that deep powder snow on our skis. The trees were adorned with the most beautiful white ornament, and I heard the snow crash to the ground from one of the low hanging branches as we ventured by.

The snow on the trees glistened in the sunshine, and the birds were chirping non stop. Every so often we saw a squirrel hopping through the deep snow on its way to the nest, full of food it collected in the fall. We stayed in a cabin someplace in the Rockies in an upscale cabin, we were even provided with a heater and a stove. It wasn't exactly roughing it, but it did get chilly during the night. The entire night, there were no sounds in the vast ranges of the mountains, not even a peep. We were only gone three days, and it was time to head back home again. Everybody had to be back at work on Monday. I was hoping to do this again some day, but the day never came.

34

THE DOUBLE EDGED SWORD

On July of 1962, the U.S. Navy issued us a rail ticket to the Great Lakes boot camp. We were recruits, all from Denver. The four of us met at school and had classes together. One day in the school cafeteria we got together and decided to join up.

Some of my friends thought they made a mistake signing up, but there was no doubt I made the right choice. I couldn't wait to get to boot camp. Had I only known what was waiting for me, maybe, I wouldn't have been so anxious.

We boarded the Rio Grande train in Denver, heading to Chicago. It took a couple of days to get there. We had a terrific time on the train as we viewed the countryside. The terrain was mostly flat, seeing waves of grain as far as my eye could see.

We traveled to Nebraska, making a stop in Omaha, where we took on more passengers while others got off. I don't remember all the other stops, but I am sure we stopped some place in Kansas as well.

The food was out of this world, and we were treated like royalty. Snacks were available day and night. The menu listed steak, lobster and many other marvelous dishes. This was a confirmation, indeed, that I made the right decision. I was proud to serve in some capacity in my new found land, and happy to be part of the greatest Navy in the world. I wasn't a U.S. citizen when I joined the Navy, and what a surprise, they accepted.

To join, all I did was to swear that I had every intention of becoming a citizen. I was anxious to do that after I got out of the service. My dream was, to become a full-fledged citizen, and to take advantage of the opportunities this great country had to offer.

At last, the train pulled into the Great Lakes Navy boot camp, and now, it was the time of reckoning. I had heard lots of stories about boot camp from other people who had gone before and they were frightening.

Should I have believed all the stories? Or did they just want to scare me? Either way, I came to the point of no return. I wouldn't let it dampen my spirits and the adventure that waited for me.

With our sea bags in hand, we stepped off the train, it had everything in we needed for the next ninety days. I brought along a set of dress blues, dress whites, and dungarees with all the necessary toiletry items.

Before long, we saw gray Navy buses pull up to take us to our new life that I would cherish, or maybe not, for the next three months. We arrived in the morning and were led to the grinder which resembled a concrete plaza. It was a plaza for recruits to be drilled.

We sat on the ground for four hours waiting for instructions, and additional supplies. I know now where the term 'hurry up and wait' had its origin. Right off the bat, we were taught basic commands, and met our drill instructor, a second class Petty Officer Randall. The man screamed and hollered like nobody I ever heard before. There was no doubt in anyone's mind who was running the show.

On my first evening on base, we were directed to the chow hall 'the restaurant'. I was hungry, and I couldn't wait to see what was for supper. We were allowed to eat all we wanted; the problem was we only had thirty minutes. From my training in the German bakery, I was able to down food in a hurry.

> Our drill instructor woke us up around two in the morning. We got dressed, made our bunks, and reported to the grinder for drills.

The first night, we were shown to the barracks, our new home. Everybody had a small locker for their personal items. I made sure I didn't leave things lying around for the fear of losing them. To my surprise, our drill instructor woke us up at two in the morning. We got dressed, made our bunks, and reported to the grinder for a drill.

It all came off surprisingly smooth. That was a miracle! Most of the guys hadn't woken up yet. Darn it, I missed my morning coffee. I couldn't do anything without having three cups in the morning. I had to adjust.

At times, I had to stand fire watch which meant I had to walk back and forth in the long hall of the barracks with bunks lined up on both sides. I had to make sure there wasn't a fire danger.

The barracks were built entirely out of wood, and if they ever caught fire, they would burn in seconds. At times, I was so tired, I caught myself sleepwalking. I don't know how effective I would have been had there been an emergency.

Understanding the English language was difficult for me. I kept my eyes on the guy next to me and copied what he did. Hopefully he was following instructions.

The Recruit Chief Petty Officer was a fellow recruit, elected to be the leader of his boot camp members. Nobody liked our RCPO, 'Recruit Chief Petty Officer', causing the guys to complain to our platoon leader who changed things in a hurry; little did I know I was part of this change. We had around seventy guys in our platoon, and our Recruit Petty Officer was now searching for someone.

The guys nominated me to lead the platoon, and that was a shocker. I wasn't ready for it. I was very shy and afraid of my own shadow, partly due to my language difficulty. I had to get over my shyness fast. Leading a platoon was no job for a timid sailor.

The instructor strapped a double edged Navy sword on my belt. It was long enough, and if not careful, I could have tripped over it. I could never figure out why a sword and not a gun; it must have been Navy tradition.

The sword was long and heavy, and at times, almost caused me to trip. The blade was so shiny, and when holding it in the sun, it almost blinded me. The edge was sharp as well. I found out the hard way, when I ran my finger along the edge and cut myself.

It appeared to be old and may have been used in one of the sea battles, fighting the pirates. I even had to sleep with it at night, and by laying it next to me in the sheath, I was safe. Needless to say, nobody messed with me. They knew, with one swipe, their head would be coming off.

The guys were issued guns, but they weren't the real thing and were only used for drills. First, we were trained to handle the weapon, and the men had to prove they were proficient in the use of the gun. In the Navy, you were never issued a gun unless you were on shore patrol or a gunner's mate aboard a ship. The officer of the deck always carried side-arm.

The guys were forced to sleep with their gun as well, and it was called, *piece*. The guns were loaded for the purpose of defending the ship in case of an attack. What would have happened if one of the guns had gone off accidentally in their bunk? That never happened, as far as I know.

One day, we went to the firing range to qualify with the weapon. I was issued a gun for the sole purpose of shooting at targets. It would have been difficult to take the sword and score. I had never held a weapon, much less shot one. I discovered aiming at a target wasn't easy. I couldn't hit the side of a barn. My instructor figured, because I was German, shooting would be easy for me, but not so.

The range master asked me, "Why aren't you hitting the target, Berger?" My reply was, "In my whole life, I never held a gun." My instructor said, "Do you see the range finder?" To which I replied, "Vat is a range finder?" He had his job cut out, but with paying close attention, I improved greatly.

One of the requirements was, to be able to score a hit, preferably a bull's eye. I didn't know shooting was part of the deal. Had I thought about it, I should have realized, in war, shooting was part of the game. With practice, I was able to hit the bull's eye, and that amazed me, as well as my instructor.

When it came to marching, I had a tough time calling out cadence. I never knew why they chose me to fill the role of an RCPO. I got

Instead of saying "parade rest," I would say "rest the parade." Calling out the command "a half step forward march, I would call out "about a half step forward march."

into big problems when it came to marching. I had guys running into each other, much like cars on LA's freeways, but with much less collateral damage. I tried hard to say the right things, but I just couldn't spit it out.

Instead of "*parade rest,*" I would say, "*rest the parade.*" The command "*by the half step forward, march,*" I said, "*about a half step forward, march.*" Instead of "forward march" I said in German *Vorwärts Marsch.* You get the point. I was frustrated, and ready to visit a shrink. The sailors were totally confused. I didn't give up though, and it paid off. Towards the end, I was getting pretty good at it.

I marched the guys all over the base until I tired them out. I had them jump across ditches, swim through a canal, climb up nets twenty feet high, and shoot their rifles on the run. Thank God, I didn't have to do that, all I did, was yell at them. If I would have had to run the obstacle course, I probably could have done it. Our drill instructor was by my side, and helped me out when I found myself in a quandary. I only did what I was told, but half of the time I couldn't understand what the drill instructor told me to do, and that was a huge problem.

I didn't have anybody to translate what my instructor asked me to do; I was clueless most of the time. Calling cadence was real tough, and marching them was a nightmare. I came to the conclusion; I had to do something different to keep my job. This isn't working.

I taught the guys to count in German and shouted out commands in my native tongue. It made things much easier for me, but I was not so sure how the sailors felt about the whole situation. Would they report and send me to the base commander? If they did, I wouldn't have understood a word.

I was the talk of the base, but I never did anything that would have given me a bad name. Let's face it; I was a mess, beleaguered, with a comedy of errors. It didn't stop me from having the time of my life. The guys had problems pronouncing the German words. I definitely had problems pronouncing English words, but we made progress, and it all worked out to everybody's satisfaction.

The men marched much brisker, and it boosted everybody's morale. This may have been the forerunner of 'Starlach Thirteen' or 'Hans's Heroes'.

I was proud of the guys for having hung in there. They felt a higher purpose in life. On the contrary, the officers couldn't believe their ears when we marched in German commands. Did they think the Germans infiltrated the base?

Talk about having fun, this was it, even though the guys directly and indirectly made fun of my accent. I had a ball hearing the guys practicing German, and hearing them pronounce the words, it was hilarious. More and more of the guys bought German / English dictionaries. I was afraid; continuing to scream at the sailors in German would not be welcomed.

One evening, I was summoned to the office of the drill instructor, and as a rule that would have been no cause for alarm. However, upon entering his office, he screamed at me, and his face turned fiery red, much like an over ripe tomato. The arteries in his neck popped out on both sides, and it wasn't hard to figure out that I was in deep trouble.

I understood the first few words upon entering his office, and they were, "What the hell are you trying to pull, Berger?" To which I replied, "I am not trying to pull anything. Vat have I done wrong?" Upon which he made me do twenty-five push-ups. That was no problem, but I could never figure out the other part of the meeting. I knew he wasn't entirely happy about something I had done.

When our meeting was over, I asked him, "Vat else can I do for you?" He replied, "Get the hell out of my office." To which I said, "Wery vell, sir." I walked briskly out of his office, my head held high, like nothing ever happened, but I knew better, and acted like the meeting never occurred.

When I got back to the barracks, the guys asked me why I had to see the drill instructor, and I told them, "I didn't understand vat he vanted from me." This bothered me later, and I would have given anything to find out what it was all about. It will remain a secret forever.

Maybe it had something to do with marching the guys and calling out the cadence in German. I was worried that The U.S. Government would send me back to Germany.

On one of the marches to the chow hall, we were wearing dress whites. One of the guys was wearing white shorts with red hearts; the red hearts were visible through the white uniform and everybody gave him a hard time. I believe his girlfriend sent him those shorts for a Valentine's present, and he was proud to show them off to everybody. The recruits were jealous that they didn't have girlfriends sending them those kinds of presents.

Over all, things went well for everybody until we had to learn how to fight ship fires, essential when on board any ship.

Fires will sink ships especially when the ammo is ignited, then it is all over. I got into this building; flames were shooting under my feet, over my head, and on both sides of me. As long as I held the nozzle in front of me, nothing would happen. There was no room for mistakes.

Any slip-up at this training exercise could have been fatal. I wasn't in the least bit scared. I didn't realize how dangerous it could have been. One of the guys singed his eyebrows when he panicked as the flames started licking at his face. They shut off the gas immediately, and transported him to the naval hospital for treatment.

I was looking for the day to hike out of this place. Each morning we had an inspection whereby the drill instructor checked everybody's locker, and also made sure the bunk was made up properly.

When our drill instructor checked the bunks, they had to be tight as a rope.

I tested it by dropping a quarter on the bed sheet, and the coin had better bounce. If it didn't, I made up the bed all over again..

If any of those things were not done properly, you'd have to do push-ups or you would be sent to some boring work detail like scrubbing floors with a toothbrush or cleaning toilets.

One of the guys didn't have his socks rolled up properly when the drill instructor checked his locker. He made him chew on the dirty socks for an hour.

We had no laundromats to wash our clothes. The Navy thought we should wash them by hand. That's one chore I wasn't too fond of. After washing my clothes, I had to give great care that all articles were square knotted when hung. Upon inspection, we made sure the clothing articles were properly hung on the line.

The clothes had to have one's name on them. If they didn't, I was reprimanded, or worse, if I lost items, I would have had to replace them and pay for it out of my pocket.

Every day I attended classes teaching us how to be good sailors. I learned all kinds of technical things about ships and how to maintain them. The problem was we had to get up early in the morning. By the time I got to class, I was dead tired.

Overall, it was a great experience, and I had a good time. Thinking back, I'd do it all over again. It made me grow up and prepared me for life. At last, it was graduation time. I had to take a written test which worried me because I still had a tough time reading and understanding English. I must have passed since they allowed me to participate in the graduation.

It was getting close to graduation and we had to do lots of training. We marched hours upon hours to get everything right. Everybody had to march in step. If just one messed up, we had to do it all over again. We were responsible for each other, and formed a unit. We finally got it right and we were ready for the big day.

We marched on the huge grinder, in front of the viewing stand with heads high and chests out. It was jam-packed with mostly parents, siblings and friends watching their sons, brothers and in some cases fathers perform, marching in step and showing off their new dress blues. None of my family came to watch me. Mama and Papa had no way of getting there, and my sisters didn't have any idea where I was at the time. We were not a close family. I was used to it, and took it in stride.

As a Recruit Chief Petty Officer, I marched in front of the platoon with my sword held high. At this point, I excelled, pointing the saber in the proper direction and careful not to trip over myself. I performed elaborate maneuvers, similar to twirling a gun.

The most difficult thing was to stay in step with the rest of the men marching behind me. I should have had a side view mirror. I was constantly afraid of dropping the sword and that would have been embarrassing.

To be part of the platoon was awesome and to belong to the finest fighting force on this planet made me proud. We ranked tops out of all the platoons that graduated that day, and maybe there was a slight chance I had something to do with it.

That afternoon, the train arrived and we jumped aboard, very happy to be on our way home. I remember we stopped in Chicago looking at the scenery and the tall buildings. It reminded me of New York a few years earlier.

We stopped to have hamburgers and French fries by the train station. The food must have been good because when I think of it, it still makes me hungry. With all the screaming I had to do, I lost my voice.

A couple of days later, I was home again and back to my unpredictable life, but somehow I felt I had a purpose in life, being part of something awesome. I have never had a routine life, things changed often, and for the most part, it was for the better.

35

WAITING ON UNCLE

I was happy to be back from boot camp. Herr Vollmer saved my job. It was a pleasure driving to work in my fabulous Buick Dynaflow. I was anxious to get in my car and drive to work at the German bakery on Broadway in Denver. It would have been tricky to take a date out on a bicycle, or on a bus. It probably wouldn't have made the best impression. Just for that reason alone, it was worth having a car. One drawback was the car cost me a small fortune to maintain. It was a good way to get around, but expensive.

While working at the Pizza Oven in Denver, I befriended June who invited me, along with her husband Sam, to go fishing in the Rockies. With eagerness I accepted the invitation. That same day, I bought me a reel, a pole and a fishing line at Sears. Now I was ready. At five in the morning they honked their horn letting me know they had arrived. I flew out of the door to their car.

We drove for three hours, high in the Rockies, at the twelve-thousand foot elevation; we arrived at the home of the big trout. It was a gorgeous trip. I couldn't get enough of the spectacular scenery. At the high elevation, granite slabs were hugging the road with short pine trees dotting the landscape.

When we arrived at our destination, Sam pulled over and we climbed out of the car. In a few minutes and several deep breaths, we were ready to hike to the Lake and fish, a distance of one mile. What a beautiful walk along the meandering creek, as the most gorgeous bright wildflowers greeted us on the bank of the creek. The birds sang beautiful melodies, which echoed off of the cliffs. The giant trees reached into the heavens with their big branches as if to praise God. What a serene place!

We didn't encounter many people in the back country of Emerald Lake. As we came closer to the lake, the water was dark blue, a reflection from the sky above. It was a perfect day for fishing. The lake was as smooth as a bath tub.

When we reached the shore, we sat down to catch our breath. The sun had barely crested the peak, the rays warmed up my body, and I was ready to catch my trophy trout. First, June showed me how to rig my pole. She was good at it and gave me one of her lures. She told me, "This lure will catch you a trophy trout." I rigged my line the way she showed me, and I was ready. The reel was working great, and I had plenty of line to reach far from shore.

I took a quick nap in my comfy plastic recliner I had purchased earlier in the year. I rigged my line and I was satisfied with my first cast. I wanted the hook and bait sink deep, where the big ones were. I had my pole fastened to my chair, just in case I dozed off. The vibration of the pole would be an indicator of a strike. I kept a close eye on my bopper, but sleep got the best of me.

The saying goes; the biggest fish always gets away. Sound asleep, I felt my pole sliding into the water, and lucky me, I just caught up with it before it disappeared into the depths of the lake. I couldn't figure out how the pole got lose from the chair.

The fish had to be huge; with great force, it pulled the rod and reel into the water. Had I not woken up, the pole, and everything with it, would have been gone forever.

By early afternoon, Sam had four beautiful trout, June had three and I had three. They were a good size, close to two feet each. June brought delicious sandwiches with ham, cheese and Coke to wash down the meal. It was a wonderful day. In the back of my mind I wondered how big the fish was I lost earlier. Life couldn't have been any better. The beauty of the mountains, the majestic peaks still blanketed with snow, were indescribable. I had never seen such beauty.

I pinched myself to see if this was real, and not just an awesome dream.

It was time to head back to Denver. We picked up our things, hoping we'd be able to carry everything in one trip. It was tough. I was carrying my fish on a stringer tied to my chair. Sam and June had their hands full as we struggled climbing uphill towards the car. We took a couple of breaks along the way, but we made it. The toughest part was the thin air as we labored to fill our lungs.

We were totally exhausted. Sam pulled onto the highway and I noticed he kept rubbing his face and sticking his head out of the window. I knew he was tired and afraid he might fall asleep. Within the hour, sure enough, Sam was sound asleep behind the wheel. June kept waking him up when she poked him in the ribs. I don't know why she didn't take the wheel.

Things got worse when Sam drifted into the opposing lane. This shook Sam up. Lucky for us, no car was coming. June told him to pull off the road and catch a brief nap. The rest of the way, he did a good job getting us home.

A week later, June asked me if I wanted to go fishing again. I politely declined the offer. A few years later, I did make another trip to Emerald Lake, caught a couple of nice rainbow trout, but it wasn't the same. I missed my friends from long ago.

There were many things to explore in this fabulous country. I discovered there was more to life than work, but at the same time, I was planning to attend the University at Boulder after serving a hitch in the Navy.

I was getting impatient waiting for Uncle Sam to call me to active duty. I knew it would be by Christmas or shortly after. I watched on TV, and heard on the radio about the Cuban Missile crisis, I was afraid I would be called sooner, than later. Sure enough, the Navy ordered me to report to Treasure Island, California.

The following week, I boarded a flight from Denver to Travis AFB. The flight wasn't long, only a couple of hours. This was the first time I had been on a jet, and with amazement, we crossed a third of the United States in just a couple of hours. Before long, the plane landed at Travis. From there, a gray Navy bus picked me and a number of other sailors up and transported us to Treasure Island.

Once there, I was to be assigned to my duty station. I spent three weeks at Treasure Island; the days were long with little to do, always keeping my ears open for my name to be called. It was boring, and it seemed as though time stood still.

Treasure Island wasn't very big. It only took an hour to walk around the whole island. The naval presence was obvious with ships tied up, mostly for training purposes. Administrative buildings lined the streets. What intrigued me were the palm trees. I had never them before, only in movies. They were tall and thin. Why didn't snap in half during the powerful typhoons in the Pacific.

The island was built around 1920 for the World's Fair. It took thousands of tons of rocks and dirt to create this manmade wonder in the middle of the bay.

It is mind boggling to think anything that huge could be built and in days when we didn't have all the technology and equipment for a huge project like this. The United States was able do just about anything once it made up its mind to do it.

After I had been at Treasure Island a week, I volunteered to help at the Acey Ducy Club. It was where non-commissioned officers relaxed with a drink or two. My job was waiting on tables, serving food and liquor. After closing time, around midnight, I helped clean up the restaurant and went back to the barracks.

I enjoyed working at the club, and to my surprise, the officers at times, gave me a tip. I didn't tell anybody about the money, if I had, my job would have been grabbed. I didn't know how I ended up with the job, but I was happy I did.

While at Treasure Island, I made friends with a few guys, and at times, we went by bus to the Big City of San Francisco. We had a great time window shopping, climbing the steep hills, and going to Fisherman's Wharf where we looked at all the touristy stuff.

My favorite place was China Town, observing the people and their culture. It appeared as if I was in a different country, not the United States. I liked the carved ivory of roses, houses and other beautiful trinkets. We didn't buy much, only small trinkets to send home to our parents. We had very little money, just enough for a bus ride into town and back.

From my vantage point at Treasure Island, I clearly saw Alcatraz. It was still occupied with the most famous prisoners, including the Bird Man. When I was there, three prisoners escaped.

> Nobody knew if they made it to shore, or became fish food, but one thing was for sure, escaping from Alcatraz was virtually impossible.

Nobody knew if they made it to shore, or became fish food, but one thing was for sure, escaping from Alcatraz was virtually impossible, even for the strongest swimmers.

When I arrived at Treasure Island, the Navy gave me a sheet to fill out; we called it the dream sheet. They asked me where I would like to serve. I selected two locations; one of the two was an icebreaker in Alaska, the other, a destroyer at Pearl Harbor, Hawaii. The Islands offered exotic beaches, and if I was going to be stationed on a ship, I had a good chance of visiting many of the beautiful South Sea Islands.

More often than not, the Navy sent you where you didn't want to go, perhaps performing some boring clerical work. At last, my name was called via the loudspeaker. I knew the time had arrived; they had selected my duty station. Would it be a duty station in Nevada or Kansas?

I couldn't believe my ears: I was told my home would be on a destroyer in Hawaii at Pearl Harbor. My dream had come true, and before long, I winged my way to beautiful Hawaii where the oceans are the bluest and the beaches the whitest.

I would not see Treasure Island again until 1966 when I enrolled in a class to prepare me to become an instructor. The training came in handy much later in my life as I became a law enforcement instructor, training peace officers on all kinds of equipment.

Just before Christmas 1962, I was on my way to Hawaii, flying on a Boeing 707 with plenty of power. The flight was smooth and uneventful. In those days, the ladies serving us were called stewardesses, not flight attendants. They served hot meals, and babied the travelers even if you weren't in first class. How things have changed over the years.

After five hours, we landed in Honolulu. I didn't have to be concerned about somebody picking me up. The Navy provided a shuttle to my new duty station.

As we approached the airport in Honolulu, I was fascinated how lush and green the islands were as they came into view, surrounded by the bluest ocean. I had never in my life seen anything that beautiful. Extinct volcanoes were ringing the island of Oahu, with eerie black cones inside of the craters.

The pilot landed the plane with precision, with hardly a bump when we touched down. It took a while to taxi to the concourse due to the traffic ahead of us. The crew announced we were free to leave the cabin.

We made our way to the terminal where a gray Navy bus was waiting to take us to Pearl Harbor. Along the way, there were beautiful beaches and gorgeous golf courses. I loved everything I saw. My adventure was about to begin. It seemed like an eternity before we arrived at Pearl Harbor.

I knew I had made the right decision joining the Navy. My dream came true, I was about to enter the most beautiful part of the world. Where is my ship going to take me? Perhaps to Fiji, or Samoa?

After we drove through the main gate, a number of ships greeted us; among them were nuclear subs on one side of the harbor. Of all the ships, which one was mine? My ship was tied up at the destroyer alley as it was called.

A couple of carriers with tankers and supply ships were tied up at Ford Island. Sailors got off the bus at various points on base. My ship, the USS Carpenter 825, a destroyer, was at the end of the pier, and the last one to get off.

My ship was a gray ghost amidst the silhouette of other ships. I grabbed my sea bag, which contained everything I would need for the next two years. I got off the bus, and approached the huge vessel which had an overpowering odor of diesel fuel.

I liked the smell of diesel ever since I was a kid. It reminded me of the gray Deutz tractor Michael's dad used for farming. I approached the ship, but didn't know at what location to board the vessel. Should I board at the front, at the back, or at midsection? I yelled to a sailor on the ship with my heavy German accent, "Ver do I climb aboard?" The sailor on the quarterdeck yelled back at me, "Walk on the gangplank leading to the quarterdeck." My reply was, "Ver is the gangplank and vat is a quarterdeck?" The sailor probably got tired of me asking him all these dumb questions.

The quartermaster, as he was called, directed me to the gang plank which led me directly to him. One had to go to the quarterdeck first to enter the ship; it's where the officer of the deck checks your documents. I showed him my papers, and I was aboard. He did ask me where I was from. Again he studied my papers, looked me over, and at last gave me permission to board. It was terrific to be on the vessel, known as the greyhound of the fleet.

One of the crew members showed me to my bunk, suspended by a pair of chains, attached to the overhead. It was already dark, with only the dim, red lights visible, showing me the way. I fell into the bunk, tired from the long trip. I noticed the linens hadn't been changed from the previous occupant. They were soiled, and I didn't want to sleep on that particular bunk.

I fell asleep among the sounds of the diesel engines, and personnel coming, and going. This particular bunk was assigned to me, and I had no choice but to claim it. In the morning, the supply people came and changed the bedding.

The bunks were next to the bulkhead and stacked three high. I discovered the greenhorns like me, got the bottom bunk; the guys with pull, slept on top. Only three feet separated the bunks. I had to be careful not to disturb the guy in the middle bunk.

The bottom bunk wasn't bad. Nobody was able to poke you from below. The guy in the middle had it the worse. The guy in the top was not harassed for a good reason. He was from supply and pressed your uniforms for inspection. It was a good idea to stay on his good side.

I wandered all over the ship, intrigued by the huge five inch guns and giant smoke stacks. Sleeping arrangements were tight. The ship needed room for all the ammo, torpedoes and rockets. When we were in heavy seas, to keep from falling out of the bunk, I wrapped my toes around the ankle irons. It prevented me from tumbling onto the steel deck.

I was supplied a small locker for my personal items which I kept under lock and key. At five in the morning was reveille, the boatswain mate blew the whistle, and everybody hit the deck.

I stumbled around trying to find my way around. Getting to the mess hall was important, where breakfast, lunch and dinner was served. I was pleasantly surprised at the variety of food. For breakfast, one had a choice of scrambled eggs, hard boiled eggs, and eggs over easy as well as omelets. You could order S.O.S.; translated, shit on the shingles. I didn't like it. Perhaps the name of the dish turned me off.

I was far from being fluent in English, and I had better learn the Navy lingo quickly. It didn't take long, and I was able to communicate with the crew effectively. I learned Navy words, and just enough to be dangerous.

I will explain some of the Navy terminology for you: the *bulkheads* are the walls of the ship, the *overhead* is the ceiling, the *forecastle* is the bow of the ship, and the end of the ship was called the *fantail*. The kitchen is called the *galley*, the staircase is called the *ladder*, and there were many other expressions that I will explain later.

The guys aboard ship were mocking me when I mispronounced words, and in turn I called them "slew cocked foot suckers." I was assigned to the deck force which meant I had to chip paint, and paint the sections after removing the rust. When coming into port, I helped the boatswain mate secure the ship. I got lots of fresh air, and enough saltwater to sink a ship.

When out in the open sea, there was nothing like the night sky, with the millions of stars greeting you. It was so clear, you could see for miles and miles, and in the daytime, I was able to see the curvature of the earth as I scanned the horizon.

As ships approached, all I could see was the uppermost part of the mast, but soon, the whole ship emerged with its splendor. I have never seen an ugly ship on the ocean, even when it was rusty it had a story to tell. Nobody knew where it came from, and where it was going.

I wish I would have had the opportunity to talk to the Captains of the vessels. They were from all over the world. Ships from China, Russia, Korea, Japan and many other nations crisscrossed the ocean. What a privilege to have had the opportunity to sail the wide Pacific all the way to China and Japan.

When I came on board, I had to stand watches, mainly during the night. I loved the night, full of splendor and on a clear night, the firmament was lit up like a giant candle. The bow of the ship sliced through the waves like a hot knife through butter. The ocean released a green and turquoise glow that changed the entire side of the ship to a myriad of bright colors. The micro organisms in the water produce beautiful shades of colors.

The reasons for standing watches were to recognize any dangers which could harm the ship and its crew. In times of war, it is essential to identify enemy ships from a great distance by the means of binoculars. We were given night vision goggles, and any small light increased greatly, since it was a light gathering device.

When standing watch on the bridge, I was assigned to the le helm, which meant I communicated with the officer of the deck and the engine room technician, the *snipe*. I had a difficult time repeating various commands. I noticed the officer had a hard time keeping a straight face after he heard me trying to spit out the speed of the ship.

When I repeated the speed of the ship to the engine room via the air phone, the guy on the other end told me to take the shit out of my mouth, so he could understand me. At first I felt insulted, but what could I do, but grin and bear it. This occurred less and less as the crew got to know me. It was obvious I had a language problem and the sailors for the most part were patient.

The torpedo men had a ball when they asked me to repeat *which way went the wild whippor will.* The whippor will is a real bird found in the Midwest grain fields. The Americans asked the Germans to repeat if they suspected he was a spy. The Germans had a hard time pronouncing w's and th's. The w's come out as v's and the th's come out as s's.

At times, I am still battling the pronunciations, even after being here for better than fifty years. The torpedo guys did this a couple of times, but gave up after I figured out why they were laughing their heads off. Then it wasn't fun anymore.

When I first arrived aboard the ship, the crew told me to watch out for the mail buoys. Finding out later, there was no such thing. Supposedly, there was a ghost on the ship who appeared to a number of the crew. A sailor tragically lost his life when his head was crushed by the five inch gun. Thank God I never saw him. Had I seen him, it would have scared the living daylights out of me and would have caused me to jump overboard. Standing watch at night gave me the creeps, afraid he might appear. At times, I heard unusual noises from the upper deck. It was dark, and I started imagining things which weren't there.

Flying fish were a common sight seeing them crash on the steel deck. As they flew past me, they produced the weirdest sound, a whooshing noise. None of them ever crashed into me, but it was close. I tell people about that, and they think I am making it all up.

When I was still on the deck force, and painting the ship, scraping off the rust, I sometimes painted over the rust spots without removing them. It didn't happen often, but I was tired of the job, and didn't pay attention to what I was doing.

It was time to paint the smoke stacks. I volunteered climbing up the chimneys. It was no different than washing windows on a high-rise. I sat on a boatswain chair, with safety lines attached, just in case. The job was dangerous, and only two of us volunteered.

It was scary as the ship rocked back and forth, and at times a giant wave would spill over the side of the ship, and reach us dangling in a precarious position. What I liked about that job was nobody bothered me. I was working at my own speed, knowing full and well, nobody was going to take the job away.

I made a game out of painting. I enjoyed climbing the sides of the ship with just the aid of a rope to repel, and climbing back up to the deck. I was painting the forecastle of the ship, using a boatswain chair, and painting away at my leisure. When I finished the job, I decided to climb back up to the deck via the rope that held my chair. The climb was approximately thirty to forty feet. I was in pretty decent shape, and only weighed around 150 pounds.

Ordinarily, I wouldn't have had a problem. Climbing hand over hand, I became exhausted, and by the time I made it to the deck, my strength was gone. I couldn't climb another inch. With nobody around, I was in danger of falling to the platform below.

A sailor, whom I had never seen before, came to my rescue and pulled me onto deck. To my amazement, I never saw him on the ship again. Where did he come from? Was it an angel who came to my rescue?

On leave, a tragedy occurred on a destroyer, tied up next to ours. One of the electricians was changing light bulbs on the main deck in the mess hall. That, in itself wasn't a big deal, but it turned deadly.

He unscrewed one of the bulbs, the current traveled through his body and exited through the main deck, and that in turn ignited the fuse of a rocket below the mess deck.

Through this, a number of other rockets ignited, and the result was, the rockets tore through the steel deck. All in all, four sailors lost their lives, and many more received severe burns. I didn't know any of the men personally, but what a tragedy!

I was attempting to work my way out of the deck force and into the galley which ultimately led me to be the ship's baker. The reason was I was afraid of being involved in an accident if I stayed on the deck force. I made it into the galley helping the cooks with their menial tasks. One of my duties was taking the trash from the galley to throw it overboard. The easiest way was emptying it off the fantail. One day, a huge wave carried me clear to the fantail, and the only thing that saved me was the railing.

Had I fallen overboard, nobody would have found me in the vast ocean. By the time they had noticed that I was gone, it would have been much too late. This only happened once. I learned not to walk on the port side when the ship was making a right turn or on the starboard side when the ship turned left. There are many tricks to being a smart sailor.

One of them was to stay out of the boatswain's way when he was working. Most of the time, I saw him holding a cup of coffee. Every now and then, I actually caught him working. When he worked, he worked hard, maintaining the ship. He was a Petty Officer First Class, and most of the work was done by peons like us. Over the years he paid the price, learning the things he was teaching us now. Jake was his name; he was passing onto us the skills needed to be good sailors.

He had a cushy job, as long as everybody pitched in and did the job properly. I don't know what it was, but boatswain mates were in a foul mood most of the time. Out at sea, they didn't have access to liquor, and that may have been the reason.

I remember a second class boatswain mate, and when he went ashore he drank until the wee hours of the morning. When he came back to the ship he was wasted, but come five in the morning, he was up and about, and you'd have never known, just a few hours prior, that he was drunk.

One of the sailors who wanted to become a boatswain mate, started to hallucinate, seeing beautiful women on the bulkhead. It was either the alcohol or the paint fumes, or both. I was intrigued by what he claimed he saw. I kept looking, but there weren't any women visible, only rust spots.

I was assigned to paint the chain locker, where the anchor chains are stored. The shaft leading to the chain locker was deep and narrow. In my days, we had lead paint with deadly fumes.

When I crawled down into the shaft to paint, another sailor relieved me at a prescribed time. We never thought the lead could harm us neurologically or even kill us. Another hazardous job was chipping paint with an incredibly noisy air hammer. We wore no earplugs, and after completing the job, I couldn't hear anything for days.

Whenever my wife calls me, I have an excuse; I blame it on the Navy when I don't hear her. Five years ago, I received a letter from the Department of Defense; I was informed that our ship was sprayed with some kind of an agent.

They didn't identify the type, but it most likely didn't benefit the crew. The letter stated: should I ever contract cancer, or have neurological problems, it might be the result of the tests conducted. I am entitled to visit the VA hospital should it become necessary. Now that makes me feel so much better, but at least they acknowledged it later.

We crossed the Equator on the way to American Samoa. I was working in the galley preparing meals, and that is when I noticed we were saving all the trash in big barrels. Nobody would tell me why, but I knew something was up. I found out later, when you cross the Equator there is a big initiation for the crew who were still Pollywogs.

Prior to crossing the Equator a sailor is known as a Pollywog, and after crossing, you become a shellback. As we neared the Equator, the Captain put the initiation into motion. The Pollywogs had to crawl from the forecastle to the fantail on all fours. Along the way, we were whipped with wet fire hoses, and that was just the beginning.

At about amidships was this fat man, naked from his waist up, who represented King Neptune of the deep. His entire belly was covered with thick wagon grease. When I passed by him, he grabbed me by the head, and rubbed my face in his fat belly. That was disgusting, and by the time I was done with the grease job, they gave me a crude haircut.

> When I passed by him, he grabbed me by the head, and rubbed my face in his grease covered fat belly.

The barber was not the traditional kind. He grabbed my head with both hands and proceeded to cut my hair with old, rusty scissors. When he was done, I didn't have much hair left, only a patch here, and there. Another guy who pretended to be a doctor attempted forcing a slimy oyster down my throat. I didn't dare open my mouth.

The next station was the garbage shoot. I had to crawl through the old, stinky garbage which we saved for days in the galley earlier. At the end of the garbage shoot I was thrown into a huge tank filled with dirty, oily water, and old garbage.

They dunked me, and when I came up, I was supposed to yell 'Shellback'. The words didn't come to me, and they dunked me several more times. I was gasping for air, and by accident, I swallowed a bunch of the polluted water. At that point, I finally spit out the word shellback.

I yelled as loud as I could, 'shellback'. It was a nightmare, and to prove I became a shellback, the certificate is hanging on our wall, signed by King Neptune himself.

The next morning while working in the galley preparing breakfast, I was cracking eggs on the grill, when I noticed the year 1942 stamped on the crate. As soon as I cracked the eggs, a putrid odor traveled throughout the ship, and that morning, we had light breakfast traffic with lots of guys going hungry.

The next morning, after everybody recovered from the horrible rotten egg episode, I cracked one of the eggs, and lo, and behold, a little baby chick ran off the grill. Although its little feet burned, we made it our ship's mascot. Some people actually believe this story and I don't tell them otherwise.

When I was still on the deck force, our ship was coming into the harbor from one of our cruises; the sailors were standing at attention in their beautiful dress whites. What a sight.

The Captain asked me to man the intercom to make a few announcements immediately after we tied up at the pier. I announced: "*All hands prepare to dump the shit cans on the pier.*"

I did not know they were called trashcans; needless to say, I was never again asked to man the intercom. What made things worse, was that all of Pearl Harbor heard my announcement.

I kept turning in my chit for a baker's position. I didn't like cooking, and working in Germany as a baker's apprentice, I was well suited for the job. To my surprise, the Commissary Chief called me into his office and asked me all kinds of questions about why I wanted to be the ship's baker.

I couldn't tell him, but the current Petty Officer Second Class was a terrible baker. He was well liked, but baking was not his forte. His rolls were like bullets, and the breads were as hard as a rock. The crew bitterly complained to the Captain about the dire situation. He was forced to make a change.

I put in for the position, and the chief assured me he would keep me in mind for the job. After he dismissed me, I didn't hear from him until the next day, when he told me, from this moment on, I would be the ship's Chief Baker.

I jumped for joy. From now on, standing watches were a thing of the past. My shift started around midnight after the crew finished watching the flick on the mess deck. There was little traffic aboard ship during the night hours and the good thing was I wasn't interrupted while working.

At first, it seemed overwhelming having to bake for two hundred guys. I was now accountable for everything that came out of the galley having the slightest resemblance to bread. My fear was unfounded. The job was a piece of cake.

I had it made, I only worked around five hours, and my job was done, but it was non-stop. I had access to excellent recipes. As long as I followed the book, everything turned out well. I baked various types of breads, Danish and other delicacies. I had an incentive to turn out good products. If I hadn't, my name would have been Jonah and chances were they would have thrown me overboard.

I even baked pizza one night, and that was a hit. I gained all kinds of friends. The officers from the bridge came down in the middle of the night to see what kind of goodies I was baking because the aroma reached the bridge.

I did favors for the guys who ironed my uniform when in a pinch during a surprise inspection. One hand washed the other, or if they rubbed my back, I'd rub theirs. I was careful to maintain my ethics and not take advantage of the situation.

Things worked out splendidly and everybody was happy. When we were out at sea for many weeks, the guys got grumpy, but good food lifted their spirits. Another morale booster was, when a helicopter from one of the carriers dropped off mail.

I had a girlfriend back home and got mail almost daily. The smell of perfume enveloped the entire living area. I passed the envelope around just to make the guys jealous; it was kind of mean to do that. One day, however, I received a Dear John, and the letters stopped.

Now the table had turned, and guys did to me as I had done to them. If you have never received a Dear John, you haven't lived. It is somewhat like crossing the Equator.

We arrived in Samoa, and it just so happened, tied up next to a diesel submarine. We discovered their food was exceptional. We traded lobsters for steak or whatever else we could find in the reefers, stocked with steaks, lamb, and other delicacies.

On weekends, we pulled out all the stops, and prepared the best meals. The ship had a printing press and produced first class menus. You would have thought you were dining at a fine restaurant.

During the day, I was free to leave the ship. The guided tours were informative and the culture fascinated me. American Samoa was once a German colony. I discovered German writings on buildings throughout the island. The church I visited was built by the Germans prior to WWI. After the armistice of WWI, the Germans lost their colonies in the Pacific.

We toured the natives' living quarters which consisted of a hut with windows, minus the glass, and a dirt floor. It was an eye opener to see how primitive the Samoans lived. At night, the natives rolled out a mat to go to sleep. If you owned a pig or two, it was a sign of prosperity. At night, the sleeping arrangements were unique, the porkers laid on one side, and the people on the other.

The men wore wraparound skirts just like the women; the fabric was colorful with all kinds of flowery designs. They were large people by our standards; remarkably, the women were bigger than the men.

The Hawaiians were similar in appearance. The South Pacific Islanders moved from island to island, and were known as great seafarers. There was much trade between them, and their journeys took them thousands of miles across the vast Pacific.

The island was very beautiful with coconut trees, surrounded by the bluest ocean you can imagine. Their houses were simple, instead of shingles on the roofs; the houses were covered with grass which hung over the side of the building. They didn't have to worry about the cold, only the typhoons.

I enjoyed it more being out in the ocean, than on land. An exception was Samoa and Japan. Whenever we came into port for an extended time, I missed the beauty of the sea with the beautiful nights, the glowing stars, and on occasion, the storms. I felt at home on the ocean.

I remember visiting the Royal Hawaiian hotel, one of only a few at Waikiki. It was a beautiful pink building, with Diamond Head in the background. The view was stunning. The beautiful beaches were covered with white sand and coconut palm trees were swaying in the wind.

I walked towards Diamond Head a few times, not far from Waikiki. It is an extinct volcano, and hasn't erupted for 150,000 years. The island was born during an explosive eruption.

The native Hawaiians know Diamond Head as Le 'ahi, the name of the native tuna. The mountain ridge resembles the tuna's dorsal fin. Diamond Head is like the rest of the Honolulu volcanoes, similar to the Punchbowl, Hanauma Bay, Koko Head, and the Manana Island. Diamond Head is part of the Ko'ola mountain range. I never attempted to climb the mountain, a strenuous exercise.

I loved Waikiki Beach, a great place to relax and get lots of sun. The white sand was marvelous and I found myself going to sleep, only to be woken up by the crashing waves. On a regular basis, I became sunburned. Falling asleep was nothing unusual, and by the time I woke up, I was as red as a lobster.

There was no place like the International Market Place. It had everything the visitors could possibly want. When we sailors visited the Market Place, we wore nothing but swimming trunks. That was the dress of the day. If I remember right, besides the swimming trunks, we wore a light shirt, that way, we didn't get sunburned. If we did, it didn't hurt so badly, but the itching never stopped, and getting into my work clothes was plain murder. After much pain and suffering, the burn turned into a tan, but I had to continue exposing myself to the sun, otherwise, it faded quickly. In those days, nobody ever talked about skin cancer. There must have been many cases, but few people paid any attention to the danger. Later in my life, I did have skin cancer of the basil variety.

When sailors violated Navy protocol, the sailors were subject of receiving

Captain's Mast. If a sailor got sunburned to the degree where he couldn't perform his duties, he'd be going to Captain's Mast. Captain's Mast is a form of judicial punishment, and at times, the sailors lost rate if the crime was severe, one was missing ship's movement. Other times, one was denied the privilege of going on liberty on weekends.

While in port, my Captain told me Mama had called the ship to see if I was okay. The Captain assured her I was just fine. She sensed there was a problem. It was amazing how she got a hold of our ship. I had a falling out with Mama before I went active, and that bothered me for a long time. I didn't write to her for six months and she was anxious to hear from me. Not writing to her was mean on my part. She worried herself sick not hearing from me and called the ship. I didn't get to talk to her, but the Captain did. He told her I was just fine. Once we wrote each other, things returned to normal.

I loved going to the YMCA, down town Honolulu, it was a great place to visit. It was equipped with a beautiful fresh water swimming pool and other amenities. It was clean, relaxing, and lying by the pool was terrific. To stay there overnight, it cost five dollars. The best price in town.

Whenever we went on liberty to Honolulu and Waikiki, we tried to hitch a ride. It saved us lots of money. People didn't mind giving sailors a ride. We didn't encounter much crime and walking around Waikiki was safe and fun. I enjoyed the Beach where I did lots of bodysurfing, and always on the look out for a big wave to ride to the beach. I am sure there were sharks in these waters, but I never gave it a thought. We were having too good of a time. I was fortunate to have seen, and experienced the wonderful things life had to offer.

We befriended many tourists from the mainland. On occasions, we were asked to escort them around the island and at times, treated us to dinner. They knew, on a sailor's salary, we couldn't afford such luxuries.

When on liberty, two or three of us guys went to Honolulu looking for things to do. We always hung out together and helped each other out. When one ran out of money, the other chipped in to buy coffee or a sandwich. When we were offered a free meal, we didn't refuse the offer. We were truly beach bums in every sense of the word and loved every minute of it.

Some of the tourists were more than willing to buy us food and an occasional drink. I had very little money to spend, everything was so expensive. My service was free as a 'tour guide', and I was happy to show my friends from the mainland around the island. The rub was that they had to provide the wheels.

On one occasion, I had the opportunity to go the leeward side of the island. The Polynesian Cultural Center was fascinating and we learned how the natives live. They performed beautiful dances, and my favorite was the hula. I don't know how the girls moved their hips without getting hurt.

One group of performers, the natives of New Zealand, performed native dances and singing that was out of this world. They harmonized beautifully.

The time went by too fast and before long we were back at the base. Our guests took us to the base and we bid them farewell. We thanked them for the wonderful time that we spent with them.

Every couple of months, our ship steamed to an ammo dump to take on ammunition. All hands helped to load various shells, rockets, and other types of ordnance. It was similar to a water brigade passing the ammo from one person to the other. You didn't dare drop one of the six inch shells or the rockets on the steel deck; that is why the steel deck was covered with old mattresses.

During World War II, a Navy ship was taking on ammunition. One of the sailors dropped a shell on the steel deck, and it exploded. The whole vessel became an inferno with many lives lost. That was known as the second Pearl Harbor.

The rusty bow of the ship protruding out of the water served as a reminder of what could happen when someone is careless. The incident wasn't talked about much.

We steamed by the U.S.S. Arizona on the way to the open sea. It was before the memorial was built which covers the breadth of the ship. During the time I was there, a small platform was built for visitors to view the remains of the ship.

Over a thousand sailors lost their lives on the U.S.S. Arizona on the tragic day December the 7th 1941. After that many years, one can still see the oil bubbles reaching the surface from the bottom of the ship. All we saw from the observation deck were the large rusty gun turrets, fore and aft, and the outline of the ship.

It was always a solemn occasion whenever we passed by. The sailors prayed softly while standing at attention with their heads bowed in reverence.

In war, a destroyer has a life expectancy of only five minutes; the explosion of the torpedoes and other ordnance would lift the destroyer clear out of the water. The bulkhead is thin, and offers little protection. That is why the Navy coined the phrase, 'tin can'.

During general quarters, my station was at the bottom of the ship, loading live rockets into the rocket launcher. In case of war, I wouldn't have lasted long.

Cne of the exercises was 'Condition Three'. In war time, the crew worked four hours on, four hours off. War time cruising was continued as long as the threat persisted. If it lasted for a week or longer, it was exhausting for the crew because nobody got much rest.

After a couple of years, I had my fill of the island and was itching to get off. It was commonly referred to as having Island fever. One of the problems was the locals didn't care much for service personnel. We had no money to spend and we were considered a nuisance.

There was a sign on one of the manicured lawns which read: 'sailors and dogs stay off the lawn', but all in all, I had a great time, and having a positive attitude helped. I was a repeat customer at the German restaurant at Waikiki Beach, 'The Hofbrau' where I unwound with a couple of bottles of dark Bavarian beer.

I got acquainted with the people working there and we were like family. On weekends when on liberty, I hauled a couple of friends from our ship to join me. We accompanied the accordion player with spirited singing, and although it was in German, the guys mimicked the words and had a good time.

I made it my business, keeping an eye on my friends, just to make sure they didn't drink too much. The Navy had patty wagons going up and down the streets looking for drunken sailors. When the shore patrol brought them back to the base, they were locked up in the brig overnight, no questions asked.

I made sure my friends made it back to the ship before the Shore Patrol caught up with them. The sailors drank beer and didn't realize the alcohol content was higher than the U.S. brewed beer, and without saying, they got drunker than a skunk.

It wasn't uncommon for a sailor to miss ship's movement because alcohol kept him on land. If a sailor missed the ship's movement, he was subject to Captain's Mast, and at times was reduced in rank and placed in the brig until the ship came back into port. One of our guys was reduced from Petty Officer second class to seaman, and was issued a dishonorable discharge to boot.

Our ship was the flagship of the Pineapple fleet, appropriately named. Our Captain was a great guy, tough when he had to be, but fair.

We even had Sunday worship service aboard ship, at sea, or if we were in the harbor. The service was conducted by our commissary Petty Officer Second Class. Our Captain was a believer as well as our XO. I know they prayed for the crew especially when we ran into bad weather.

Our fleet consisted of three destroyers, a tanker, a couple of frigates and a carrier. We operated with the U.S.S. Enterprise, the Hornet, the Hancock and the Constellation at various times.

To receive mail, a helicopter from one of the carriers dropped it off on the fantail. Food was received the same way from one of the supply ships via high lining.

239

The Navy arranged activities for us on the base to keep us busy, and perhaps keep us from getting into trouble. We had famous entertainers performing for us, and we weren't even charged a cover fee. There was no way you could beat a deal like that.

The funny thing was that I can't remember any of the entertainers. If Elvis Presley had performed, I would have remembered. We also had athletic competitions, pitting ship against ship, and that was fun. We were furnished soft drinks, hot dogs and hamburgers, all you could eat.

We'd do sit-ups, push-ups, and play baseball against the crews of other ships. I left playing baseball to others but I set a record doing the most pull-ups. I am sure that the record has been broken many times by now.

In a couple of weeks, our ship left for Asia. How exciting! I had never been there. On Monday morning, we set sail. A total of seven ships left that morning and the channel was crammed with ships, including the carrier Kitty Hawk, four destroyers, a supply ship and an oiler. The sailors were standing at attention with their dress whites on the decks. The National Anthem was played when we passed the U.S.S. Arizona. It was a solemn occasion.

Soon, we cleared the channel and steamed into the open Pacific. I looked back one more time as the Diamond Head drew fainter and fainter, eventually disappearing from sight. We were out at sea for a couple of days when rations were transferred to our ship. It was routine when at sea to obtain rations and personnel aboard via high lining.

That is something to see! A couple of ropes were launched by a rocket, and attached between the ships, building a bridge so to speak.

I remember high lining a Chief Petty Officer, when one of the waves between the ships soaked him, but we managed to get him to our ship without drowning the guy. When he came aboard, he was soaked from head to toe, but happy to be alive.

We also received our fuel the same way, connecting both ships with huge oil hoses which carried diesel fuel from the carrier or tanker, to our ship. Between the ships, the waves were churning, at times reaching our bridge. The sea water was compressed between the vessels and produced a huge amount of energy.

We were receiving diesel fuel from the Kitty Hawk, when one of the ships drifted too far. The oil hose stretched, snapped, and ricocheted back to our ship. The situation was extremely dangerous. Our vessel was covered with heavy bunker oil and if one of the crew members had been close to the hose when it snapped, it would have cut him in half. What was annoying. The sailors from the carrier thought it was pretty funny.

We were about as big as a postal stamp next to them. We promised we'd get even with them someday, but before we could, the carrier was decommissioned. It took us forever to get our ship cleaned up, we scrubbed, and scrubbed, and scrubbed some more with some type of detergent which dispersed the oil.

Our ship may not have been the biggest, but it had lots of teeth, so to speak. She would have been a match with any submarine or even a surface vessel with our five inch dual guns and rocket launcher.

When I was off duty, I used to visit the guys in the sonar room, partly because it was nice and cool. That was one of the places on the ship, where air conditioning filled the area, as was the officer's quarters.

It was fascinating to watch objects under the surface of the water, especially when a sub was prowling the ocean. The system was able to identify the various sounds submarines produce. Each ship or submarine has a fingerprint by the type of echo it produces.

Destroyers are able to detect foreign subs by the calling card they leave behind. The key of a sub is to have it operate as silently as possible. The sonar room was off limits to me. I was not yet a citizen, but rules were broken. They knew who had the key to the reefer.

On the way to Asia we ran into a typhoon, what an awesome experience. The storm was severe as the ocean was churning, and letting us know who was the boss. We were like a cork floating, and trying to stay upright.

The destroyers around us were like submarines, submerged most of the time, and every so often I caught a glimpse of them as they climbed out of the angry waves. Everybody was scared including me, but I was too busy trying to stay on my feet, to worry what might happen.

During the storm, we discovered an Albatross sitting on the bridge minding its own business, just relaxing, and getting out from under the storm. What a magnificent bird with its huge wings and beak. It stayed with us for a couple of days, and then took off again, its destination, the ocean, its home. The bird took our minds off the storm as we marveled at its presence. We hated for the bird to leave. We saw the albatross glide to the depths of the black, ferocious waves.

The bird very seldom reaches land, and if they do, it is to lay eggs and rear their chicks. Observing the Albatross in stormy seas reminded me of a ballet as it glided across the waves with such elegance. You'd think the waves would pluck them out of the air, but no chance. Their flight is nothing but spectacular. I have seen them land, and taking to flight, it is a comedy. They appear awkward, they tumble as they land, and taking off isn't much better. It shows God has a great sense of humor when he created animals like the Albatross.

On the bridge, a spectacular panorama unfolded in front of our eyes, the giant waves as tall as mountains. The ocean embraced our ship with its giant arms. At times we were straddling the waves, and were suddenly plunged into one of the deep valleys, making the ship shudder, and as this happened, it lifted the two huge screws clear out of the water.

We inspected the suspension at amidships, hoping and praying the ship would not break in half. At one point we were listing almost at 90 degrees, and thank God, we came back up. I walked on the bulkhead instead of on the deck. I didn't dare climb up a ladder as the ship went down into a trough, the force would have jettisoned me to the top of the ladder.

We had been in rough weather before, but this had it all beat. I didn't have to cook for a couple of days, giving me a break. I could always get into the reefer and get food out for the guys, but who wants to eat frozen meat?

In a couple of days we were back to normal, we outran the storm, and were ready for a well-deserved break. Being seasick is no fun. The guys told me they wished they could have died. Soon, everything returned to normal operations, and I was able to bake my breads and pastries again.

Early one morning, I was about ready to wrap everything up in the galley; all I had left to do was to get the bread out of the oven. At that particular point, the ship was struck by a huge wave that caused the bread to slam against the side of the oven with terrible consequences.

I opened the doors, and saw what I suspected. The loaves of bread were flatter than a pancake. Needless to say, I had to start all over again, and worked clear into the late morning hours, but it all worked out okay. I was happy the guys had warm, fresh bread to eat in time for breakfast although a little late.

I pushed my luck when I baked a peach cobbler. It was time to take it out of the oven to let it cool. I was gingerly carried the cobbler to the serving line, when a giant wave made the ship list to port. Due to the motion of the ship, it threw me, along with the cobbler into the serving line. I lost my balance, but couldn't let go of the cobbler, and if I had, it would have been a disaster.

I held onto the pan as the fiery hot juice ran down my arm. Like hot lava, it burned through my skin. I reached the serving line alright, minus my skin. Our corpsman checked my arm and saw that the juice burned clear down to the muscle. He bandaged me up, but it burned like crazy for several days.

I had a scar for the longest time, and when people asked me what happened to me, I told them what occurred. I could have told them I received the scar in a fierce battle at sea, and that would have made it a juicy story. It was a juicy story alright, but with a peach flavor.

Our ship was conducting plane guard, and it was fascinating to watch the jets land on the carrier in the night. It was as though we were at some airport with all the noise of the jet engines. The whole ship was lit like LaGuardia Airport.

The pilots were practicing landing and takeoffs, and that lasted a good part of the night. A tragedy occurred when one of the jets came in too low while making a landing approach. The plane slammed into the fantail of the carrier. There wasn't much left of the plane or the pilot. They never did find the pilot, he was lost at sea.

It was dangerous landing on a carrier. The ship moved from one side to the other and the forward motion of the ship made it a tricky maneuver. I was told it was like attempting to land on a tiny stamp out in the vast ocean.

Trying to sleep while on patrol was impossible, the jet engines screamed, the tires screeched, and the noise of the deck was deafening. It was a recipe for a restless night. I felt privileged to have had those experiences, and to have been part of the incredible displays of bravery by the pilots was awesome.

Another exciting story was, one of our chiefs was picked up by the Navy via helicopter to protect him from the syndicate in Asia who had a contract out to have him killed. Lucky for the chief, he made it back to the States alive.

The cruise to Asia was an awesome experience for any young man just joining the Navy. Our first port of call was in Japan at the port of *Yokosuka.* We extended our stay for two weeks. Yokosuka became the homeport of the Seventh Fleet beginning in 1945. The town had a great history dating back to the year 1063 when the Kinusaga Castle was built. It is an industrial center, home of Nissan. During the time of WWII, Japan built two carriers at the port city and many other naval vessels.

When on liberty, I walked all over the place looking at the shops and viewing the surrounding area. It was a very cold November in 1963. To be ready for this type of weather, we wore our Navy pee coats which kept us nice and warm. After we left Yokosuka, we steamed to Sasebo, Japan and stayed there two weeks. It wasn't any warmer.

While in port at Yokosuka, I heard in the morning of November the 22nd 1963, that our president John Fitzgerald Kennedy had been assassinated in Dallas. At first, I thought what a cruel joke, but it was true. It was a very sad day for us all. There wasn't much to say. We prayed for our nation. Our flag was flown at half mast, we were somber, hoping and praying we would get through the crisis.

We were either in Yokosuka, or Sasebo, when a few guys and I took a taxi to Tokyo and for a dime the driver took us all over the city. That was one heck of a deal. We couldn't tell the driver where we wanted to go. He didn't speak English and we couldn't speak Japanese and as a last resort I tried German, and that didn't work either.

He drove us through town, and after a few miles, we ended up at a river where we boarded a small boat which took us on an excursion trip. We had a marvelous time and saw beautiful sights along the way. One thing stood out, the farmers grew their crops on terraced hills. The hills were beautifully maintained with lush green plants and the terraces gave it a manicured appearance.

There was little room to grow things, and they utilized every inch of land. Japan was a clean and pristine land. The people were polite, and forever smiling. One weekend, we decided to go skiing in the Japanese Alps. We took a train to Yokohama where we caught a bus and traveled up into the Japanese Alps. It was a marvelous experience! The Japanese Alps reminded me of Bavaria. The mountains were absolutely beautiful; the peaks were covered with snow, and it was like a winter wonderland. I saw why they called them the Alps.

We stayed in a beautiful alpine motel and it had all the amenities anybody would want. We were tired and slept until nine in the morning. When we woke up for breakfast, we hurried to the dining room and to our surprise, there were no chairs, so we sat on the floor eating. I don't remember what we ate, but it must have been okay. After breakfast, we rented a pair of skis, and after a short walk we arrived at the ski lift which took us up the slope.

The slopes weren't very challenging, but enough to give us a nice ride down. It was so quiet, and all I could hear was the sound of the ski lift. The Japanese are a quiet people, and I felt embarrassed by all the noise we were making.

The next day, we had a slalom race with the native folks, and if I remember, we came in first. That was a fun day. The Japanese people were so gracious and told us to come back tomorrow for another slalom race. Well that didn't happen due to our time constrains.

One of the problems was, ordering food. Many dishes included sea food, not my favorite. The waitress came to take our order and we never knew what we were going to get. That reminds me of another chapter in my book.

I didn't like fish, and fish were served a million different ways in Japan. I ate the stuff, but I didn't enjoy it much.

The people were just wonderful and made our stay very pleasant. When we ate, we sat on the floor with our legs crossed, and ate with chop sticks. It is really tough to eat soup with those little sticks. I am just kidding, but I had a tough time getting the food to my mouth and with practice, it would have made eating much more enjoyable.

I had a marvelous time skiing and talking to the Japanese people and to my surprise, many conversed in English. They observed us and thought the Americans were a little strange.

The second day of our trip it was time to return to port. The first stretch of our trip was by bus, and it was marvelous riding through the white mountain landscape, laced with snow, and waterfalls, partially encased with ice.

The bus took us to a train station where we boarded a train that took us to Yokosuka where our ship was berthed. We settled in and were getting comfortable, and by luck, we had a little money left to buy food. After we were on the train for an hour, we heard lots of giggling and carrying on in the next car.

That was worth investigating, and discovered, there were French stewardesses filling up the car. We hit the jackpot for sure! Young women were just waiting to meet us. We filtered into their car and the booze was flowing. The sailors ordered so much liquor, the bartender ran out of the stuff. He told us he had no more. Maybe it was best to close the bar. Our sailors, including some of the women, were feeling pretty good by then.

I didn't have any alcoholic beverages. I made sure I didn't do something I might regret later. I met this girl by the name of Monique Laundry who was working at the French embassy in Tokyo. She spoke Japanese, English, German and her native French.

I was impressed by her beauty and charm. It was obvious she was bright. We liked each other and before leaving the train, I told her I would be making a trip to Tokyo at a later date, and perhaps have lunch with her. I kept my word!

The next weekend, while on liberty, I took a taxi to the train station in Yokosuka, jumped on board, and before long the train arrived in Tokyo. I wore my civvies for obvious reasons. It was recommended when traveling off base so as not to attract attention.

I was afraid I might run out of money on the way to Tokyo. I counted the money over and over, just to make sure there was enough to get me there and back plus pay for the lunch.

I flagged down a taxi, gave him the name of the restaurant, and he took me right to the place. The taxi was cheap, and the ride was dangerous, and scary. The driver never stopped at any of the traffic lights, and just blew his horn as he drove through the intersections, something I wasn't used to. I closed my eyes and prayed.

When I arrived, I walked into the restaurant looking for her, when I saw her waiting for me at a table in the corner of the restaurant. We started out making small talk either in English or German, and I learned her parents were from Alsace Lorraine, formerly known as Elsass Lothringen, when it was part of Germany. She was familiar with the area in Germany where I grew up, and that brought another denominator into this equation.

She ordered for me, and her Japanese was excellent as far as I could tell. Can't remember what I ordered, but it wasn't fish. I observed her closely, and came to the conclusion she must have come from an aristocratic family.

Her English was impeccable, and a notch or two above mine. I was nervous and stumbled all over myself attempting not to look uninformed. When she spoke, she ran her fingers through her hair, and judging by her body language, she told me, "I like you, and want to see you again."

She only had an hour or so for lunch, before going back to work. She told me she was eager to see me sometime in the near future. I pondered the idea for a while. Our ship was leaving port soon, and my money was running low.

Had we stayed in Japan longer, I would have made an effort to see her again. I discovered long distance relationships don't work.

The thought of meeting her again was exciting, but on a sailor's salary, I would have had only enough money to take her to McDonalds, and there were none in Japan at the time.

Our diplomatic relationship with France wasn't the best under Charles De Gaulle's reign, and traveling up to Tokyo to meet a French woman from the embassy could have aroused suspicion. I wasn't a U.S. citizen yet, and seeing a French woman may have raised some eyebrows. The Navy had their spies and I am sure they were keeping an eye on us.

As sailors, we were prohibited to divulge our ship's movements. The old saying goes like this: 'loose lips sink ships'. I spoke with her a couple of times on the phone and promised her that my trip to see her was still on my agenda, but I knew the chances were next to nil. That concluded my romance in Japan.

After Japan, we visited Hong Kong, and stayed there two weeks. We anchored out in the harbor alongside other naval vessels. The harbor was jammed with U.S. Navy ships. What an experience! When on liberty, we took a water shuttle. The U.S. Navy was generous and picked up our tab from our ship to Hong Kong.

There was a group of us, who visited the Tiger Balm Garden, and that was fascinating. Not knowing the rich history of China, I missed out on the significance of the attractions. The Garden was built in 1935 by Aw Boon Haw as a theme park with statues of warriors and dragons. In the 1980's, it was converted to an amusement park.

I believe there must have been dragons on earth when man arrived on the scene. There are too many stories about the slaying of dragons. Many countries have a dragon in their folklore. Germany for instance, in the *Niebelungen Lied*, Siegfried, the Germanic warrior slew the dragon.

In the early 1960's, nobody, or very few people were carrying credit cards and everything was paid for in cold cash. The dollar was mighty, and everybody was eager to receive the currency. In Hong Kong, like everywhere else, the U.S. dollar was king.

One night, we stayed in the heart of Hong Kong; the rates of the hotel were reasonably priced. We had just enough cash to pay for one night which we split three ways. The stay was pleasant. It was an upscale hotel where foreign diplomats were staying. I saw fancy limos taking guests into the city, and I knew then, we weren't staying in a Motel 6.

We had a steak dinner before heading back to our ship, but the next day, we were all very sick from food poisoning. It prevented us from working the next three days, and the rest of the week, it was a struggle.

I would have given anything for a Big Mac, but there weren't any American fast food chains around. While still in Hong Kong, I took a ferry to

Kowloon, known for its many tailor shops. I strolled down the main street of Kowloon, with stores on both sides of the street displaying men's apparel. I went into a shop, and told the clerk what I wanted. The tailor measured me for size, and quoted me $40.00 a suit. I decided to buy two: one was blue, and the other gray. Later I discovered gray was not my color. Within a couple of days, I made another trip to Kowloon and picked up the two suits I had ordered a couple of days earlier.

The tailor did a great job and the suits fit like a glove. I had never owned two suits at any one time, and it made me feel wealthy. I detected much later, the suits were sown with cheap yarn, and in time, they fell apart. I had them re-sown. I wore them for many years and got rid of them when my midsection expanded.

In Germany, a man's wealth was measured on how many suits he owned, not how much money he had in his pocket, but it didn't hurt if you had a little fortune accumulated.

The U.S.S. Carpenter sailed back to Japan, patrolling the Sea of Japan in the dead of winter, and Ivan was watching. We were off the Siberian coast. It was very cold, and when I touched the bulkhead, my hands froze. The ship had no insulation, and sleeping next to the bulkhead made it a very cold experience. The ocean was around freezing, and it was like floating in an ice tub. I couldn't get warm. The Navy didn't supply us with portable heaters.

We were just off the coast of Siberia, not far from the secret Soviet sea port of Vladivostok. One afternoon, we were shadowed by the Russians who were, I am sure, out of the port of Vladivostok. Vladivostok is close to Japan and is Russia's foremost Arctic port in Siberia. A Russian bomber TU16 Badger did several flyovers, and had its eye on our carrier fleet.

While conducting anti submarine warfare exercises, on our port side, a Russian diesel submarine of the Whiskey Class surfaced. That was an exciting event to see their submarine surface with sailors of both ships eyeing each other.

The Soviets were prepared for this type of weather, and were wearing heavy coats, and fur hats with earflaps to protect them from the arctic cold.

We watched with amazement as the diesel broke through the ice and surfaced only a couple of hundred feet to our port side.

Our destroyer was free of ice, but where the sub surfaced, ice was all around. The Russians, I was sure, thought we were crazy, just wearing tee-shirts. It was obvious that we were not prepared for the arctic conditions. I hated the thought of something unfortunate happening to our ship, and had we been forced to abandon ship, we would have frozen to death.

Later, we were shadowed by a Russian Kotlin class destroyer, but our Captain had spotted their armada long ago, and we weren't surprised at their presence.

Our Navy did this on a regular basis to sharpen our skills. In case it came to war, we would be up to the task of defending our ships and men. The whole carrier taskforce, including the U.S.S. Hornet, kept a wary eye on the Russians with our planes and helicopters.

We had another surprise; a Russian Badger was conducting surveillance. The Badger was their frontline heavy long range bomber, similar to our B-52. Our long range B-52 bombers were much more powerful with eight jet engines, and carried many tons of ordnance.

I am sure, at times there were close calls, and I am surprised no shots were ever fired accidentally. We dropped depth charges, and giant explosions lifted the water fifty feet into the air behind our ship as we played cat and mouse with the Russians. The men fired large torpedoes with dummy warheads. I compared them to dolphins slicing through the surface of the water with a big splash. Had these torpedoes been armed, they could have blown any ship out of the water.

Before we reached the Japanese port of Yokosuka, still out in the open sea, we were met by a boatload of women who offered their services. It is not what you are thinking; they came prepared to paint our ship from top to bottom if we gave them food to feed their families.

In a matter of a few hours our ship looked like new. I had never seen anything like it in my life; they put us guys to shame. There were around ten women, equipped with brushes, ready to work. Our Captain consented, and allowed them to board. They spoke very little English, and of course, none of us knew Japanese, but somehow we communicated. We supplied them with buckets of our gray Navy paint, and the entire ship had a fresh look. They did a magnificent job. When the women were finished, we gave them the best of our food. I was concerned as I saw the freezer getting low.

The women took off with their boat loaded down with precious food. After a week, we pulled into the harbor of Sasebo, Japan. With the new paint job, heads turned as we steamed into the harbor. The U.S.S. Carpenter was transformed into a polished fighting ship.

While in port, our crew bought lots of merchandise to take back to their families. I purchased a set of dishes at a very reasonable price. Our ship was full of all kinds of merchandise, mainly electronics. The gangways were packed with gifts as we steamed back to Hawaii. It was a safety issue. In case of fire, it would have been a huge problem. The passageways were blocked and we had to climb over boxes to get around.

In Sasebo, as well as in Yokosuka, the call girls were manning the bars. Our sailors dropped a lot of money, and that wasn't all. Come Monday morning, there was a long line at sickbay. I never engaged in these risky practices, even though it was tempting at times. Not visiting the bars kept me out of trouble.

On the way back to Hawaii, the Captain gave the okay for us to dive off the ship to do some recreational swimming. The boatswain mate was standing by with a gun, just in case a shark decided to join the party.

It wasn't long before huge sharks showed up to investigate. For good reason, our guys hurried out of the water to evade these killing machines. We thought everybody was out of the water, but one was still swimming in close proximity to the sharks. It was now a rescue operation. They threw him a line, and pulled him alongside the ship. Lucky for him!

As he pulled himself up on the rope, a huge shark was going to get a piece of him. It missed the sailor by a foot or less, with jaws wide open; the shark was ready to devour him. We saw the huge fish disappear under the water with its huge mouth still wide open and displaying tens of white sharp teeth ready for a meal.

After we had the sailor safely aboard, another shark was seen at port side of the ship close to the forecastle, and we estimated that it was twelve feet long. Another couple of sharks were on the starboard side of the ship. It was not the time to be in the water. The gunner's mates emptied the gun locker and started shooting the sharks at close range. The water turned bright red.

Before long, a feeding frenzy ensued! Sharks began attacking each other. All I saw were fins on the surface. It resembled red foam as the water churned from the sharks attacking each other. The sharks attacked everything and anything.

After this recreation stopped, we made our way to the harbor of Kaohsiung, Taiwan. Kids, about ten years of age welcomed us as we anchored outside of the harbor. We threw coins into the water, and the kids dove after the money. They were excellent divers and caught the money every time before it sunk into the deep. They only went after quarters, dimes, and nickels, but if it was a penny, they let it go. We watched them hour after hour. We lost money hour after hour, but it was fun watching them perform incredible feats.

Kaohsiung was a large town. After getting off the liberty boat, sailors in their dress whites occupied the entire street. My friend Dennis and I were following behind them, and by the time we reached the end of street, they had all disappeared. I was naive, and couldn't figure out what could have happened to these guys. Not one of them was left on the street. I was hoping the rapture hadn't taken place.

Did moray eels attack them and pull them into their deep caves? This scenario occurred whenever we went ashore, no matter where. Monday morning, the guys were lined up at the sick bay to get their life saving penicillin shots.

To me it was inconceivable that none of them ever figured out how dangerous it was to engage in these risky practices. Kaohsiung was a city with much prostitution where 60,000 young girls of thirteen to seventeen years of age were working as prostitutes. They were brought to the island from China and other places in the Pacific. Parents sold their daughters to the highest bidder. It was sad to see this happening to young girls, still children.

My friend Dennis and I wandered into the city to locate a restaurant, but first I had to use the restroom. I found the restroom and settled down to do my business, when a lady began talking to me from the adjoining stall. Needless to say, I wasn't in the mood any longer, and left the restroom. I wasn't used to that kind of arrangement.

We were seated at the upscale restaurant, and looked the menu over. It came time to order, but we had a problem, we couldn't read the menu. This happened on previous occasions, and we took our chances hoping we would be served a scrumptious meal. At last, the waiter came to our table with the meal. I saw a fish like creature staring at me on my plate. Fish wasn't my favored food anyway, and there was no way I would have eaten it. That was my dining experience at Kaohsiung, Taiwan.

Every time we left home port and sailed to another part of the world, one of the sailors pulled off his wedding band as soon as we exited the harbor. I asked him why he did that, and he told me nonchalantly that he had a family in Japan as well as in the States. How a man could do that is beyond anything imaginable. It probably caught up with him in the future.

On our last visit to Yokosuka or Sasebo, we were offered a tour of Nagasaki. A group of guys signed up, and we boarded a bus to Nagasaki. It was very emotional when we saw how the nuclear bombs affected the city.

I witnessed how horrible the war was, and how it affected the civilian population. This brought back memories of my family, and the near misses we had fleeing the enemy.

A cable car carried us to the top of a mountain outside of Nagasaki, and from there, we had a spectacular view of the whole valley. Scores of people perished the day the bomb was dropped, and there were still isolated ruins, a testimony of that awful day. Most everything was rebuilt by now. It was only eighteen years after the war, and the Japanese had most of the cities rebuilt.

You couldn't help but feel for the people living there. Nagasaki and Hiroshima rose from the ashes.

A couple of weeks later, after we crossed the vast Pacific, we arrived at Pearl Harbor. I had missed the place and looked forward to going ashore. This was my last hurrah so to speak and I was determined to have a good time. A couple of my friends, Keith and Paul came along. We hitched a ride to Waikiki, and while there, we befriended a couple of girls. One of the ladies was a stewardess for Delta, enjoying her vacation on Oahu. As it happened, her girlfriends didn't live far from the beach. Sandy invited us to her place, and later in the evening we went back to the beach. There was no need to wear my street shoes so I left them at Sandy's place.

We were at the beach listening to music and watching the white breakers, when we decided to head back to her apartment to pick up my shoes. When we arrived, we found the place ransacked. My shoes were gone, and the suspect thief left his old pair. How thoughtful!

At least he had class and didn't want me to go barefoot.

While we were in the process of checking what other items were missing, her former boyfriend showed up. He introduced himself as such. We suspected he might have been the person who broke into her apartment. There was no sign of forced entry. He was our guy. He had her key in his hand.

He couldn't have been very bright, coming back to the scene of the crime. Her jewelry and cash was missing. In the meantime, the cops showed up, but prior to their arrival, he approached me and wanted to fight.

He caught me off guard and punched me in the face, but it didn't hurt much. I didn't have time to return the favor as he ran from the scene of the crime. I was hoping to get even with the creep, one way or the other. The cops were very thorough, and asked me if I could identify him if I saw him, and the answer was, an affirmative yes.

The cops asked me if I wanted to go with them to help them locate him, and take him into custody. I certainly could do that. The policemen and I patrolled the Waikiki Beach area, checking out the hangouts along the way without leaving any stone unturned.

I reckoned they ran his name and he most likely had committed other crimes in Honolulu. When we walked into one of the restaurants, he was sitting at the counter having a drink. Now that was way too easy. One of the officers asked me if I was certain it was him, and I affirmed it was the guy. The officer wasted no time, walked up to him, and slapped the handcuffs on him.

All I was wearing were swimming trunks and sandals, what a sight! That was the usual attire at Waikiki Beach; I barely weighed one hundred and fifty pounds. How things have changed over time. I wouldn't be caught dead running around in my swimming trunks in public now.

The cops had him secured in no time. In those days the officers didn't have to read the Miranda rights to the suspect. The last thing this thief told me before they took him away was, one day he would find me and kill me.

I felt uneasy about that, but what were the chances? I am sure; they locked up him up for a long time. This was like 'Hawaii Five O' series with all the excitement.

I was getting close to my separation date, and hoping it wouldn't delay me from leaving the island. The prosecutor could have delayed my departure if he wanted me for a witness. I should have thought about that, but my departure went off without a hitch. The end result was, another thief was in custody, and I was on my way back to the States.

I flew from Honolulu to San Francisco and from there caught a plane to Denver, Colorado. After arriving at Mama's and Papa's home, I discovered my sister Helga had in the meantime sold my car. That upset me, but I was happy somebody else had use of the car. Otherwise, it would have just sat around and not benefited anybody. My next car was a 1962 Mercury; it was an even more elegant car than the first.

In December of 1963 I was separated from active duty. I received an honorable discharge after serving another four years in the Naval Reserve. After forty years of my discharge, I received a letter from the Department of Defense. At first, I was puzzled as to why I heard from the government.

I found out that while operating off the Hawaiian Islands, the government selected our ship to be part of a secret mission. I had no clue we were bombarded with iodine radiation which could lead to all kinds of medical problems later in life. In a way, I was glad I didn't know of the exposure until much later. It would have caused me to worry for the rest of my life. Thank God, I am healthy thus far, and hope and pray I'll stay that way.

36

ELUSIVE DREAMS

I was not welcome at my former home after arriving from Hawaii. This was not a total surprise, and having a little money in the bank, I had enough for an apartment should the need arise. The money I had saved was for my education. I traveled to Boulder, Colorado and enrolled at the University of Colorado. I packed up, and moved to Boulder. I moved into one of their dorms and it all worked out great. It wasn't long before I started getting into a rhythm of studying.

My roommate's home was in Chicago where his family ran a small business. We got along well and he encouraged me to be diligent in my studies. I majored in history, and English, for foreigners such as I was. The university offered English courses for students who recently came to this country which was a great benefit. My English still gave me lots of trouble, but I made progress.

After six months at the university, my confidence took a nosedive, and I left school. My roommates tried to talk me out of leaving. I didn't listen to them. It was difficult for me to keep my mind on my studies. I had a taste of California after I got out of the service and I was hooked. I was in love with the state.

I had never seen any place where one could be at the ocean one day, and the same afternoon be in the mountains. California was an incredible place to live. I also knew my shoveling snow days were over. I realized later, it was a big mistake to leave school. I should have listened to my friends.

I came back home for a short time, but I was not welcomed by Mama. She told me she had high hopes for me; my actions told her that I wasn't serious about making something of myself. One morning when she left for work, she told me I wasn't welcome anymore, and I had better be out of the house when she returned in the evening. I was not at all shocked by her demand.

This had happened to each of my sisters. I wasn't the exception. I still had a little money in my pocket, and that afternoon, I took a taxi to the train station, and caught the Rio Grande via California.

I didn't know if Mama was bluffing, but I took her up on her request. The trip to California was absolutely beautiful traveling through the Rockies, and then the Sierra Nevada Mountain Range. I left in February, and there was much snow. I saw the ice covered peaks, and the breathtaking sunsets. It was a lifetime experience for me, and a great delight.

Many years later, I spoke to my sister Gerlinde who lives in Greely, Colorado. She told me our mother tried to commit suicide, walking barefoot and with light clothing to Golden, Colorado in the month of January. I remember when I was still at home, Mama told me, she wanted to commit suicide, and preferred freezing to death. We wanted to help her, but she wouldn't listen.

When the doctor prescribed her pills, she flushed them down the toilet. He was not amused by her actions. Golden was approximately thirty miles from Denver, and I was puzzled how she made it to the town. She almost succeeded in her wish.

Out of the blue, Gerlinde received a call from a doughnut shop. Apparently Mama had her phone number, so one of the employees called my sister. My sister climbed into her car and rushed to Golden. She found Mama on one of the stools half frozen. She walked her to the car and on the way home, Mama recovered somewhat.

The war took its toll on my mother and left her broken. My dad didn't have an easy life living with her, and frankly, I don't know how he survived. Mama became irritated without much provocation. There was a time when she threw objects at Papa and luckily for him, she missed. He was an angel, in spite of everything. He was always kind to her and did everything to make her happy.

I was heart broken when my mother disowned me at the age of seventeen. Throughout my high school days, it was touch and go. I never knew from one day to the next if I was still welcomed. When I finally left home for good at the age of twenty-two, I had very little contact with my parents. She wrote me, "if I ever attempted to visit them, something awful would occur". I didn't know exactly what she had in mind, but I was not anxious to find out.

Many years later, I was elated to learn my father became famous for his work. I regretted that I didn't share his good fortune with him. In 1974, while doing research at the hospital, he completed his scientific work: Silver permanganate method to demonstrate axis cylinders and myelin sheaths on frozen sections. Pathologists were using gold to determine the cause of brain damage. Papa was able to substitute silver for gold. It was a huge money saver for hospitals worldwide.

Papa's discovery created enormous excitement in the medical world. The Medical University of Colorado, at Denver, honored Papa, picking him up in a black limousine, and took him to a conference room on the hospital grounds. Decorated tables, covered with all kinds of food and wonderful desserts greeted him. Dad loved sweets and wasn't about to leave hungry.

Dignitaries from far and wide attended this grand occasion. The hospital staff introduced Papa to the audience who showered him with accolades. Papa was treated like celebrity.

It was a special moment when the hospital presented him with an honorary doctor's degree. Being a humble man, he couldn't believe what was happening. Two hours later, he was brought back home from the grand occasion in the same elegant black limousine. With enormous pride, he held tight the framed certificates. The next day, the phone never stopped ringing, receiving calls from all over the globe congratulating him on his achievement.

Papa had a problem! Mama thought she should have been invited as well to the party. This was not the case! Only medical doctors attended the function, no wives or girlfriends. This infuriated her! The next morning, Mama hollered at Papa, "These certificates mean nothing, and you ought to be ashamed accepting these meaningless, cheap forms of appreciations." She took his certificate, the honorary doctor's degree, and threw them down the staircase. They ended up torn to shreds, intermingled with shards of glass.

Papa was devastated, and couldn't believe his wife would do something this horrific. He felt abandoned! The rest of the day, he sat in his office chair, holding his head in his hands, slumped over; joy escaped him like a dove leaving the nest for the last time. Was this the same woman who he loved so much? But now he wasn't sure what to think. Over and over, he asked, why she reacted the way she did. There was no explanation! He was consoled, knowing that she couldn't erase his name from medical journals and remove the plaque mounted in the hospital.

She was devastated by the events of the past. I didn't walk in her shoes and will never know everything she lived through. To me, she will always be my hero. She went way beyond the call of duty. She stood up to tyranny when it counted, but later lost her will to live.

EPILOGUE

I gave my life to the Lord while I was in the Navy, which turned my life around. I have a greater purpose in life, serving the Lord.

Psalm 146:5
Blessed is he whose help is the God of Jacob, whose hope is in the Lord his God, The Maker of heaven and earth, the sea, and everything in them-the Lord, who remains faithful forever.

John 3:16
For God so loved the world that he gave his only begotten Son and whosoever believeth in Him shall not perish but have everlasting life.

Papa was happy living in the United States and enjoyed life. He worked at the Colorado University Medical Center in Denver as a pathologist until he retired at the age of sixty-five. He continued drawing and painting, and kept his hands in medical research. In 1989, he passed away in Loveland, Colorado at the age of eighty.

Mama was a housewife and passed away in 1993 at the age of eighty-four in Loveland, Colorado. The doctors in Germany didn't expect her to live past twelve. She proved them wrong. She never did recover from the devastation of war. There wasn't anything we could do to make her happy. Her dreams were to free herself from the past after coming to America. I am sad to say, that never happened. My parents sacrificed much, so we children would have a better life, and we did.

My sister Herta lives close to Munich and keeps herself busy writing books and doing art work. She has a daughter, Dagmar and a son, Hans.

Gerlinde lives in Greely, Colorado. Her six children are grown and left home long ago, with the exception of Gianni who lives with her. She is a successful business woman who owns and manages a number of apartments.

Helga is married and lives close to Denver, Colorado. She has three children who live close by and she enjoys her grandchildren. Most of her working life was in the medical field.

After my separation from the U.S. Navy, I settled in sunny California. I was married in 1965, and became the proud father of two boys, Jeff, and

James. Jeff is married to Stephanie and lives in northern California. They have two wonderful boys, Blake, and Dylan. Jeff works for a computer company as an engineer and Stephanie does freelance work from home.

James lives south of Fresno. He has no children, but is blessed with three dogs and three cats. He works for a health insurance company as a supervisor.

In 1991 I was divorced from my first wife. Later, in 1994, I married Jeanette and gained two stepsons, the youngest is Brent who lives in Fresno, California and has two beautiful girls, Lindsey and Jenifer. Norman was the oldest and passed away unexpectedly on February 15th 2012 at the age of forty-nine.

Life has been good and I consider myself very blessed and honored to have had the privileges given to me. I became a U.S. citizen in California, in 1968. This was one of the most memorable, and awesome experiences in my entire life. People risk their lives to come to America. It is the best country where dreams can still be fulfilled.

I was involved in the apparel industry, and later the police business which took me all over the western United States as well as the East Coast. Since retiring, I am enjoying life to the fullest. I help around the house doing my honey-do projects which laid dormant for a number of years.

I am writing this book, and took art classes. I recently built a gazebo in the back yard which was a miracle especially since I am not a handyman by any stretch of the imagination.

I learned to play the accordion somewhat. In my spare time, I am involved in our church and volunteer at the Community Regional Medical Center in Fresno. My dreams were fulfilled in this blessed country, the greatest nation on planet earth. I am free to worship the way I choose, and pursue happiness.

In short, I am having the time of my life. Yes life is good.

SOURCES

My mother's war journal covers our flight from Hitler and the Soviet forces in detail.

Guido Knopp 'Die Grosse Flucht'. A poignant book. His book confirmed what my mother told me.

Anne-Rose Froehlich wrote the book 'Kindheit in Truemmern'. She is my sister, and her stories vary from mine somewhat.

Antony Beever wrote many books, one of which was 'Stalingrad'. He is deceased.